August Wilson's
Fences

August Wilson's
Fences

A Reference Guide

SANDRA G. SHANNON

Greenwood Guides to Literature

GREENWOOD PRESS
Westport, Connecticut • London

Library of Congress Cataloging-in-Publication Data

Shannon, Sandra Garrett, 1952–
    August Wilson's *Fences* : a reference guide / Sandra G. Shannon.
        p.   cm.—(Greenwood guides to literature, ISSN 1543–2262)
    Includes bibliographical references and index.
    ISBN 0-313-31880-8 (alk. paper)
    1. Wilson, August. *Fences*.   2. Historical drama, American—History and criticism.   3. Conflict of generations in literature.   4. African Americans in literature.   I. Title.   II. Series.
    PS3573.I45677 F434   2003
    812'.54—dc21   2002035222

British Library Cataloguing in Publication Data is available.

Library of Congress Catalog Card Number: 2002035222
ISBN: 0-313-31880-8
ISSN: 1543-2262

First published in 2003

Greenwood Press, 88 Post Road West, Westport, CT 06881
An imprint of Greenwood Publishing Group, Inc.
www.greenwood.com

Printed in the United States of America

The paper used in this book complies with the Permanent Paper Standard issued by the National Information Standards Organization (Z39.48-1984).

10 9 8 7 6 5 4 3 2 1

Copyright Acknowledgment

All quotations from August Wilson's *Fences* are used with permission of Penguin USA and August Wilson.

To my daughter, Kristen Michelle Shannon

Contents

Preface   ix

Acknowledgments   xv

1   Introduction   1

2   Content   29

3   Texts   49

4   Contexts   63

5   Ideas   97

6   Art   129

7   Reception   153

8   Bibliographical Essay   175

Works Cited   191

Index   197

Preface

August Wilson's Fences: *A Reference Guide* is a companion piece to what has clearly become the signature play of one of America's most prolific and most gifted writers. The elevated status afforded this 1950s domestic drama is due to a number of rarefied features that have for the last fifteen years endeared it to a national as well as global audience. During its 1987 Broadway run at the 46th Street Theatre, *Fences* broke the record for nonmusical plays by grossing $11 million during its first year in New York. It went on to garner four Tony Awards, including Best Play, and to earn the prestigious New York Drama Critics Circle Award. It also captured the John Gassner Outer Critics Circle Award and ultimately the Pulitzer Prize.

Apart from its commercial success, however, the importance of *Fences* may be determined by what it reveals about the changing American psyche as the country continues to grapple with long-standing constructs of race, class, and gender and attempts to situate itself within the twenty-first century. As a popular nonmusical Broadway play of the late 1980s that featured an entire cast of African Americans, *Fences* signaled a shift in America's theatrical taste. That shift also involved risk-taking by producers who gradually began to financially back African American plays other than popular cash cow musicals. Just as its predecessor *Ma Rainey's Black Bottom* proved in 1984, Broadway audiences and, by extension, Americans were more willing to gaze through the window of African American experience and see aspects of their own diverse cultures.

Fences is the story of a responsible yet otherwise flawed black garbage collector in pre–civil rights America who, in August Wilson's hands, rises to the level of epic hero. As Troy grows in stature, we are correspondingly more able to connect our own circumstances to those expressed in the colorful stories he tells of victories and defeats over various forms of oppression. Likewise, as the play transcends the confines of the Maxson household, the struggles of Troy's devoted wife Rose, his determined son Cory, his shiftless son Lyons, his wounded brother Gabriel, and his steadfast friend Bono tap into our shared experiences. As reviewer Brent Staples notes, "[T]his play, with virtually no concessions to the middle class, has enfolded the universal in the particular, in a way that results in total accessibility."[1] As such, *Fences* cuts across class, race, and gender to raise issues familiar to the human condition.

Proof of *Fences*'s appeal and its endearment lies in its influence beyond the theater and into the classroom. Deemed a "generational play," its staying power is largely attributed to its ability to mirror the classic struggles between status quo, tradition, and age on one hand and change, innovation, and youth on the other. *Fences* is a story that frames the narratives of three generations of Maxson men: Troy's father, Troy himself, and Cory. It presents an archetypal conflict that is ever relevant to adolescents, adults, and older individuals of all races and nationalities. White students in Des Moines, Iowa, read and discuss *Fences* and react to the mirror image it casts back at them. African American students in Washington, D.C., hear the voices of their parents and grandparents and are moved to engage the characters in terms they know best. Asian adolescents in Beijing, China, who "rush into society,"[2] against the wishes of the older guard who favor a state job, insurance, and housing were struck by the similar conflict revealed by the African American play when it premiered there in 1996. Like much of Shakespeare's canon, *Fences* transcends time and location and continues to afford space for contemporary dialogue.

Not surprisingly, then, *Fences* has become a familiar item on reading lists, syllabi, and exams in high school and college curricula. An increasing number of anthologies and various teaching resources feature the play, thus facilitating its continued presence in classrooms across America and beyond. Not only is the play one of August Wilson's most critically and commercially acclaimed works, but it is also one of the most read and discussed, the most performed (nationally and internationally), and the most accessible of his eight-play repertoire. By all accounts, it has been inducted into the canon of classic American literature.

In response to the proven appeal and classic nature of the play, *August Wilson's* Fences: *A Reference Guide* serves as a helpful companion for both students and teachers entering the dramatic world of August Wilson by way of this Pulitzer Prize–winning play. Aimed specifically at an audience more in tune to practical rather than theoretical issues of the text, this reference work will overview a number of textual, contextual, and thematic sites of interest in *Fences*. As a reference tool, it is a cognitively friendly companion piece for the introductory-level reader or spectator, providing a well-informed base of knowledge certain to lift the level of written and oral discourse about the play.

August Wilson's Fences: *A Reference Guide* provides an introduction to the playwright's creative process, emphasizing what went into the making of *Fences* both practically and aesthetically. In addition to examining what inspired the artist's creativity and imagination, this reference book takes a brief behind-the-scenes look at Wilson's nonlinear process of writing and revising *Fences*—a process that revolved around the central theme of responsibility. Toward this end, this study gives significant attention to the eclectic muses that inspired Wilson as he wrote and honed *Fences* to its now-definitive form and examines influences that will likely shape the so-called "bookend plays."[3]

August Wilson's Fences: *A Reference Guide* follows a simple organizational strategy. Chapter one, the "Introduction," overviews fundamental aspects of August Wilson's aesthetic and carefully delineates his dramatic agenda. Inasmuch as *Fences* is but one of eight plays informed by these principles, the play has been contextualized here within the larger visionary framework that supports the body of Wilson's work. In addition to creating a portrait of Wilson as an individual artist, the "Introduction" also gives a brief look into Wilson's early life, paying attention to the forces that propelled him beyond a potentially troubled life in his native Pittsburgh to his current status as one of America's most gifted voices in theater. Further, it situates him within European, African, and American literary traditions that undergird his writing. Representatives of these traditions, according to Wilson, include Euripedes, Aeschylus, Sophocles, Shakespeare, Shaw, and Ibsen alongside O'Neill, Miller, and Williams.[4] Clearly Wilson suffers no anxiety of influence from his literary predecessors and unabashedly pays homage to them. In a controversial landmark speech in 1996, he told a theater community gathered in Princeton, New Jersey, "The foundation of the American theatre is the foundation of European theatre that begins with the great Greek dramatists; it is based on the proscenium stage and the poetics of Aristotle. This is the theatre that we have chosen to work in."[5] But the bedrock of Wilson's literary aesthetic is defined by an even more powerful tradition: activism. Those whom he credits most for sustaining the revolutionary tone of his work include, first, his grandfather followed by Nat Turner, Denmark Vesey, Martin Delany, Marcus Garvey, the Honorable Elijah Muhammad, and Amiri Baraka. While Wilson concedes to the influence of American and European dramatists, he does not miss an opportunity to make known his ties to Africa and to acknowledge the dominant place it occupies in his aesthetic: "I learned the language, the eating habits, the religious beliefs, the gestures, the notions of common sense, attitudes towards sex, concepts of beauty and justice, and the response to pleasure and pain, that my mother had learned from her mother, and which you could trace back to the first African who set foot on the continent."[6]

Chapter two, "Content," provides a helpful summary of the action of *Fences* from the play's jocular opening scene between Troy and best friend and working partner Bono to the final atavistic funeral dance by brother Gabriel in Troy's honor. The basis for chapter three, "Texts," is a sound critical assessment of *Fences* and an overview of its distinguished production history. Building upon an image of a man holding a baby in Romare Bearden's 1969 work titled *Continuities*, Wilson stretched his creative genius to form the basis for his depiction of a *responsible* black man: Troy Maxson. In addition to discussing what inspired Wilson artistically to write the play, chapter three delves into commercial and political motives that brought the play into existence.

Chapter four of *August Wilson's Fences: A Reference Guide*, "Contexts," examines the forces of history that determine the conflict as well as the resolve of African Americans in this 1950s play. Its time frame spans several major historical moments for African Americans in the twentieth century including Reconstruction, Great Migration, Great Depression, and the Civil Rights era. Thus, this chapter examines the extent to which historical, cultural, and sociological forces of these eras impact upon *Fences*; that is, how such forces manifest in the play. Chapter four also points to biographical parallels between August Wilson's *Fences* and real-life conflict he experienced with his late stepfather. And, finally, chapter four explores how *Fences* relates to the African American experience, noting the play's commentary upon two recurring themes in Wilson's work: "deprivation of possibility"[7] and the responsible black man.

Chapter five, "Ideas," explores the numerous intersecting themes that run through *Fences*. This essentially entails an examination of ideas that spring from certain historical realities for African Americans living in the

1950s. It also entails a look at August Wilson's own perspective on the inaccuracies and unfairness of history in recording these "realities." This is in addition to his desire to foreground mistakes that African Americans have made during the twentieth century.

August Wilson's most compelling dramatic strategy in *Fences* is to create a three-dimensional, complex protagonist. To do so, he relies upon the artwork of Romare Bearden and the lingering influence of a paternal role model that he found in his stepfather. Chapter six, "Art," provides insight into his efforts along these lines. The result of these major influences lead to a more tightly controlled drama that "[raises] a single character to a much grander scale."[8]

Chapter seven of *August Wilson's* Fences: A Reference Guide, "Reception," surveys the critical and scholarly landscape that *Fences* has inspired since its inception. It also includes an assessment of the play's overall reception among theater reviewers, academic critics, and ultimately African American audiences—those who experience the text as well as those who sit for the performance.

Chapter eight, "Bibliographical Essay," the book's final chapter, synthesizes the arguments set forth in the most critically poignant and useful studies to date on *Fences*.

NOTES

1. Brent Staples, "'Fences': No Barrier to Emotion," *New York Times*, 5 April 1987, 39.

2. Margaret Booker, "Building Fences in Beijing," *American Theatre*, May/June 1997, 51.

3. August Wilson has, to date, completed eight plays in his proposed ten-play agenda to write one play per decade about some aspect of the African American experience in the twentieth century. To date, the completed plays are set in decades from 1911 to 1985. Plays yet to be written, or his so-called "bookend plays," are to be set in the 1900s and the 1990s.

4. August Wilson, *The Ground On Which I Stand* (New York: Theatre Communications Group, 2001), 11.

5. Ibid., 41.

6. Ibid., 15–16.

7. Director Lloyd Richards coined the term "deprivation of possibility" to describe the "pride, frustration, exploitation, and internecine aggression" in August Wilson's *Ma Rainey's Black Bottom*. See Ishmael Reed's "In Search of August Wilson," *Connoisseur*, March 1987, 93.

8. Sandra Shannon, *The Dramatic Vision of August Wilson* (Washington, D.C.: Howard University Press, 1995), 90.

Acknowledgments

I wish to say "thank you" to August Wilson for writing *Fences*, for this was the play that first kindled my interest in perusing the body of his work. This was also the play that ultimately led me to explore the evolution of his playwriting genius. I appreciate as well his permission to quote extensively from *Fences* in this study. It is only fitting, then, that I return to this starting place to look more closely at what makes this particular play so appealing—so personal for me and yet so universal.

I also wish to thank Dr. Margaret Booker, who in 1996 carried *Fences* across the globe to Beijing, China, and directed a successful all-Chinese production at the Chinese People's Art Theater. In addition to offering me encouraging words as my work on *August Wilson's* Fences: *A Reference Guide* progressed, she was instrumental in helping me secure several riveting photos from that production. My gratitude also extends to officials of the Chinese People's Art Theater for granting permission to publish these shots as part of this study. I also owe a special acknowledgment to my Salzburg Seminar fellow associate and dear friend Dr. Joanne Brown of Des Moines, Iowa, who shared with me her students' thoughtful written reactions to *Fences*. Observations about the play offered by students enrolled in her undergraduate course titled "Family in American Drama" helped shape my thinking about the play's impact upon varied cross-sections of America's theatergoing audiences.

The publication of *August Wilson's* Fences: *A Reference Guide* was greatly facilitated by support from Howard University's Faculty Research Support Grant Program, which sustained my research and writing for approximately two years. Finally, I wish to acknowledge my wonderfully supportive husband Michael and my "little lady" of a daughter Kristen, both of whom gave me space and solitude when I needed them most.

1 Introduction

Ever so often a writer discovers a way to erase borders, transcend particulars, and communicate in a language understood by a majority. This special talent allows the writer, sometimes unwittingly, to construct a one-size-fits-all world where key moments of recognition forge bonds between different races, cultures, genders, and ages. This special talent indicates the writer's mastery of the delicate balance between the world that he knows (i.e., the ground on which he stands)[1] and a world that points to cultural landscapes beyond his own immediate recognition.

Pulitzer Prize–winning playwright August Wilson is just such an artist. To date the author of eight plays (his ultimate goal is to write ten) that explore the black experience since 1900, Wilson most clearly achieves this quality in his 1985 play *Fences*.[2] Although this play set in the 1950s is but a part of the playwright's overall ten-play mission to re-write the distorted historical narrative for twentieth-century African Americans, it is distinctive on several counts. Aside from being Wilson's most commercially successful work, *Fences* is most unique among his other plays in its adherence to a more traditional structure. This is all the more noteworthy because Wilson at first was not at all inclined to adhere to Western standards of tragedy. In fact, he found the strict Aristotelian paradigm calling for beginning, middle, and end (in that order) stifling as well as antithetical to his Africanist aesthetic. Yet despite his initial reluctance to adhere to a prescribed form, Wilson eventually yielded to the advice of several playwrights and close friends from his theater community that by doing so, he could write a better play.

By most accounts, *Ma Rainey's Black Bottom*, Wilson's previous play to open on Broadway, was a runaway success. But that success was largely gauged according to ticket sales and positive responses of its audiences. Yet the play still troubled some members of Wilson's inner circle of professionals who were concerned about the lingering bifurcated, scattered focus of *Ma Rainey* and its lack of a singularly clear protagonist. Neither did some of New York's toughest and most respected critics join in the praise heaped upon the play. Instead, they pointed to what they deemed to be recurring problems in Wilson's work: excessive characters and split focus. One such critic noted that *Ma Rainey* was "split figuratively just as the set is split literally."[3]

Wilson's Achilles' heel had been exposed. In the wake of fanfare surrounding *Ma Rainey's Black Bottom*, he had to contend with the paradoxical nature of success. On one hand, he was pleased at the various visible signs of approval heaped upon the play. Yet on another, the play's internal structural weaknesses tugged at his confidence and made him reconsider his friends' concerns. Ultimately *Fences* became the fruit of his decision to wrestle with his so-called demons that plagued his writing. As Wilson conceived and wrote *Fences* in the early 1980s, his guiding principles were (1) to adhere to the more traditional, tightly unified structure of the well-made play; (2) to create a single clearly defined protagonist; and (3) to make the audience care about what happens to this protagonist by drawing from universal themes and by elevating his stature from individual to epic hero. Wilson did not consider these variations to his playwriting approach as mere concessions. Rather, he perceived them as challenges that tested his determination to write the best play that had ever been written. In 1989 he told an interviewer, "After telling people that I knew how to write that kind of play, I asked myself 'Do I really know how to write that kind of play?' So I wrote *Fences* in answer to the challenge that I'd given myself."[4]

In the final analysis, August Wilson's now-classic drama *Fences* not only significantly quieted his detractors, but—much like Lorraine Hansberry's *A Raisin in the Sun*—it also forced a redefinition of the term *universality*. Although the play's conflict is grounded in experiences peculiar to African Americans in post–World War II America, it also resounds with themes that ring familiar to both readers and audiences alike. The forces of history conspire to deprive an ambitious man of life's possibilities. A young man wants to break free of his father's rule. A faithful wife is wronged by a philandering husband. A woman decides to nurture a motherless child. On the surface each of these scenarios may elicit some degree of familiarity—perhaps even empathy. Yet there is little about either situation that is identifiably African American—or Asian, African, or European for that matter. What are at stake in each instance are human experiences that invite universal recognition. As Hansberry observed, "One of the most sound ideas in dramatic writing is that in order to create the universal, you must pay very great attention to the specific."[5] Wilson achieves this delicate balance in *Fences*, thereby earning its place among classic works of literature.

When measured against Wilson's seven other plays, each of which is noticeably grounded in African and African American cultural signifiers, *Fences* most lends itself to open-ended interpretation. From the archetypal showdown between father and son to the altruistic gesture of a mother toward a dead woman's child, the play taps into the wellspring of human emotion. To what may we attribute the universal resonance of *Fences*? To what may we attribute its concurrent and equally intense focus upon the African American experience?

When asked to identify his biggest source of inspiration for playwriting, August Wilson invariably credits the blues. *Fences* captures the dynamics of this universal language in its searing conflicts as well as in its healing resolutions. For the unenlightened, the blues may simply denote the sounds that emerge from musical instruments, such as the guitar or harmonica, or perhaps they may consider the blues to be that which emerges from a singer's soulful wailing about life's disappointments. However, the blues operates on a much more expansive scale that informs a way of thinking, a way of healing, a way of coping, a way of creating, and a way of living one's life. Ralph Ellison defined the blues as "an impulse to keep the painful details and episodes of brutal experience alive in one's aching consciousness" and regarded it as an "autobiographical chronicle of personal catastrophe expressed lyrically."[6] August Wilson defines the blues aesthetic as "a philosophical system at work," "a way of passing along information," and "an emotional reference."[7] Ma Rainey, the real-life blues prima donna depicted in Wilson's *Ma Rainey's Black Bottom* (1985), sees the blues as "life's way of talking."[8]

As Amiri Baraka argues in *Blues People* (1963), the roots of the blues have their origins in Africa and endured throughout slavery in the United States to achieve its first wave of popularity during the 1920s. The pervasive "feelings of exasperation, indeed *blueness*, that might have been tied to the master's request to a slave to pick three hundred pounds of cotton a day or to plow ten acres could easily have led to the songs we now know as the blues. . . . The *condition* of the blues, then, interceded the name."[9] Now, in the twenty-first century, as a result of increasingly diminishing cultural borders, the blues as a performative art form enjoys extremely wide appeal. Once clearly a cultural signifier, now the blues have become the shared domain of a multicultural society. It is not uncommon to see Asian or Hispanic blues artists who render blues lyrics by way of song or musical instrument with just as much finesse as legendary African American blues greats. Ironically, a major drawback of widespread popular identification with blues music and the entire blues aesthetic is the diffusion of the concept's original meaning and impact. For example, the expression "having the blues" has been diffused of its onetime intense emotional significance and now simply has become synonymous with the likes of melancholy. Hence, whereas the lyrics of African American blues singers of the 1920s told stories of destitute poverty, homelessness, and Jim Crow slanders, many of today's references to the blues come in the form of lighthearted parody or as marketing ploys. Also, the massive global appeal of the blues suggests that it communicates on levels that transcend culture and race.

As an essentially nonverbal medium, the blues operate in *Fences* on several complex levels. It surfaces most obviously in lyrical tunes rendered at emotionally explosive moments during the play or during what seem to be the nadir of a particular character's life. During such low points, mere images can suggest meaning and preclude the need for culturally specific language—hence increasing potential for universal empathy. For example, the beginning of act 2 of *Fences* turns on the now-familiar image of a black man holding a baby captured in one of collagist Romare Bearden's works. That image as context comes into focus as Troy returns from the hospital where he learns that his mistress and mother of his child has died in childbirth. He stands in his front yard holding a tiny bundle in his arms. That bundle contains his newborn daughter who, as we learn later, turns out to be Raynell. While he musters enough nerve to communicate with his wife, he engages the infant in a playful but revealing conversation about homelessness. This blues moment culminates in lyrics that reference the familiar image of the train as Troy indirectly plays upon the sympathy of the audience: "Please, Mr. Engineer let a man ride the line/ Please, Mr. Engineer let a man ride the line/ I ain't got no ticket please let me ride the blinds" (*Fences*, 2.3.79). Troy knows that at this juncture, both he and his daughter stand on the periphery of the Maxson family circle. To find a means of persuasion not possible in a simple explanation, he resorts to singing the blues. Immediately following this blues verse, Troy begins to petition Rose to take his child in her care: "She's my daughter, Rose. My own flesh and blood. I can't deny her no more than I can deny them boys" (2.3.79). The contrast between the implicit emotional plea in the blues lyrics and his own logical—albeit pathetically inept—words is great.

In *Fences* the blues dynamic that informs the play is not limited to song lyrics. The blues also marks its presence by establishing an appropriate emotional context to compliment the down-and-out predicaments of deeply troubled characters, such as Troy. That blues context comes into play as several profoundly moving circumstances align as they do in *Fences*. For example, six months after Troy staggers his wife Rose with the double blow that he has had an affair with Alberta and that they have conceived a child, he is engulfed by a supreme sense of loneliness. He sits alone on the steps of a home that is technically not his; he built it with money diverted from his brother's payment for a war injury. He has handed over his two-month-old daughter to his wife from whom he is now estranged. She has vowed to have little or nothing to do with him and spends much of her time caring for the infant and attending church affairs. Because of a deep-seated rift between the two and knowledge of Troy's infidelity to his mother, Cory has severed ties with Troy. Thanks to his big brother's intervention, Gabriel now lives in an institution. This is a low moment for Troy; he is utterly alone. In a manner that recalls 1920s American poet T. S. Eliot's principle called "objective correlative," blues moments, such as the one described above, occur when a cluster of images or a sequence of events converge to produce profound human emotions that are understood by a majority.

Wilson's attraction to the blues goes beyond the emotional spark that it supplies to inspire his writing. For a young man estranged from his German father and embraced by his mother's African American heritage, it became his segue to the cultural and communal bonds he sought to establish with African Americans and, by extension, Africa. In an often-repeated anecdote, Wilson explains his introduction to the blues and the indelible impact that it left on him personally and professionally. He told journalist Bill Moyers:

> I listen to the music of the particular period that I'm working on. Inside the music are clues to what is happening with the people. . . . The blues are important primarily because they contain the cultural responses of blacks in America to the situation that they find them-

selves in. Contained in the blues is a philosophical system at work. You get the ideas and attitudes of the people as part of the oral tradition. This is a way of passing along information.[10]

Thus the blues, at first, took on a deeply personal meaning for Wilson, especially during the 1960s when he came into manhood *without* the guidance of his German father but *with* Daisy Wilson's African heritage as his moral and cultural anchor. Eventually the blues became his ontological guide as he claimed his African heritage, established principles of manhood, and discovered his artistic voice.

In an attempt to negotiate his private past and address certain wrongs that have been perpetrated against African Americans in America since 1900, August Wilson works through his writing. The blues assists him as he immerses himself in the African legacy left by his deceased mother Daisy Wilson and—much like Herald Loomis, the protagonist of his play *Joe Turner's Come and Gone* (1988)—tries to reconnect the fragmented pieces of his past.

In addition to employing the universal language of the blues, *Fences* inherits the philosophy of universalism from a number of artists and intellectuals who, as a result of Wilson's association with them and acceptance of their ideas, have influenced the play. Most notable among such individuals is Lloyd Richards, who for several years worked closely with Wilson in shepherding at least four of his plays from the Yale Repertory Theatre to Broadway. During a June 2000 interview at his New York home, Richards explained, "[T]he art of the world belongs to all of us. Artists are not just speaking to a narrow group of people. When their ideas are profound, they affect and relate to everyone."[11]

Richards's views, in retrospect, reveal fundamental philosophical differences between him and Wilson. Having been schooled in the theories of Aristotle, Konstantin Stanislavsky, and Paul Mann early in his professional career, having successfully directed numerous European plays, and having held pivotal administrative roles in mainstream theater organizations, Richards seems destined to embrace a more global perspective. That is not to suggest, however, that as an African American he lacks consciousness about contemporary realities of politics, race, and culture. Rather, it is to submit that he chooses not to foreground such issues in his professional activities, choosing instead to regard racism as a given and opting not to expend his energies railing against it. Several years following the expiration of his tenure as Dean of Yale School of Drama, he regrets missed opportunities to train dramaturgs to extend their creative sights beyond Western cultures:

> Our training and the training of most American dramaturgs was centered essentially in western culture. We were not sending them out with the knowledge that would permit them to suggest an oriental play, to suggest an African play, to suggest a South American play or a play other than western culture theater. And that was one of the things that I never got started but wanted very much. So that we were training people who would go out into the theaters of our country with the knowledge that went much beyond their own cultures, the usual culture.[12]

But even though Richards and Wilson had fundamental differences on matters of race, culture, and politics, they managed to share a surprising amount of common ground as black men. In fact, it was while fine-tuning *Fences* in 1987 as it made its way to San Francisco and then on to New York that they realized just how much the elder Richards and the maverick Wilson had in common. Richards—the seasoned theater veteran that he was—was not naïve to the hardball politics associated with succeeding on New York's Great White Way. Under pressure from the play's producer to edit Gabriel's final scene where he unsuccessfully attempts to blow his horn, Richards and Wilson showed extreme solidarity in their refusal to do so. Apparently while the producer was concerned that audience puzzlement over the finale would impact ticket sales, Wilson and Richards insisted on retaining Gabriel as the embodiment of African ritual. Wilson scholar Harry Elam concurs on the importance of Gabriel's gesture in his pronouncement that

> Gabriel's ritualistic and spiritual enactment is an exhibit of a syncretic cosmology, the presence of African tradition within New World religious practice. . . . Gabriel invokes a racial memory, and African inheritance. His actions again reinforce the impact of the past on the present as the family's African heritage provides a benediction for their African American present.[13]

The influence of collagist Romare Bearden in both general and specific ways may also shed light on what makes *Fences* Wilson's most universal and widely accepted work. "The truest artist feels that there is only one art," Bearden asserts, "and that it belongs to all mankind."[14] In a world populated by "conjure women, trains, guitar players, birds, masked figures, winged creatures, and intense ritualistic activities: baptisms, women bathing, families eating together at their dinner tables, funerals, parades, night club scenes,"[15] Bearden demonstrates this belief on canvas.

Much as August Wilson has done in all of his plays to date, Bearden chose as his focus the daily rituals of black people or the "continuity of a culture's ceremonies, marking the traditions and values that connect one generation to another."[16] Instead of sweeping landscapes, Bearden's canvas zooms in on the unsung heroism found in day-to-day existence of African Americans. His fragmented, eclectic artistic medium achieves spiritual dimensions, often suggesting the process of reassembling, healing, and making sense of the loose pieces of African American life. This is all the more pertinent when one considers the disjointed nature of the African American psyche still reacting to a history of slavery. The results of this process are a heightened sense of dignity, heroism, and grandeur in their existence. Wilson often admitted imitating this aspect of Bearden's style in his plays as he tried to capture the essence of what the much-acclaimed artist did on canvas in the text of his plays.

Thus, the Bearden image of a black man holding a baby featured in the collage titled *Continuities* does more than evoke the edifying principle of the responsible black man. Also presented in this carefully pieced together domestic pose are images that suggest the limitations of this man's life and the lives of his family on one hand and their boundless sense of honor and dignity on the other. Clearly Bearden's definition of responsibility during the post–Emancipation era in African American history that we may assume is depicted in this collage has much to do with preserving the family intact. It also demonstrates that, for African American men, in particular, the faithful execution of rituals is a large part of being responsible.

The most prominent symbol of responsibility in Bearden's *Continuities* is the infant. The powerful visual message of a small child being cradled in the arms of its father strikes a sharp contrast to a historical backdrop of African American men who neglect their role as fathers, ultimately giving in to the so-called walking blues. In this inspiring frame, the representations of an African American man and woman standing next to each other in *American Gothic* style[17] defy the stereotype of the disjointed black family. Also contributing to this family portrait is the child nestled comfortably against its father's shoulder and held securely by its father's unusually large hands, a recurring image in much of Bearden's work.

Fences begins with the image of a man holding a baby. The source of that image is Romare Bearden's collage titled *Continuities* (1969). © Romare Bearden Foundation/Licensed by VAGA, New York, NY. Photograph by Colin McRae.

Strewn about the landscape are ritual reminders of responsibilities to be fulfilled in order to provide for this young life. The harnessed mule waiting in the background, the house in obvious need of repair, the broom leaning against the side of the house, and the chicks in the front yard all suggest rituals of responsibility to be performed—rituals that have been suspended but momentarily to pose for a picture. Thus, Wilson's rationale for building *Fences* upon the foundation provided by this Bearden work seems quite fitting. Although a great part of the play's appeal lies in its open invitation to empathize the nature of the characters' lives, it is equally appealing for its faithfulness to African American cultural experiences. Indeed, as Peter Wolfe argues, "Although the characters and their complications are American, the play's resolution comes from Africa."[18] Like Bearden, August Wilson invites us to peer through universal lenses at the culturally specific narratives present in his work. But also like Bearden, his work remains chiefly about the African American experience.

The universality of *Fences* raises an interesting paradox that is at the center of much of August Wilson's well-publicized political stance on black theater. The source of his political stance may be traced back to a speech Wilson gave in 1996 at an annual Theatre Communications Group conference.[19] One of several premises of this speech was an outright rejection of the concept of universality as defined by one of the most outspoken critics of Wilson's plays: Robert Brustein.[20] At issue here were comments Brustein made in a 1993 article insinuating that the proliferation of minority artists would lead to lower standards.[21] Among other highly accusatory statements, Brustein notes, "It's disarming in all senses of the word to say that we don't share common experiences that are measurable by common standards. But the growing number of truly talented artists with more universal interests suggests that we may soon be in a position to return to a single value system."[22]

Wilson took offense to the above statement as well as to similar statements by Brustein that seemed to equate universalism with common standards. According to Wilson, Brustein's call for "a single value system" was tantamount to devaluing cultural differences and upholding a single standard of excellence. He abhors Brustein's concept of universalism as it stands to lessen or even negate particular aspects of African American culture and art. Needless to say, August Wilson's Africanist, blues-informed, ritual-based aesthetic is antithetical to Brustein's notion of a "single value system," for it evolves from an entirely different worldview. Thus, to assess Wilson's plays such as *Joe Turner's Come and Gone*, *The Piano Lesson*, *Two Trains Running*, *Seven Guitars*, or *King Hedley II* using only a European yardstick, for example, would mean missing much of what these works convey.

The currently popular practice of color-blind casting, which Wilson has detested publicly, sheds even more light on the inherent paradox of universalism, especially as it relates to Wilson's art and politics. Proponents of the trend of tearing down racial and ethnic boundaries on stage hail it not only as a way to increase employment opportunities for actors and actresses, but also as a means of defamiliarizing classic works that increasingly elude contemporary audiences. To put on an all-black production of *Romeo and Juliet*, or to mount a multicultural presentation of Rogers and Hammerstein's *Cinderella*, they would argue, is to elicit new meaning and thus create new relevance for such classic works.

But Wilson, who regards the practices as "an aberrant idea," and likens it to "assimilation that black Americans have been rejecting for the past 380 years,"[23] adamantly opposes interpolating actors and actress of different ethnicities into works initially imagined for race-specific casts. His argument does not rest on economics but upon what he terms artistic integrity. Based upon sentiments expressed in his June 1996 "The Ground On Which I Stand" speech, August Wilson's contention with color-blind casting takes into consideration the unique history that black actors and actresses carry with them—a history that problematizes color-blind casting in ways not experienced by members of other racial groups. When these actors step into roles where they must also assume identities of their historical oppressors, Wilson cries foul: "Our manners, our style, our approach to language, our gestures, and our bodies are not for rent. The history of our bodies—the maimings . . . the lashings . . . the lynchings . . . the body that is capable of inspiring profound rage and pungent cruelty—is not for rent."[24]

But as with other difficult positions August Wilson has taken, he is not closed to compromise. In 1997, for example, he granted permission to white American female director Margaret Booker to stage *Fences* in Beijing, China. Booker did so with an all-Chinese cast and an all-Chinese technical staff. Furthermore, as Booker noted in an article summarizing her experiences, "Not one actor had been to America, knew an African American, or even spoke English."[25] Did this represent a reversal in Wilson's position on color-blind casting? What was it about the circumstances of this production that helped gain Wilson's approval? Perhaps it was because Chinese actors who stepped into a black world—if but for a matter of hours—did so without the weight of their past upon them. Their connections to *Fences* seemed to have had more to do with the

Troy (Liang Guanhua) realizes he must ask Rose to be a mother to his orphaned baby girl. Rose (Gong Lijun) lingers in the background. Beijing People's Art Theatre.

The ultimate showdown between Troy and Cory. *Left to right:* Cory (Cong Lin), Troy (Liang Guanhua), and Rose Maxson (Gong Lijun). Beijing People's Art Theatre.

shifting of a powerful nation's economic and generational center from one determined by tradition to one responding to the trappings of modernization. In *Fences*, that shift is played out on a much smaller scale appearing as an insurmountable conflict between two close relatives within a single family unit. Thus, younger Chinese audiences were more likely to see their plight in that of Cory, who wants to strike out on his own. Representatives of the old guard, however, could just as easily see the uncompromising Troy Maxson as their chief spokesperson for upholding Chinese tradition. To be sure, the issues presented by the play served to help the Chinese negotiate an impending generational shift or what amounts to an all-out challenge to the hegemony—a battle that is waged within all cultures.

Just as *Fences* distinguishes itself among Wilson's other works in its across-the-board appeal, the play is also able to pinpoint its focus upon particularities of the African American experience. Many of these particularities respond to historical realities for African Americans in 1950s America as well as the decades preceding and immediately following the play's 1957 setting. Although Wilson repeats the popular disclaimer that his plays are

Gabriel (Wu Gang) strains to announce Troy's arrival in Heaven. In the background *from left to right:* Rose (Gong Lijun), Raynell (Tang Ye), Lyons (Zhang Yongqiang), and Cory (Cong Lin). Beijing People's Art Theatre.

not buoyed by historical research, it is possible to recognize historical parallels in the familiar reflections cast by his use of time, place, and character. Accordingly, because *Fences* is a generational play, it is essential to review the history of the decade in which it is set. It is equally important to contextualize *Fences* within key decades that frame the play. An examination of the cultural and political realities for African Americans during the 1900s, 1940s, 1950s, and 1960s significantly illuminates the complex causal chain connecting many of the Maxson family's conflicts.

For example, Troy Maxson's father hails from the earliest historical era represented in the play: Reconstruction (1865–1915). This problematic juncture for African Americans was largely defined by hundreds of unskilled laborers, frustrated sharecroppers, poverty, illiteracy, Ku Klux Klan violence, and fragmented families. Black intellectuals Booker T. Washington and W.E.B. DuBois theorized on how best to address the so-called Negro Problem of this era and joined the public debate on what should be done to address the fate of a population facing desperate times. This monumental task before them was charting a reasonable course to improve the quality of life for the masses of newly freed slaves. Options were limited: learn a trade, work the land, and pose no threat of resistance to southern whites, according to Washington, or agitate for total justice and equality, according to DuBois.

Troy and Gabriel's father, Cory and Lyons's grandfather, appears to be a disciple of Booker T. Washington's thinking, especially in the weary sharecropper's emphasis upon the agrarian work ethic and his nonresistance to oppression from his white employer. The senior Maxson resigned himself to a failed life, and, therefore, was but an emotional shell to his wife and children. Troy recalls, "He ain't knew how to do nothing but farm. No, he was trapped and I think he knew it."[26] Clearly this man had become a victim of the Reconstruction politics so prevalent among vengeful southern white practitioners who begrudged the status of black freedmen. Moreover, there was little love spent between Troy and the burly, brutish man known as his father whose cruel ways drove away his family.

Although long deceased by 1957, the senior Maxson patriarch looms large as an ever-present influence in *Fences*. Despite his absence, he still plays a key role as the largest determining factor in Troy's personal history and as the most obvious explanation for the brash, selfish, and unfaithful man Troy turns out to be. This was a man whose raison d'etre was harvesting cotton for his white boss. This was a man who would consume several whole chickens and leave his children mere scraps. This was a man who would run off his son and attempt to rape the girl he leaves behind. Unlike Lorraine Hansberry's Big Walter Lee (*A Raisin in the Sun*, 1959), the deceased Maxson patriarch leaves a very distasteful legacy against which his family must struggle.

Fences also prompts us to examine the racial dynamics of World War II (1939–1945), especially as they relate to the fate of thousands of African American soldiers who willfully enlisted to defend the United States on hostile foreign soil only to return to equally hostile Jim Crow restrictions and various racially motivated hostilities levied against them. Like Charles Fuller—author of *A Soldier's Play* (1981), a work that treats more extensively than *Fences* the institutional racism African Americans faced in WWII—Wilson captures the cruel irony of one honorable and well-meaning soldier measured against a drastically forgetful and ungrateful nation. According to editors of *Call and Response: The Riverside Anthology of the African American Literary Tradition* (1998),

Many of the eight hundred thousand black American soldiers were eager to fight in World War II to uphold American democratic principles abroad. Paradoxically . . . these soldiers fought in segregated units against both the systemic racism of their own democratic government and the genocidal racism of a fascist German regime. Back in the United States, black civilians battled against poverty, joblessness, racial violence, and legal segregation in virtually every aspect of American life.[27]

In 1948, A. Philip Randolph, organizer of the Brotherhood of Sleeping Car Porters, the first black labor union, threatened to advise young African Americans not to enlist in the armed services if the United States government did not ban discrimination and segregation throughout the ranks. Still, it was not until October 1954 that the Defense Department issued an order abolishing federally sanctioned segregation in the United States armed services.

In order to appreciate the bitter ironies that Wilson presents in his depiction of the mentally impaired Gabriel and in order to understand Troy's constant battle against becoming "a leftover from history,"[28] it is helpful to know the overall treatment black men endured as soldiers and as civilians during and after their tenure as privates in World War II. The army that provided a mere $3000 to compensate Gabriel's head injury is the same army that sanctioned various racist acts on the Fort Neal, Louisiana, base, which is the setting of Fuller's play. Because of the dual-edged sword of racism Gabriel faces, a once mentally sound and promising black man is reduced to refuse at the play's end. Thus, Gabriel magnifies the same regretful condition that noted director and Wilson's onetime mentor Lloyd Richards labels as "deprivation of possibility"—a condition that also psychologically cripples his brother Troy and contributes mightily to the tragic tone of *Fences*.[29] That condition, as Lloyd Richards explains, is very much like the deferred dreams that dominate the lives of the cast of Lorraine Hansberry's 1950s domestic drama *A Raisin in the Sun*. There is, however, one notable exception: Whereas the Youngers' tenacity is eventually rewarded in the form of a home big enough to accommodate their growing family, Troy and Gabriel Maxson cannot even pursue any of their dreams. Simply put, they have been deprived of the possibility because of age and irreparable mental damage. While the Younger family moves from their crowded flat to a modest home in Chicago, Gabriel moves to an institution, and Troy is completely shut out of the major leagues.

Fences also draws upon the very real plight of Negro League baseball players who, from 1898 to 1946, were barred from all-white major-league teams and forced to play a segregated game in the style of nomads and traveling circus performers. Despite the segregation and the sporadic nature of their baseball contests, however, Negro League players were fiercely proud of their capabilities. In fact, it is that pride, confidence, and the sheer love of the game that, for many, deflected their attention away from the legally sanctioned apartheid that characterized the sport at the time.

The conflict of World War II subsided in 1945 with the annihilation of Hitler and his Nazi camps in Europe. During that same year, America took on another major issue: integration of major-league baseball. As historical records that date as far back as Reconstruction show, legislation upheld the actual separation of "colored" and white baseball players.[30] During the bloody Civil War years, baseball became a popular pastime in America—so popular that the newly formed National Association of Base Ball Players (NABBP) saw fit to draw up legal restrictions barring the commingling of blacks and whites in the sport. This move was in response to the country's preoccupation with the so-called Negro Problem or deciding the fate of the masses of newly freed slaves.

Negro Leagues flourished throughout the United States during this period touting rosters of exceptionally talented black ballplayers, whom sports historians and surviving Negro Leaguers frequently compared favorably to white major-leaguers who occupied similar field positions. Negro League pitcher Satchel Paige, catcher Josh Gibson, and base-stealing center fielder James "Cool Papa" Bell were the frequent topics of the popular baseball lore that flourished in both black and white camps. But for all of the world-class talent relegated to the Negro League, much of that talent went unrecognized, untapped, unrecorded, and ultimately forgotten. Because of marked inadequacies in the organization's infrastructure, many statistics from past games simply do not exist. As Robert Peterson notes in *Only the Ball Was White* (1970),

> Few generalizations are possible about the organized black leagues during the three decades in which they flourished so to speak. Perhaps three general statements might be advanced with some degree of temerity: (1) that the leagues (and most of the teams) were consistently underfinanced; (2) that, except for a brief period at the beginning, they lacked leadership; and (3) that, due chiefly to points 1 and 2, the Negro leagues never approached the level of white organized baseball in stability or discipline.

On October 23, 1945, after much political wrangling, Jackie Robinson,[31] a popular member of the Negro Leagues, signed a contract offered by Branch Rickey, head of the Brooklyn Dodgers' farm system, to play the 1946 season with the Montreal Royals. With the stroke of his pen, Jackie Robinson had, in effect, confronted and, to some extent, overcome the demons that taunt major-league hopeful Troy Maxson to his grave. Yet unlike many African Americans at that time, Troy is not impressed by the league's selection of Jackie Robinson as their token of integration. Obviously unaware that Robinson's draft was part of a carefully orchestrated strategy that had just as much to do with his political savvy as his talent at the plate, Troy jealously resents him and insinuates that his talents are mediocre at best: "Hell, I know some teams Jackie Robinson couldn't even make! What you talking about Jackie Robinson. Jackie Robinson wasn't nobody."[32] Neither is Troy humbled by palliative comparisons to his rival: power-hitting catcher Josh Gibson,[33] again insinuating that if he had the fortune afforded by both age and opportunity, he, too, could be a home-run hitting hero.

Still, Troy's animosity toward Jackie Robinson goes beyond his own green-eyed envy and even overshadows the historical relevance of Robinson at this politically significant juncture in African American achievement. Troy's grumbling serves to foreground the voices of the nameless masses; that is, he turns attention to African Americans who have been silenced and whose stories have been deemed insignificant. In essence, Troy speaks for those Negro League players who, despite the number of extraordinary obstacles they faced, persevered and even excelled at the sport. Most importantly, he speaks for those who, like him, never got the chance to prove their talents; they were deprived of possibilities. Troy is 53 years old when *Fences* opens in 1957, and 61 when he dies. When African Americans were allowed access to major-league ball, Troy was 43 years old, an age deemed past the prime for handling the physical demands of the sport. Troy's tragedy, then, as one might argue, is that he was born too soon.

The insurmountable odds against Gabriel and Troy Maxson do not just defer their dreams; they preclude them altogether. As such, the circumstances of these Maxson brothers very much recall the hopelessness and fatalism so characteristic of Greek tragic heroes who persevere in the face of certain defeat or, quite possibly, death. According to Wilson's perspective, however, such moments of abject defeat become perfect opportunities to introduce the blues dynamic in the play. Such low points in the play allow audiences to better approximate the enormity of the emotional conditions that African Americans experienced during pre–civil rights

America. As with the blues, emphasis upon logic and words become subordinated to pathos.

In taking stock of the postwar era in America's economic and political history, one truth becomes painfully obvious: African Americans and white Americans enjoyed starkly different qualities of life. It is particularly important in discussing *Fences* to imagine the world with which African American *men*, such as Troy Maxson, had to contend in the 1950s. Inasmuch as the play evolves from and is centered upon a decidedly male worldview, it is helpful to discuss it within the context of masculinist sensibilities. This approach should not to be construed as an oversight of womanist concerns in the play suggested by Rose or, for that matter, Alberta. However, it is in keeping with the design of August Wilson, the playwright, who writes from "the ground on which he stands." That is, as an African American male, he writes about the world he knows best.

Quite helpful in teasing out the historical and psychological realities for black men of this decade is an investigation of how Troy negotiates this world fully aware that it is not he but members of an hegemonic white society that make the rules by which he must play. In what ways do Troy's aspirations for a better life for himself and for his family differ from those of more privileged whites? What kind of husband, father, and friend could Troy have been had he been able to realize his dream? This knowledge of the so-called rules and clarity about who makes these rules provide a basis for understanding—though not necessarily for condoning—Troy's thinking and his actions. For example, as Troy buys furniture for his home, fights for dignity on his job, seeks alternatives for his deferred dream of playing major-league ball, and stirs Cory away from possible victimization in college sports, contextual knowledge of what African American *men* endured in the 1950s becomes invaluable.

Call and Response anthology editors aptly characterize the general plight of African Americans in the wake of World War II:

> With rare exceptions, public signs particularly in the South and private behavior nearly everywhere in the nation reflected the disparity between the American dream for whites and the blues realities for blacks. The signs still read: NO COLORED. WHITES ONLY. Because of racial discrimination, the vast majority of African Americans, many of whom were unemployed, made up a large portion of America's lowest economic class. Many of those who were employed

held menial jobs, working as domestic servants, maritime workers, common laborers, sharecroppers, and farmers. African Americans were still the last to be hired and the first to be fired.[34]

Moreover, in the advent of World War II, fierce competition in the labor market pitted newly arrived European immigrants against African Americans, both of whom often sparred over the same jobs. In many instances white supervisors opted to hire immigrant labor—in effect, forcing African American men and their families into destitution. Troy Maxson was one of the lucky ones; however, his circumstances are far from exemplary.

Clearly, as a result of conditions, such as those described above, the National Association for the Advancement of Colored People (NAACP) and other such civil rights organizations had their marching orders. Thus, they monitored treatment of African Americans across the country—especially in the South, one of the last bastions of Jim Crow law—and, in many instances, called for legal intervention. It was not until the "hot winds of change"[35] blew over America in the 1960s that more organized, more resistant, more massive grass-roots campaigns against different types of racism and oppression spread throughout the country.

In popular culture of the 1950s, African Americans were largely presented as the invisible other; that is, seldom were their lives portrayed as worthy of investigation. The invention of television only served to dispense these stereotypes to a wider national, even international, audience. In light of these conditions, *Fences* may be perceived as a competing subversive narrative on the general postwar optimism that did not extend to African Americans.

Commonplace during this decade described by Barnard Hewitt as "Prosperity—Strictly Limited"[36] was the large number of white American men who secured well-paying jobs, married, settled their families into picturesque suburban neighborhoods, and sent their children off to colleges. The nationalistic image that white America strove to project was that of an idealized middle-class family conscientious about their child-rearing obligations and just as concerned about their status within their community. Such families consisted of wise, breadwinning fathers; perpetually pleasant and attractive stay-at-home mothers; and bright, academically inclined children.

During postwar 1950s, the increasingly popular medium of television capitalized upon the country's need to promote propagandistic notions of uniformity, complacency, and security within the family structure and, by extension, within postwar America. Classic situation comedies of the era, such as *Ozzie and Harriet* (1952), *Father Knows Best* (1954), *Leave It To Beaver* (1957), and *The Donna Reed Show* (1959), fit this bill perfectly. Family values, model citizenship, temperance, and overall model behavior were the dominant messages conveyed by each.

African American men, on the other hand, continued to boost unemployment statistics, often failed at securing home mortgage loans, and, realistically, had neither the option nor any foreseeable means of purchasing real estate. Moreover, the majority of African Americans in the 1950s lacked funds to educate their children beyond high school. As *Fences* confirms, in 1957 television was still considered a luxury within the average African American household. Troy not so subtly conveys this truth to his son Cory in one of his more responsible moments: "While you thinking about a TV, I got to be thinking about the roof . . . and whatever else go wrong around here."[37] More pressing issues of survival far outweigh the Maxson's need for in-house entertainment. Thus, the misleading image of America as the land of pervasive and inclusive postwar prosperity did not reach African Americans. The Maxsons provide a convincing challenge to this myth.

Although written in 1983, *Fences* fits comfortably among major American drama of the postwar era. Its adherence to certain dramatic conventions of the times earns it a place alongside works by a cadre of notable Anglo American playwrights of the so-called Silver Age of Drama. Critic Gerald Weales's pronouncement that "American drama, particularly in the fifties, has concentrated on the private instead of the public problem, has been psychological rather than social, has been explanatory rather than dramatic"[38] is just as applicable to *Fences* as it is to Arthur Miller's *Death of a Salesman* (1949), William Inge's *Picnic* (1953), and Tennessee Williams's *Cat on a Hot Tin Roof* (1955). In similar fashion, *Fences* exposes the private world of Troy Maxson and reveals the inner source of his blues. While the play's characters are not entirely divorced from the social milieu in which the play is set, greater emphasis is placed upon penetrating the psychological impetus of their experiences. This fuller presentation makes it just as possible to identify with Troy Maxson's humanity as it does the moving life experiences of Willie Loman, Madge Owens, or Brick Pollitt.

But *Fences* is a play about African Americans. As such, it also upholds the well-wrought tradition begun by Lorraine Hansberry's *A Raisin in the Sun* (1959). That is, *Fences* moves beyond those stereotypical representations of black Americans that had been so popular throughout much of the country's early history toward images that show them as pensive, compassionate, and ultimately complex individuals. In taking stock of the comparatively few significant postwar plays by African Americans, such as Alice Childress's *Florence* (1949), Louis Peterson's *Take a Giant Step* (1953), James Baldwin's *The Amen Corner* (1954), and, of course, Lorraine Hansberry's *A Raisin in the Sun* (1959), what becomes clear is that none fall outside of Gerald Weales's sweeping statements about drama of this decade. That means *Fences* is in good company as a domestic drama—one that conforms to 1950s structural conventions but that does so while capturing a more realistic cultural profile of African Americans.

That *Fences* evolves out of both Euro-American and African American dramatic traditions is not debatable. In fact, August Wilson publicly proclaims this truth in the very memorable public stance he took in delivering his 1996 speech, "The Ground On Which I Stand." Then, he asserted, "In one guise, the ground I stand on has been pioneered by . . . the American dramatists Eugene O'Neill, Arthur Miller and Tennessee Williams."[39] But one would do well not to interpret this praise song too literally. Although Wilson proudly credits three of America's most accomplished white playwrights in his acknowledgment, apparently his allegiance stops there. He is publicly forthright in admitting that he has not read the works of these playwrights. This denial, as one might well imagine, has been the source of considerable discourse that either insinuates or charges outright that August Wilson's *Fences* appropriates much from Arthur Miller's *Death of a Salesman*.[40]

The canon of now classic dramas by white American playwrights of the postwar period suggests that African Americans were inconsequential to the affairs of the white hegemony that, at that time, determined the nation's ideal domestic image. Given the prevalence of this trend, African Americans were essentially out of sight and out of mind and did not have similar aspirations for the American Dream—good jobs; supportive family; comfortable, safe homes; and access to institutions of higher education. All things considered, then, *Fences*, in effect, may be read as a subversive narrative that stands in accordance with August Wilson's artistic mission: "to simply restore that experience [the African American experience] to a primary role, thereby giving the facts of history a different perspective, and creating, in essence, a world in which the black American was the spiritual center."[41]

Fortunately, the 1950s was a pivotal decade—one that saw increasing organized resistance by African Americans to status quo racist practices in the United States. It also was a decade of significant legislation against discrimination. For example, in 1954 the Supreme Court agreed that separate education for black and white students produced significantly unequal opportunity for minorities, thus effectively destroying the legal basis for segregation within public schools. No doubt, Cory Maxson reaps the benefits of this legislation as the athletic scholarship offered to him is from a traditionally white college. Also in 1954, Malcolm X (formerly Malcolm Little) became minister of Black Muslim Temple No. 7 in Harlem, New York. While holding this position, he was catapulted into national limelight as the fiery, powerful spokesman for the Nation of Islam and a symbol of resistance for African Americans.

Two years prior to the 1957 fictional setting of *Fences*, an unforgettable Rosa Parks refused to give up her seat for a white rider and, thereby, precipitated a series of events that led to the civil rights movement. Also in 1955 the Reverend Martin Luther King, Jr. led Montgomery, Alabama, blacks in a boycott of the city's segregated buses. In 1959 lunch counter segregation was challenged. This spirit of resistance also manifests in several of Wilson's characters—most notably Troy, Cory, and Rose. Troy resists the semblance of emasculation that came with being shut out of major-league baseball. Cory resists his father's will to dictate his life. Rose ultimately resists her subordinated marital role that eclipses her sense of identity.

The 1960s mark a transformational phase in the life of August Wilson as a twenty-year-old African American male coming of age and finding his voice as an artist in urban America. In addition to defining the formal beginnings of his career as a writer, the year 1965 marked Wilson's aesthetic crossover to his cultural heritage as an African in America. This affirmation was the result of serendipity when, in that same year, he stumbled upon the lyrics of Bessie Smith's "Nobody Can Bake a Sweet Jelly Roll Like Mine" in a specialty record shop. The effect was profound. The year 1965 yielded two other profound changes in the young poet's life: his estranged biological father passed away, and the young man moved out of his mother's Pittsburgh house and into a rooming house on Bedford Avenue in that city.

The mid-1960s also found Wilson immersed in beliefs espoused by cultural nationalists. From 1965 to 1968, he encountered other black writers at Pittsburgh's Halfway Art Gallery and formed Pittsburgh's Center Avenue Poet's Theatre Workshop. According to Wilson, he and fellow black artists were about the business of "politicizing the community, or, as we [i.e., other artists] used to say in those days, 'raising the consciousness of people.'"

The culminating scene in *Fences* is set not so coincidentally in 1965—a watershed year in civil rights history. Dominated by the gunning deaths of Malcolm X, Medgar Evers, and Martin Luther King, Jr., and marked by the synergy of the Black Arts Movement, the decade saw marches and sit-ins as well as witnessed a very vocal campaign for a separate black aesthetic. On the national scene, the Vietnam War raged on and "Queen of Soul" Aretha Franklin basked in the title while regularly topping the charts.

But *Fences* does not draw our attention outward from the play to the very real political skirmishes of the 1960s involving African Americans and whites. In largely subtle ways, Wilson interprets the story of this revolutionary decade through the internal wars raging within his characters. The "hot winds of change," therefore, announce their presence in the impact they have upon the individual rather than upon the masses, thereby restricting our gaze to the Maxson family circle. For example, Troy Maxson's defiance against the discriminatory practices on his job anticipates Supreme Court rulings on employment conditions for African Americans. His noncompliance with the Jim Crow rules forced upon him by his employer is quite antithetical to the unfair, dehumanizing labor policies that his sharecropper father accepted without question. Cory's opportunity to attend college on an athletic scholarship is an indicator of pending legislation to relax college admission for African American youth. With such relaxed policies, schools became sites of promise for African American youth—the promise of continued challenge against the white hegemony. Further, Rose's articulation of discontent with her all-consuming roles as wife and mother is but a prelude to a larger scale national movement for women's rights. Each character seems detonated with the potential for revolution and resistance that so characterized the 1960s and beyond for at least ten more years.

While the year 1965 brings the death of *Fences* protagonist Troy Maxson, it is a year filled with signposts for August Wilson and a year that just so happens to be a significant marker in the annals of civil rights–related events for African Americans. Troy Maxson's passing paradoxically signals the beginning of a series of advances for African Americans. For example, the assassination of Malcolm X on February 21, 1965, delivered a stunning blow to his legions of followers who shared his belief that America had reneged on its promise to African Americans. In the wake of his death, however, fellow cultural nationalists and legions of followers who sympathized with this position galvanized forces to continue his legacy of resistance by any means necessary. A twenty-year-old August Wilson was among this notable group of artists along with Rob Penny,

Amiri Baraka, Ron Milner, Ed Bullins, Philip Hayes Dean, Richard Wesley, Lonne Elder III, Sonia Sanchez, and Barbara Ann Teer. These African American poets and playwrights rallied around the subversive position set forth by critic Larry Neal in what became a landmark proclamation of a new black aesthetic. Titled "The Black Arts Movement" (1968), this essay pushed for cultural self-sufficiency in the arts. Affirming Etheridge Knight's position, Neal writes,

> Unless the Black artist establishes a "Black aesthetic" he will have no future at all. To accept the white aesthetic is to accept and validate a society that will not allow him to live. The Black artist must create new forms and new values, sing new songs (or purify old ones); and along with other Black authorities, he must create a new history, new symbols, myths and legends and purify old ones by fire. And the Black artist, in creating his own aesthetic, must be accountable for it only to the Black people.[42]

Fences traces the historical roots of the Maxson family back to an era appropriately referred to as "the Nadir of the Black Experience."[43] Over the course of two acts, the play then takes its readers and spectators to the threshold of positive change for African Americans and concludes with a redemptive sign that all hope for the Maxson clan has been entrusted to another generation. Cory and Raynell inherit a world that had essentially cheated their father and their grandfather, but they would do well not to inherit their bitterness toward it. The play, which spans some 100 years, probes tense psychological battles that African Americans waged within individual family units. The intimate look at the dynamics that kept this black family together during this century is just as affirming of their humanity as an exploration of what unfortunately sets it asunder. As such, *Fences* chronicles Troy Maxson's psychological and ultimately physical emancipation from the effects of poverty, from paternal neglect and abuse, from physical incarceration, from his deferred dreams of major-league baseball, from workplace frustration, and from alienation within his home to complete spiritual and mental freedom, then death.

NOTES

1. This phrase coined by August Wilson describes the close correlation between his identity and his politics. It later became the title for the controver-

sial speech that he delivered at the 1996 annual conference of the Theatre Communications Group in Princeton, New Jersey.

2. In addition to *Fences*, as of this writing, August Wilson has completed seven other plays in his project to write ten plays about the African American experience in twentieth-century America. These include *Ma Rainey's Black Bottom* (1985), *Joe Turner's Come and Gone* (1988), *The Piano Lesson* (1990), *Two Trains Running* (1993), *Seven Guitars* (1996), *Jitney* (2001), and *King Hedley II* (written in 1999; currently unpublished).

3. Stanley Kauffman, "Bottoms Up," *Saturday Review* 11 (January/February 1985): 83.

4. Dennis Watlington, "Hurdling Fences," *Vanity Fair*, April 1989, 110.

5. Lorraine Hansberry, *To Be Young, Gifted, and Black: Lorraine Hansberry in Her Own Words*, adapted by Robert Nemiroff (New York: New American Library, 1970), 128.

6. Ralph Ellison, "Richard Wright's Blues," in *Shadow and Act* (New York: New American Library, 1964), 90.

7. Bill Moyers, *A World of Ideas* (New York: Doubleday, 1989), 168.

8. August Wilson, *Ma Rainey's Black Bottom* (New York: New American Library, 1985), 82.

9. *Call and Response: The Riverside Anthology of the African American Literary Tradition*, ed. Patricia Liggins Hill (Boston: Houghton Mifflin Company, 1998), 537.

10. Moyers, *World of Ideas*, 168.

11. Lloyd Richards, interview by author, tape recording, New York City, 1 June 2000.

12. Ibid.

13. Harry Elam, "August Wilson," in *African American Writers*, 2d ed., vol. 2, ed. Valerie Smith (New York: Scribner's, 2001), 848.

14. Kinshasha H. Conwill, introduction to *Memory and Metaphor: The Art of Romare Bearden, 1940–1987* (New York: Oxford University Press, 1991), ix.

15. Ibid., 9.

16. Ibid.

17. Similar to Leonardo Da Vinci's *Mona Lisa*, Grant Wood's regionalist painting *American Gothic* (1930) has been the subject of much speculation. Despite the anonymity of the familiar dour-faced white couple bearing an upright pitchfork, the work has become an American symbol of Puritan idealism, agrarianism, and what some perceive as early American traditions.

18. Peter Wolfe, *August Wilson* (New York: Twayne, 1991), 73.

19. Theatre Communications Group (TCG) is a New York–based national service organization that exists to strengthen, nurture, and promote the not-for-profit American theater.

20. Robert Brustein has been August Wilson's longtime adversary, harshly criticizing the playwright for writing plays that repeatedly emphasized the African American experience instead of the so-called "human experience." Brustein also

publicly disapproved of the well-known Lloyd Richards–August Wilson collaboration, especially while Richards held posts as Dean of the Yale School of Drama and Director of the Yale Repertory Theatre. Brustein regarded the partnership as a breech of Richards's contractual duties. Brustein is currently director of the American Repertory Theatre at the Loeb Drama Center, professor of English at Harvard, and drama critic for the *New Republic*.

21. Robert Brustein, "Unity from Diversity," *The New Republic*, 19–26 July, 1993, 29.

22. Ibid.

23. August Wilson, *The Ground On Which I Stand* (New York: Theatre Communications Group, 2001), 29.

24. Ibid., 31.

25. Margaret Booker, "Building Fences in Beijing," *American Theater*, May/June 1997, 50.

26. August Wilson, *Fences* (New York: New American Library, 1986), 51.

27. *Call and Response*, 1066.

28. Wilson, *Ma Rainey's Black Bottom*, 57.

29. Ishmael Reed, "In Search of August Wilson: A Shy Genius Transforms the American Theater," *Connoisseur*, March 1987, 93.

30. See Robert Peterson, *Only the Ball Was White* (Englewood Cliffs, NJ: Prentice-Hall, 1970), 16–18.

31. Jackie Robinson (born Jack Roosevelt Robinson in Cairo, Georgia, in 1919) is best known as the first African American baseball player to be admitted to the major leagues, thereby marking an end to segregated baseball.

32. Wilson, *Fences*, 10.

33. Josh Gibson, the right-handed batter and famed member of the Negro League, was touted in 1930s baseball lore and documented in sports coverage as the rival of white baseball legend Babe Ruth. Born in Beuna Vista, Georgia, in 1911, Gibson was known as a powerful home-run hitter whose awesome right-hand swings reportedly sent baseballs to distances far in excess of those hit by Ruth.

34. *Call and Response*, 1069.

35. Wilson, *Fences*, xvviii.

36. The origins of this phrase may be traced to Barnard Hewitt's expansive study *Theatre U.S.A.: 1665 to 1957* (New York: McGraw-Hill, 1959). In a chapter titled "Prosperity—Strictly Limited, 1940 to 1957," Hewitt gives a clear account of the art and politics of the postwar period in American theater.

37. Wilson, *Fences*, 32.

38. Gerald Weales, *American Drama since World War II* (New York: Harcourt, Brace & World, 1962), viii.

39. Wilson, *The Ground On Which I Stand*, 11.

40. For further information on the suspected influence of *Death of a Salesman* on *Fences*, see Michael Awkward's essay "The Crookeds with the Straights:

Fences, Race, and the Politics of Adaptation," in *May All Your Fences Have Gates*, ed. Alan Nadel (Iowa City: Iowa University Press, 1994), 205–29. Here, Awkward distills the issue in a note to his essay:

> [W]hatever the differences between Wilson's and Miller's family dramas (and they are significant), a recitation of some of the most central of *Fences'* concerns—intergenerational male conflict; the motivations for and far-reaching impact of marital infidelity; the consequences for the patriarchal figure of not achieving the American dream; a wife's victimization in and complicity with her husband's self-delusional efforts to maintain a positive sense of self despite evidence of his failures; paternal socialization of male offspring through sports; the thematic centrality of death; and finally, a concluding requiem in which mother, close male friend, and sons assess the meanings of the patriarch's life just before attending his funeral—suggests that Wilson's play would not have been possible in its present form without the precursoral presence of Miller's canonical white American middle-class family drama. (228)

See also Robert Massa's "Fence Mechanisms," *Village Voice*, May 1985.

41. August Wilson, "Characters behind History Teach Wilson about Plays," *New York Times*, 12 April 1992, sec. H5.

42. Larry Neal, "The Black Arts Movement," in *The Black Aesthetic*, ed. Addison Gayle (New York: Doubleday, 1971), 258.

43. The source of this phrase is Rayford Logan's *The Negro in American Life and Thought: The Nadir, 1877–1901* (New York: Dial, 1954).

2   Content

Garbageman Troy Maxson and Bono, his friend of 30 years, amuse themselves with work-related stories as they put another hectic workweek
behind them. It is Friday, and despite Troy's vivid recollections of friction
on his job, he and Bono are ready to celebrate. Troy possesses the unmistakable gift of storytelling, and he puts it to good use while entertaining
Bono with both humorous and serious events of his day. In one instance
he recounts in burlesque style an incredible story involving a fellow
employee's success at smuggling a huge watermelon past Mr. Rand, his
immediate supervisor. But in another instance, Troy shifts his thoughts
from this humorous incident to much more serious recollections of the
politically volatile racial circumstances that exist on his job. Troy, who
functions as an agent of change in his blue-collar job, has confronted his
garbage company's white officials and questioned the manner in which
they routinely assign African Americans to the backbreaking, more physically demanding labor of hoisting refuse and emptying it into trash com-
pactors. This is all the more disturbing, as Troy sees it, when white
workers routinely serve in the obviously less strenuous assignment as driv-
ers. It is only this scenario that temporarily sobers Troy and Bono from
their Friday night drinking ritual, but it also foreshadows a glimpse of
other demons that plague the 53-year-old ex–Negro League baseball
player.

Following Troy's passionate narrative about job-related woes, Bono
gently maneuvers the conversation toward Troy's increasingly apparent

philandering with "that Alberta gal."[1] As if exposing a raw and painful nerve, Bono picks away at Troy's tough exterior and ever so discretely compels him to confess to the more than casual friendship with this woman who has "stuck onto" him (1.1.63). Apparently Bono for some time has watched Troy show increasing affections for Alberta. As only a true friend could, Bono forewarns Troy of the potentially devastating results that his infidelity could bring to his marriage. But Troy, who openly admits to the affair to his cohort, repels Bono's warnings and continues to rendezvous with his Alberta in a relationship that soon becomes sexual.

Despite his affair and judging by all other accounts, Troy loves his wife Rose. In fact, professing his love for her in racy verbal foreplay becomes a distinctly male ritual—one that is made all the more risqué on occasions when Bono is present to witness Troy's playful allusions to his sexual prowess. His immediate goal in invoking this ritual is to leave no doubt in Bono's mind that he and Rose are as sexually active as they were some twenty years before when they first met. Less obvious goals, however, are to reverse temporarily the symbolic emasculation Troy experiences at his workplace and to regain some of the virility he has lost by being denied his dream of playing major-league baseball. His open and much exaggerated sexual exploits with his wife appear to partially compensate these losses. In addition, Troy's Neanderthal-like means of summoning his wife—although performed in jest—appears to bolster his wounded male ego. In language that may easily rile the most liberal of today's feminists, Troy summons Rose to him with "You suppose to come when I call you, woman" (1.4.43), and "This is men talk, woman" (1.1.5).

As Troy and Bono wrap up their post-workweek drinking party, Rose delivers news that, again, sobers up her husband: Their son Cory, who is adept at playing football, has caught the attention of college recruiters. But Troy adamantly opposes Cory's interest in the sport, arguing that "the white man ain't gonna let him get nowhere with that football" (1.1.8). It soon becomes clear that Troy, who feels that the game of baseball has not served him well, harbors deep-seated resentment for how African American men fare in this game and fears that his son would experience similar disappointment. He is quick to belittle the accomplishments of any baseball player—black or white—while noting that if he or any other member of the alternative Negro League team had been given the mere opportunity to play major-league baseball, then they, too, would have excelled at the sport.

Yet aside from Troy's personal motives for disliking the sport, Cory considers his father's rejection of his football aspirations to be evidence of

Troy stands ready to take a swing at Death. Rose (Mary Alice), Bono (Ray Aranha), and Troy (James Earl Jones). © 1987 Ron Scherl.

jealousy and a fear that his son might surpass him. Cory's deductions are, in fact, conceivable, for it is no secret that Troy's virtual shutout of major-league baseball dominates his psyche and has embittered him to anyone's inclinations to pursue the sport as a career option—especially his own son. So all encompassing are Troy's beliefs that he cannot see past them to consider that Cory's participation in college football will also make possi-ble the college education that he most assuredly cannot afford.

In the shadow of Troy Maxson's gigantic presence and domineering demeanor stands his supportive and extremely altruistic wife Rose. Her introduction to the play casts her in the role of Earth Mother as she pro-vides sustenance, wise counsel, and overall domestic stability. While Troy rants about Cory's recruitment opportunity, she becomes the quiet voice of tolerance and mediation. She listens to Troy's larger-than-life stories about bouts with "Death," but has no reservation to rein him in with her favorite dismissal "Troy lying" (1.1.13). She humbly endures Troy's embarrassing public details of their sex life. And, now, she uses her wiles to convince her husband to let Cory realize his dream.

At the height of one of Troy's trademark stories chronicling how he wrestled with and won a battle with Death, his older son from a previous marriage comes to borrow money. Lyons's visit is not coincidental. On the contrary, it is timed to coincide with Troy's payday. In the well-rehearsed ritual that follows, Lyons asks for money, Troy balks, and then offers a lecture on the benefits of getting a job. This is followed by exaggerated complaints about Troy's pitiful financial state, references to the poor maternal guidance Lyons has received, and finally, surrender of his entire $76.42 paycheck to Rose. As the designated accountant of the family, she peels off a ten-dollar bill and presents it to Troy's older son. Having once again succeeded in coaxing money from Troy, Lyons exits, but not before thanking Rose and prompting loud protests for doing so from Troy, the family's proud sole provider.

Troy's weekend ritual of surrendering his paycheck and handing over money to his older son sheds light on the complex father-son relationship between them. It also provides a portrait of Lyons, who essentially grew to manhood in a single-parent home. Troy, as we later learn, spent the bulk of Lyons's early life in jail serving time for robbery and murder. Consequently, Troy's long-term absence away from Lyons during his formative years awakens a sense of guilt in him and moves him to make compensatory gestures toward his now-adult son.

While the impact of the broken father-son relationship compels Troy to overcompensate his debt to Lyons—both in terms of tolerance and money—Troy's paternal aloofness manifests in Lyons in other noticeable ways. Although Lyons appears to be an all-around decent and likable guy, at thirty-something he is but a shell of a man. In stark contrast to his father, Lyons possesses no such concern for the responsibility that his father regards so highly. While Lyons has no reservations about borrowing money from his live-in girlfriend, Bonnie, Troy makes it poignantly clear that it is he who provides for his wife and family. While Lyons feigns inability to find employment and resigns himself to the relatively stress-free world of music, Troy methodically reports to work five days a week and just as methodically brings home his earnings along with a sack of potatoes when he punches out on Friday.

Troy's battle on his job escalates to a meeting with management. As friction on this front increases, Rose stays comfortably in the background of her home. While often humming a favorite religious song, she cooks, she cleans, and from time to time, she stops to diffuse domestic squabbles or to encourage Troy's efforts against inequities on his job. The only payment she commands for her selfless efforts is a fence to encircle her home. Between going to his job and making regular visits to Taylor's bar where he sees his mistress Alberta, Troy's often-interrupted task is to construct for Rose the wooden fortress she so craves.

Once the drunken revelry between the two hardworking African American men subsides, Troy's attention turns to domestic affairs. In particular, he intends to resume his sporadic efforts to fence in their yard for Rose. Yet his nerves are still frayed from the tension of his job, and Cory's absence makes him all the more irritable. Angered that Cory is not around to help saw wood for the fence and equally miffed by his son's neglect to do chores, Troy's emotions get the better of him. Rose steps in, as she so often does to harness his anger, but her soothing, indisputable logic is no cure for what really perturbs her husband. What lies beneath Troy's displaced anger is resentment that it is football that occasions his son's absence. Whether he realizes it or not, Troy attempts to live vicariously through his son. His biggest fear, then, is that Cory, who aspires to emulate his father's mastery of a sport, will, like him, be subjected to the racist whims of coaches, team owners, and fellow players. He also worries that, like him, Cory would be unfairly sidelined when someone else deems that his son is no longer useful in the sport. He fears that Cory would eventually become a leftover.

Just as Troy's orneriness over Cory's absence reaches its climax, his younger brother Gabriel enters singing a fruit vender's song. A severe injury to the head while enlisted in military service during World War II has reduced the mental capacity of this 46-year-old man to that of a child. One of the most profound effects of the metal plate that was surgically implanted in Gabriel's head is a distorted sensibility. Gabriel fantasizes that it is his responsibility to chase away hellhounds. Furthermore, he is convinced that he is Archangel Gabriel, whose task is to open Heaven's Pearly Gates to admit its newly deceased entrants. He delights in telling Rose about his close relationship with St. Peter and relishes reminding Troy that he has seen his name in St. Peter's heavenly ledger.

Gabriel lives with Troy, Rose, and Cory in a modest Pittsburgh dwelling purchased largely by the $3000 payment the government issued as reparation for his wound. Ever the opportunist, Troy gains control of Gabriel's money and invests it as a down payment on the home they now occupy. From time to time, Troy experiences fleeting moments of guilt for using Gabriel's money as he does, and at certain low points, he indulges in self-loathing for his actions. Although, at first, Gabriel occupies a private room in the Maxson home, he decides to move in with a neighborhood boarder, Miss Pearl, where he has access to two rooms, his own key, and the right to come and go as he pleases. Sensing that his brother was upset with him (and rightfully so), Gabriel opts to move out on his own. As befits her character, Rose worries that Gabriel "ain't eating right" (1.2.27), and offers him sustenance at every opportunity that she gets. She argues to Troy that he would receive better care at a mental institution, while Troy adamantly refuses to even consider confining his brother.

Tensions continue to smolder between Cory and his father as the aspiring football player returns home from practice. Aware of the potential for a verbal battle, Rose immediately moves to avert it by rushing Cory to complete his chores before his father returns. But it seems that flack about Cory's undone chores merely serves to illuminate Troy's larger campaign against his son choosing sports as a career. The friction between the two continues unabated as their conversation moves from Cory's neglect of chores to the very responsible decision not to purchase a television set. Cory's question "Hey Pop . . . why don't you buy a TV?" (1.3.31) sets in motion one of Troy's most memorable speeches underscoring the dominant theme of responsibility. To make his point, he presents Cory with a hypothetical dilemma: If you had $200 and a roof in dire need of repair, would you fix the roof or buy a television set? As a teenager never before faced with such real-life issues, Cory responds rather naively as expected. He would buy a television set. Then he would only worry about fixing the roof when it actually sprang a leak. Troy makes his point effectively (albeit ostentatiously) and ends with a compromise. He challenges Cory to earn one half of the $200 price tag for the television set and agrees to match it with the other $100.

Following Troy's illustrative lesson in responsibility and resumption of their fence building ritual, Cory turns the conversation to one that automatically riles his father: the goings on in major-league baseball. Cory's mere mention of the Pirates's winning streak unleashes in Troy a well-rehearsed and bitter response in which he, without exception, undermines baseball feats by all-white teams. His basic premise is that, if given a chance, African Americans, Hispanics, or other minorities prohibited from the game at that time could surely excel at it.

As they work together, Troy revisits the issue of Cory being sought after by college football scouts. As do each of Troy and Cory's conversations, this one leads to a lecture on work ethics, responsibility, and, most importantly, self-sufficiency from white control. But Troy soon learns that his advice to his son to "get your book-learning so you can work yourself up in that A&P or learn how to fix cars or build houses" (1.3.35) is futile.

Bent on playing football, Cory has, without Troy's knowledge, already quit his job at the grocery store.

In the wake of this revelation is one of the most emotionally charged scenes between the two generations of Maxson men. Cory interprets his father's obstinacy about football as an indication that he has never liked him. Troy's now-classic response, "Who the hell say I got to like you?" (1.3.37), exposes his most basic and lifelong beliefs about what constitutes responsibility. For him, love, duty, and responsibility need not necessarily be compatible. In the post–Civil War environment in which he was reared, love for an African American man was a sign of his vulnerability rather than his humanity. He imposes this ideology upon Cory and makes no concessions—even when it is clear that Cory aspires to emulate him. Yet lurking beneath the explosive rhetoric that Troy unleashes upon Cory are signs of Troy's own defeat. Inwardly he concedes to deprivation of his life's possibilities—what amounts to his deferred dreams.

Against Troy's mounting protests, Cory stubbornly forges ahead with after-school football practice. However, he still does so at the expense of neglecting his chores at home. Just as he heeds his mother's advice and slips away to clean his room, Troy and Bono enter the yard savoring recent news of Troy's unexpected promotion. While Bono expects that Mr. Rand will fire his friend when he summons him to his office, Troy ironically receives news of a promotion instead. The sweet reward for persistent complaints lodged against his supervisor is that Troy now moves into a driver position. Notwithstanding his illiteracy and his lack of a driver's license, Troy plans to accept this new post as "the first colored driver" (1.4.45)—a well-deserved honor for his proactive role on behalf of fellow African American laborers.

Troy gladly shares his news with Lyons, who surprisingly shows up to repay his father the $10 loan made earlier. By settling his debt with Troy as promised, Lyons catches his father off guard. So prepared is Troy to extend the terms of the loan or to add to it, he seems reluctant to accept the money outright from his son. At first, he insists that Lyons keep the money so that a future loan will not be imminent, but Lyons also insists that he be allowed to erase this obligation. Rose finally intercedes to end this verbal tug of war. She takes both Lyons's $10 payment *and* Troy's entire weekly paycheck.

Just as Rose settles financial matters between Troy and Lyons, Gabriel enters singing. He warmly greets "Troy's boy" (1.4.47) and offers an elaborate explanation of his imagined religious mission. According to

Gabriel, his day has been spent chasing away hellhounds and continuing his vigil of waiting for Judgment Day. At that time, he will discharge his duty to alert Saint Peter to open Heaven's gate. Aside from this vigilance, Gabriel holds onto the belief that Troy does not like him and offers this as his chief reason for seeking alternative accommodations. Of course, this admission draws a quick reaction from Troy, who is already sensitive about how he has mishandled his brother's affairs: "Hell, he could come and go as he please here. I wasn't stopping him. I ain't put no rules on him" (1.4.49). Ironically, Troy seems resentful that Gabriel pays rent money to Miss Pearl, especially considering that he has finagled his brother's entire disability pay to his advantage.

As she has done so many times before, Rose offers food to her company during what, at first, seems to be a most politically incorrect moment. Troy's mentally challenged brother Gabriel has sought alternative housing in reaction to Troy's totalitarian rule. Lyons invites Troy to be his guest at an upcoming performance that underscores his pursuit of a dead-end music career that his father, in actuality, deplores. Troy discovers that Cory has deceived him into thinking that he has convinced the store owner to reinstate him in his job at the A&P. Instead of work, Cory pursues football, minus the after-school activity that he regards as an unnecessary obstacle to his football stardom. At the very juncture at which these issues converge in this scene and appear destined to erupt into an all-out battle, Rose diverts the potential chaos by offering to the warring parties short ribs and sandwiches. Because her kind hospitality begs a civil response, her offer of refreshments serves to quell rising tensions and reminds her guests that regardless of their issues, they remain family.

What evolves instead out of this atmosphere rife with tension is a history lesson that illuminates Troy's own dysfunctional relationship with his father. In light of Cory's insubordination, Troy uses the opportunity to expound on the consequences of disobedience. In doing so, he provides further information about his own troubled past, which makes possible empathy, if not support, for his militaristic approach to fathering.

Troy and Bono temporarily digress from the circumstances at hand to reminisce about poor relationships that each has endured with their less than exemplary biological fathers. Bono reveals that because his womanizing father carried on numerous affairs, he never had the chance to bond with him. Because his father so freely engaged in "searching out the New Land" (1.4.50), as it was called, rather than performing any fatherly duties, Bono carefully avoids becoming a father himself. In his apparently successful marriage to Lucille, he redefines and reconstructs the male role in the nuclear family to include the responsible, loving husband and the devoted wife—sans the adorable children.

Troy's recollections of his father are no less despicable. He recounts an episode from his past when, as a young boy entering puberty, he met with his father's fury and discovered what manner of man he really was. Underscoring this is a shocking incident that marked the beginning of his independence from the selfish, brutal, emotionally sterile, despotic rule of his father. When the young Troy Maxson shirked his duty to plow in favor of a sexual liaison with a young girl who has captured his attention, he sets off a chain reaction that ends in an exchange of blows between his father and him. When the mule that he takes to the field escapes and makes its way back home, Troy's father comes to investigate. In addition to the unturned earth, he finds his son nestled on the ground on the verge of sexual intercourse. What happens next so greatly confounds the young Troy that he never returns to his father's house. Instead of unleashing his fury upon his son, the senior Maxson runs Troy away and attempts to rape his young female acquaintance. Troy steps in to defend her and unfortunately remembers nothing more of this battle. He awakens with his trusted dog Blue licking his swollen face. At fourteen, Troy literally walks away and tries to become a man without his father's help.

But choosing to become a man at such a young age exacts its price on Troy. Following the split with his father, he gave up on life in the South and hitchhiked his way up North where jobs were scarce and decent housing was equally hard to come by. It was during this initiation phase that Troy met Lyons's mother, and the two soon became parents. Desperate for food, he resorted to petty stealing, but later faced with the support of a wife and infant son, he found it necessary to graduate to larger-scale operations. Troy responded to this added responsibility—not by finding employment—but by stepping up his criminal activity. On one occasion as he attempted to rob his victim, Troy was shot. Because he retaliated by killing his attacker, he was convicted of homicide and sentenced to fifteen years in prison. Unable to cope with their separation, Lyons's mother abandoned Troy while he served his time. At the end of his sentence, Troy came out certain that fifteen years behind bars had "cured me of that robbing stuff" (1.4.55). It was then that his life took a major turn for the better; he met and married Rose.

The warm and fuzzy atmosphere left in the wake of Troy's and Bono's bonding tales of paternal neglect soon dissipate with the onset of a more immediate father-son showdown. Cory comes home livid that Troy has paid a visit to his school and let it be known among coaches and school administrators that his son could no longer play football for his team. Cory's explosive anger emboldens him to stand face-to-face with his father to verbalize his absolute disgust at what Troy has secretly done: "You don't never want to listen to nobody. And then you wanna go and do this to me!" (1.4.57) ". . . Just cause you didn't have a chance. You just scared I'm gonna be better than you, that's all" (1.4.58). But Troy feels perfectly justified in stymieing the boy's efforts on the basis that Cory lied to him about maintaining his job at the A&P. Cory, on the other hand, interprets his father's devious actions as proof that Troy feels threatened that his son will most assuredly surpass him in an arena that Troy regards as exclusively his. Cory's tough talk changes the rules between the two Maxson men. Now that he has gathered enough stamina to verbally confront his father, the dynamics of their initial father-son relationship shift and turn completely adversarial. Troy likens these new circumstances to being "in the batter's box" (1.4.58). There is no way to reverse or to erase what has happened between them.

Still upset at Troy's preemptive move against him, Cory sulks while he idly swings a bat in his yard. Despite the recent confrontation with his father, he announces that he fully intends to stay with his team. He soon learns from Rose that his chief adversary, once again, is off attending to the business of bailing Gabriel out of confinement for disturbing the peace. Promising to further reason with Troy, Rose engages Cory's help with household chores.

Troy, too, remains defiant. As soon as he returns home from paying the obligatory $50 fee to release Gabriel to his custody, he demands that Cory "get his butt out here" (2.1.59) to resume work on the fence. Bono joins Cory and Troy as the three prepare the wood for the job at hand. But as is often the case, their talk of immediate and tangible things evolves into more philosophical ruminations. Such is the case as Troy and Bono quibble over the type of wood that best suits this outdoor construction. The issue is whether to use hardwood, which is, according to Troy, better suited to withstand the elements, or to use pinewood, which is, according to Bono, just as dependable. When Bono argues that the relative longevity of pinewood qualifies it as a more than appropriate building material, Troy interprets Bono's view as a sarcastic commentary upon his own mortality. He retorts, "How you know how long I'm gonna be here, nigger? Hell, I might just live forever" (2.1.60). Troy's extreme sensitivity to even remote references to his physical stamina foreshadows his ongoing battle with Death.

Cory provides additional cause to continue the philosophical moment between Troy and Bono. In questioning what is behind his mother's

Troy and Cory in one of many standoffs. James Earl Jones and Courtney Vance.
© 1987 Ron Scherl.

desire for a fence, he elicits a response from Bono that clearly underscores one of the play's most pervasive themes. When Troy admits that
he, too, is at a loss to explain Rose's designs for a fence, Bono puts the
matter into helpful perspective: "Some people build fences to keep people out . . . and other people build fences to keep people in. Rose wants
to hold on to you all. She loves you" (2.1.61). Failing to grasp the profundity of Bono's figurative analysis, Troy quickly dismisses it and presses
Cory to go locate a saw.

Bono uses this intuitive assessment of what drives Rose's need for a
fence as a segue to resurrect his concern that Troy's relationship with
Alberta appears to have taken a serious turn. As Bono explains, up to this
moment, the lifelong friendship between Troy and him has been based on
his certainty that Troy "knows what he's doing" (2.1.62). Because of his
high regard for Troy's usual levelheadedness about life's choices, Bono
admits that he set out to emulate him. However, Bono's nostalgic admis-
sions about what sustained their friendship belie a powerful subtext.
What Bono conveys in his characteristically subtle way of putting his
friend in check is his fear that Troy has lost sight of what is important to

him and is fast moving toward inflicting irreparable damage upon his marriage and, most importantly, hurting Rose.

Bono's tactful strategy of raising the issue of Troy's illicit affair pays off. His friend drops all defenses and acknowledges what they both know to be true: he is hopelessly in love with Alberta, and he has no intentions of ending the relationship. In response to Bono's alarm, Troy tries to explain the selfish logic that he constructs to support this extramarital sexual fling, even as he admits to loving his wife. Troy confides with Bono that Alberta provides him with certain comforts that are not possible in his current marital arrangement. While his marriage to Rose prompts ever-present thoughts of responsibility, his affair with Alberta places no such demands upon him. He appears comfortable in his decision to continue the affair, for he governs himself according to his own personalized code of ethics that sanctions such behavior as long as it "feels good." He admits, "I can sit up in her house and laugh out loud . . . and it feels good. It reaches all the way down to the bottom of my shoes" (2.1.69). Despite Troy's warped, self-serving rationale for continuing to cheat on Rose, Bono beseeches him to reconsider the consequences of his actions.

After absorbing Bono's advice, talk between Troy and Bono turns again to completing the increasingly elusive fence. They both realize that at Troy's current rate, something more is needed to motivate him to bring closure to this project. That "something more" turns out to be an outright wager from Bono. He challenges Troy by agreeing to buy his wife Lucille a refrigerator upon Troy's completion of Rose's long-awaited fence. For years they both have bragged about providing these luxuries for the women they love, but, so far, neither has delivered. Troy accepts Bono's challenge, and willingly accepts that his friend may no longer assist his efforts. The thrill of competition, then, puts Troy back on track to keep his promise to Rose.

Gabriel's pitiable circumstances are again emphasized as Troy explains to Rose the exact details of his recent apprehension and subsequent detention down at police headquarters. With each episode of this nature, Troy is faced with an issue that looms even greater: whether he should commit his brother to a mental institution. Outwardly Troy appears to detest any notion of confining his brother, arguing, "The man done had his life ruined fighting for what? And they wanna take and lock him up. Let him be free. He don't bother nobody" (2.1.65). On one hand, Rose struggles with the need to maintain Gabriel's health with regular meals that go along with a hospital setting. On the other, she acknowledges this gentle, confused man's need to be unrestricted and free to move about on his own. Rose offers Troy lunch, and the matter is temporarily suspended.

Nothing can prepare Rose for what Troy interrupts his lunch to tell her. Their eighteen-year marriage suffers a major setback with Troy's admission that he and some woman are expecting a child: "I'm gonna be somebody's daddy" (2.1.66). His announcement rips the foundation out from under Rose, shatters her domestic tranquility, and transforms her into a vocally defiant woman. As the initial shock of Troy's ruthless philandering settles in, Rose realizes the full ramifications of his actions. Not only has he been involved in this affair for some time, but he also did so while carrying on his husbandly duties with her. And now he has the gall to come to her only after a child has been introduced to their illegitimate union. Rose seethes with anger, but she is able to keep that anger at bay long enough to gently nudge Gabriel into the house away from the explosive scene that is about to occur.

The usually loquacious Troy now fumbles for words to lessen the sting of his news. However, all that he can muster are weak, insensitive remarks that underscore his unilateral thinking. Ironically, he tries to console Rose by informing her that this woman provides things that she cannot. To make matters worse, he admits to Rose that his affair with Alberta represents his last-ditch effort to squeeze from life some of the joy and passion that baseball had denied him. The baseball imagery he co-opts to explain himself seems laughable given the gravity of his transgressions: "Then when I saw that gal . . . she firmed up my backbone. And I got to thinking that if I tried . . . I just might be able to steal second. Do you understand after eighteen years I wanted to steal second" (2.2. 70).

Troy's woefully inadequate words pale significantly when measured against Rose's carefully aimed verbal blows. In no uncertain terms, she lets Troy know how much she has invested in their marriage, even at the expense of neglecting her own personal growth. For eighteen years she has held onto Troy. Along the way she has stood beside him, fully satisfied to be eclipsed by his massive shadow. During this time, she also held onto the belief that their lives together would improve. However, long after it became clear that she and Troy were "[standing] in the same spot" (2.1.70), she chose to remain.

This moment of reckoning for Troy reveals much about both him and Rose. In Troy's case, we learn that, for whatever reason, he has become oblivious to the laws of cause and effect. Hence, he also appears oblivious to the consequences of his actions. His egotistical way of thinking explains how he can subvert Cory's football plans under the guise of doing what is right for his son. It also explains how he can now boldly confront his wife with not only the news that he has cheated on her, but also the shocking revelation that he and his mistress are expecting a child. In an exercise that further dismays Rose, he carefully tries to justify his affair in the face of a woman who has, for nearly two decades, been a good and faithful wife to him and who has also born him one son and functioned in somewhat of a surrogate role to the son of a previous marriage.

Troy's reckoning also lures Rose Maxson completely "outside of the box" of the 1950s wife and mother. At the risk of breaking with the pre-vailing image that both culture and society prescribed for the black woman of this era, Rose steps out of her well-defined role and finds her own voice. That voice allows her to clearly articulate the extent to which she has consciously subordinated her will to that of her husband. That voice also allows her to locate a space of her own now that the space that she had shared with Troy has been violated. Rose's explosive response to Troy provides cathartic release as well. Her passionate, soul-searching speech makes it impossible to consider her as his helpless victim.

Troy appears attentive for much of Rose's testimony. However, when she accuses him of being anything but the responsible man that he so repeatedly and so vociferously claims to be, he reacts violently. As Rose concludes her verbal assault, she takes a parting shot at Troy's cherished image as giver and provider; she accuses him of being a taker also. This triggers immediate anger in Troy, who responds by grabbing Rose's arm and squeezing it to the point of hurting her. Her painful protest brings Cory to her defense, and, as expected, Cory intervenes on behalf of his mother. But in doing so, he strikes out at Troy only to deliver a misfired blow to his chest. Stunned by his son's physical retaliation, Troy upgrades Cory's aggressiveness toward him to "strike two." Troy knows that strike three or a climactic confrontation between Cory and him is inevitable.

Six months lapse after domestic mayhem infiltrates the Maxson home, yet the family's tensions remain. Troy has taken to making fleeting appearances at his home only to dash out shortly afterward to go to his favorite bar or to Alberta's place. This pattern upsets Rose, who having grown increasingly weary of their sham of a marriage, complains to Troy that her tolerance for what has become status quo has worn thin.

As Troy prepares to leave the house again—this time to visit the very pregnant Alberta, who has gone into the hospital, perhaps to have their baby—Rose again confronts him. This time, however, she seeks answers to an unconfirmed rumor that he had completed and signed necessary paperwork to finally have Gabriel committed. In addition to bearing the weight of Troy's gross infidelity and his behind the scenes maneuvers against Cory, Rose now contends with Troy's latest action. Just as she is about to lash out at him one more time, the telephone rings.

The telephone call brings news of Alberta's death in childbirth, but not before she delivers a healthy baby girl. The separate life that Troy constructs outside of his home comes crashing down. Grief stricken, he temporarily displaces his reaction to this news by verbally chastising Rose for wondering out loud who would take care of the details of Alberta's funeral. His anger soon moves away from Rose toward his constant foe, Death. In an elaborate apostrophe, he personifies Death and challenges this antagonistic nonentity to a future match between just the two of them:

> Alright . . . Mr. Death. See now . . . I'm gonna tell you what I'm gonna do. I'm gonna take and build me a fence around this yard. See? I'm gonna build me a fence around what belongs to me. And then I want you to stay on the other side. See? You stay over there until you're ready for me. Then you come on. Bring your army. Bring your sickle. Bring your wrestling clothes. I ain't gonna fall down on my vigilance this time. You ain't gonna sneak up on me no more. When you ready for me . . . when the top of your list say Troy Maxson . . . that's when you come around here. (2.2.77)

Troy goes down to claim his now-motherless baby daughter, but soon realizes that he must turn to Rose, of all people, for help in raising her. As he approaches his home, the weight of the moment is so pronounced that only the blues can fully capture the profound emotions he bears. The combination of his ruthless, self-serving definition of responsibility combined with his unconditional pursuit of what makes him feel good has now rendered Troy a tragic figure of his own making. The image of a big strapping man standing alone in his yard cradling a wee infant in his arms with no prospect for his next move is indeed tragic and humbling. Even more tragic is that he must bring home the emblem of his infidelity to the very same woman whom he has so humiliated.

But Troy does manage to muster up the nerve to plead his case before Rose:

> Rose . . . I'm standing here with my daughter in my arms. She ain't but a wee bittie little old thing. She don't know nothing about

Troy finally realizes the consequences of his actions. James Earl Jones as Troy Maxson. © 1987 Ron Scherl.

grownups' business. She innocent . . . and she ain't got no mama. . . . So, I guess what I am saying is . . . I'd appreciate it if you'd help me take care of her. (2.3.78–9)

In a not soon to be forgotten moment of supreme altruism, Rose accepts Troy's proposition to become a mother to the daughter she later names Raynelle. Yet the condition under which Rose concedes to Troy's request carries with it a major stipulation: She will love the child and mother it as if it were her own, but as far as marital relations are concerned, she will have nothing further to do with Troy. With this extra clause in her agreement, new rules have been set, clear boundaries have been drawn.

Rose enjoys her new role as mother but goes about her daily business while giving Troy only a glancing acknowledgment. This whole new scheme of things that came in the wake of his reckless actions begins to take their toll on him. He is bothered that no one is home to greet him and that the once gregarious family has now become splintered. Of course, Gabriel is now living in an institution; Rose busies herself with the baby and with church activities; Cory stays out of his father's way as much as he can; and Lyons's visits are as infrequent as ever. Even Bono's visits have noticeably tapered off. Troy is often alone.

But Bono does return to check on his old friend. He finds Troy singing a favorite song about a trusted dog to comfort himself in his loneliness. In an effort to avoid discussing the quagmire that Troy's life has become, Bono initiates small talk about the workplace and about honoring previous wagers they made to each other. In sharp contrast to the numerous drinking bouts he used to share with his friend, Bono now refuses Troy's offer to share his bottle of gin. The conversation is strained, and Bono soon bids Troy farewell.

Strike three for Cory comes quickly when he and Troy spar for the third time. This time Cory unceremoniously tries to get past his father on the steps of their home. Cory's tone of disrespect, which Troy quickly intuits, reflects simmering animosity between the two of them as well as Cory's renewed hatred of him for running roughshod over his mother's emotions. Before he gives Cory access to the house, Troy demands that he speak to him in a respectful tone. However, being just as adamant, Cory refuses to acquiesce because he feels that Troy "don't count around here no more" (2.4.85). The battle lines are drawn here, and the war of words that erupts between them soon turns physical.

Cory now has no reservations about pressing his father to respond to a list of violations committed against the Maxson family. Clearly this becomes Cory's moment; for the first time Troy has to listen. Cory has essentially lost respect for his father and now he seizes this opportunity to point out what he finds most problematic about this man whom he has tried to emulate all of his life. In the heated exchange that follows, Cory manages to take a few verbal swipes at Troy including what he saw as Troy's extortion of Gabriel's money to buy the house that he brags is his. Like Rose, he troubles Troy's deluded concept of responsibility, arguing that rather than doing anything for him, Troy had actually been more of an obstacle in his life. But what really riles Troy during this showdown is Cory's mention of recent events concerning his mother. When Cory spews "I don't know how she stand you . . . after what you did to her" (2.2.87), Troy quickly becomes more defensive wanting to keep Rose out of their battle.

A shoving match ensues, and Cory becomes increasingly brazen in the so far verbal battle against his father. Cory's adrenaline increases as he taunts his father by calling him crazy and refusing to leave the yard. Finally, in an act of total defiance, Cory yells "I ain't going nowhere! Come on . . . put me out! I ain't scared of you" (2.2.88). It is at this point when any demarcation between father and son is erased, and the verbal battle becomes physical. Cory grabs Troy's prized bat—the most visible symbol of his father's deferred dreams—and swings it at him. Realizing the gravity of his son's gesture, Troy wrestles the bat from Cory and stops short of bashing his head in with it. This is the third strike, the final straw. Cory walks away in complete disgust. Troy summons his old friend Death and notifies him that he is now ready.

Apparently Death decides to accept Troy's invitation, for the final scene of the play opens with the Maxson family preparing to attend Troy's funeral. As Rose tells it, Troy fell over and died while swinging at the familiar rag target that hung from a tree in the front yard. It is 1965 and much has happened since that no-holds-barred struggle between Cory and Troy. Raynelle has grown into a precocious little seven-year-old girl. Cory, who is about to marry, has gone away to become a respected corporal in the United States Marines. Lyons is serving a three-year jail sentence for forging checks. While away, his girlfriend leaves him for good.

Rose is busy readying Raynelle and herself for Troy's funeral when Cory makes a surprise appearance. Apparently he has been gone for some time because she scarcely can contain her enthusiasm at seeing him. After making a fuss over Cory, she stops only to introduce Raynelle to her brother and to offer him food. She repeatedly has to coax Raynelle inside to finish dressing. However, Raynell is both curious and inquisitive, stalling to check her newly planted seedlings in the garden and to chat with the strange man, whom she later learns is her brother. She and Cory bond immediately and seal their new relationship by singing together one of Troy's favorite songs about his good old dog named Blue.

As if Rose does not have enough to contend with, Cory soon reveals that he does not intend to go to his father's funeral. His shocking statement slows her process of dressing considerably as she tries to reason with him. Despite how their marriage disintegrated because of Troy's transgressions, Rose defends him admirably before Cory and holds him in high esteem. In a moving narrative of her past with Troy she explains to him how and why she allowed herself to be subsumed by Troy. She also sheds light on her decision to accept Raynelle as her daughter and to raise her as best she knows how.

Her patience with Cory pays off, for shortly after her talk with him, he begins making gestures that indicate a change of heart. Rose's honesty moves him to his decision to honor his father by attending his funeral. A final telephone call from Reverend Tolliver affords Cory and Raynelle one more opportunity to catch up on lost time as brother and sister. When Rose leaves to answer the call, they discuss the identity of the dog whose name recurs in Troy's favorite tune and wind up singing the complete song just before they depart for the church.

Contrary to what most believed, Gabriel gains release from the mental hospital that houses him to attend his brother's funeral. Entering from the alley with "Hey, Rose!" (2.2.100), he is well received by all gathered. The Maxsons feel a sense of completeness with Gabriel's arrival, and they embrace him in the warm glow left by Cory's reconciliation. They all respond to the healing atmosphere so lovingly established by Rose, who demonstrates her own reconciliation with the past as well. The family is now poised to pay their last respects to their brother, husband, and father, Troy.

But Gabriel must first perform the duty for which he has trained much of his life. It is a duty that many have regarded as affirmation of his dementia, but it is a job that Gabriel does not take lightly. He grabs his trumpet and assumes a stand that allows him to deliver an unmistakable blast. Yet no sound comes from the instrument, and Gabriel stands baffled for a moment before beginning "a slow, strange dance, eerie and life giving. A dance of atavistic signature and ritual" (2.2.101). After throwing off Lyons's attempt to console him, Gabriel tries to deliver a song, but, just as his trumpet had failed him, his voice seems not up to the task.

But Gabriel seems to have entered a spiritual realm that his witnesses cannot fathom through their senses. While mute to their ears and invisible to their eyes, this world seems to have a direct line to Gabriel, who having failed at his trumpet, now resorts to body movement and song. Apparently these alternate forms of supplication prove to be effective measures, for as he concludes his dance and awkwardly attempts to speak, the Pearly Gates fling open. As the play so ends, we are led to believe that the flawed but very human Troy goes through them. Gabriel puts a period on it all with "That's the way that go!" (2.2.101).

NOTE

1. August Wilson, *Fences* (New York: Plume, 1986), 3. All other references to *Fences* will be made within the text.

3   Texts

The definitive version of *Fences* (1987) is the product of a number of issues that August Wilson faced head-on in an effort to hone his skills as a playwright and come to terms with his own aesthetic position. As the third play in his developing ten-play dramatic series featuring issues pertinent to twentieth-century African Americans, *Fences* marked a milestone for Wilson in the commercial arena and unquestionably affirmed his mastery of the art of playwriting. So well received was the play for its artistic merit that in 1987 the renowned Pulitzer Committee bestowed upon it the highly prestigious Pulitzer Prize for Drama. During that same year, it received the Tony Award for Best Play and the Drama Critics Circle Award.

But for Wilson, even more important than major awards and an impressive 526-performance run of the play during the 1987 Broadway season was the assurance that his work was continuous and increasingly prolific. Even after receiving a host of major awards, he still considered himself as a struggling playwright and disciplined himself as such. Determined not to suffer the fate of the one-play playwright, Wilson began *Fences* on the heels of his whirlwind success with *Ma Rainey's Black Bottom* (1984) an earlier play that had been recently successfully staged at the Eugene O'Neill Theater Center's National Playwrights Conference in Waterford, Connecticut. As Joan Herrington notes, "[O]n the bus heading home from the Conference, he wrote the first scene of *Fences*."[1]

It would not be too much of a stretch of the imagination, then, to draw parallels between tensions surrounding the genesis of August Wilson's

Fences and the tension that precedes the oyster's singular masterpiece, the pearl. From the outset of his career as a playwright, Wilson pushed himself toward greatness and longevity in the profession. As he began to enjoy some measure of success in the theater, he shunned mediocrity, kept a low profile, and was determined to be well on his way toward completing his next play even as he enjoyed the spotlight for a work that, at the same time, played to huge Broadway audiences. *Fences* follows such a course as its inception coincided with *Ma Rainey's* move from the O'Neill Center in Waterford, Connecticut, to increased attention at the Yale Repertory Theatre School in New Haven. Thus, Wilson was extremely conscientious about being taken seriously as a playwright—so much so that he looked past certain exterior indications such as box office receipts and standing room only audiences in favor of focusing upon internal structural weaknesses that more than one critic cited as *Ma Rainey's Black Bottom's* most troublesome flaws. In particular, reviewers charged that *Ma Rainey's Black Bottom* was bifurcated in its focus. That is, they felt that the play presented blues great Gertrude "Ma" Rainey seemingly competing for center stage with members of her all-male band. Wilson's detractors were also troubled by the play's crowded cast of characters and its refusal to present at least one three-dimensional character on whom audiences could focus their concern.

These seeds of irritation from critics of *Ma Rainey's Black Bottom* equally irritated Wilson and eventually prompted him to write a better play. That better play turned out to be *Fences*, a resounding answer to his chorus of doubters. To convince them as well as himself that he could produce a more complex, more human figure, than, say, Levee, Ma Rainey, or Toledo, Wilson imagined a character who both epitomized working-class African Americans of the 1950s and, at the same time, assumed the tragic stature more commonly reserved for aristocracy.

Unquestionably *Fences* is about Troy Maxson, and that truth resounds throughout the play as we are immersed in his severely limited world and gain insight about his egotistical pattern of behavior. Other characters, such as Bono, Cory, Lyons, and even Rose, serve as mere backdrop to Troy's massive presence. That is to say, much of what they are about in the play is determined by their relationships with Troy: Bono is *Troy's* friend; Alberta is *Troy's* mistress; Gabriel is *Troy's* brother; Cory and Lyons are *Troy's* sons; Raynelle is *Troy's* daughter; Rose is *Troy's* wife. With the notable exception of Cory, it appears that Troy is the center of each of their universes. Thus, *Fences* allows Wilson to succeed admirably in challenging the opinions of critics who had earlier scoffed at his thinly drawn characters. Perhaps more than anyone, James Earl Jones, who brought Troy to the Broadway stage, can attest to the multidimensional nature of Troy's character. In an interview following a 1985 performance of *Fences* at the Yale Repertory Theatre, Jones noted,

> It's been hard to modulate Troy's levels of energy, to measure the extent to which he is deeply angry and the extent to which he is just loud-mouthing. I have not found yet where his depths and his highs are. He's like a manic-depressive; he's up and he's down.[2]

To address issues pertinent to the uneven, scattered focus so characteristic of Wilson's previous plays, he looked to the family structure as a means of containment and organic unity. Rather than the gregarious settings and transient characters that defined his earlier works, *Fences* takes place in the front yard of a home occupied by a single African American family unit sharing the same last name (if not the same mothers). According to Wilson, "What you have in *Fences* is a very specific situation, a black family which the forces of racism have molded and shaped but you also have husband-wife, father-son."[3] Troy's conflict, and indeed that of his entire family, emerges out of his concept of responsibility as it relates to core family values within this unit.

On a cultural level, *Fences* is symptomatic of an even deeper irritation that haunts Wilson. That is white society's tendency to profile African American men as irresponsible, lazy, shiftless—tendencies that Wilson flatly rejects. He vents in a 1989 interview,

> White America looks at black America in this glancing manner. They pass right by the Troy Maxsons of the world and never stop to look at them. They talk about niggers as lazy and shiftless. Well, here's a man with responsibilities as prime to his life. I wanted to examine Troy's life layer by layer and find out why he made the choices that he made.[4]

This methodical approach is part of Wilson's larger campaign to expose false and misleading stereotypes about African Americans by "stripping away layer by layer the surface to reveal what is underneath—the real person, the whole person."[5] The genesis of *Fences*, therefore, was inspired not only by Wilson's desire to create a more complex character but also by an even greater mission to deconstruct the prevailing myth of the irresponsible black man.

No doubt, the myth of the lackadaisical, irresponsible African American male has its roots in the era in African American history immediately following the Civil War and the subsequent emancipation of slaves. During that time many of the negative images of newly freed slaves that were promoted by whites in various public positions grew out of ignorance, fear, and a need to portray African American men as nonthreatening and docile. His supposed lack of a work ethic and his aversion to roles that required sustained diligence made him predictable to nervous antebellum white southerners who feared that their historical claims to intellectual and moral superiority would be challenged. Harriet Beecher Stowe's *Uncle Tom's Cabin* did much to solidify this image and to actually endear it to white society in the later half of the nineteenth century as well as in the early years of the twentieth century. Wilson's work in *Fences* is to challenge this lingering, more-than-a-century-old stereotype.

Wilson was so determined to analyze and lay to rest the myth of the irresponsible African American male that his commitment to do so greatly influenced his processes of writing and revising *Fences*. Demonstrating that Troy Maxson, with all of his flaws, is a responsible black man commanded a great deal of Wilson's attention and put his playwriting skills to the test. Joan Herrington notes in her study *I Ain't Sorry for Nothin' I Done* that advancing the theme of responsibility was the guiding principle during numerous revisions of *Fences*. What each character says and does is carefully orchestrated to portray Troy Maxson as a responsible African American man. For example, Lyons undergoes several changes before he becomes the perfect foil to his dogmatic, indeed ostentatious, counterpart Troy. As Herrington notes, "Wilson's efforts to define Troy's actions and attitudes began by using Lyons, the son of his first marriage, to highlight Troy's sense of familial responsibility."[6] While Lyons apparently has no concept of a work ethic, preferring instead the spiritual satisfaction that comes with his music, Troy is as dependable as clockwork in reporting to work each day and turning over his $76.42 paycheck to Rose at the end of each week. Whereas Troy boasts of his ability to provide for his family, Lyons depends on his gainfully employed girlfriend Bonnie for subsistence.

At some point during the conceptualization phase of writing *Fences*, August Wilson discovered a symbolic equivalent that effectively portrayed in a single visual image the theme of responsibility that he so persistently sought to impart in the play. As he examined a 1969 collage by Romare Bearden, he realized that herein was the face of the responsible black man. Bearden's patchwork canvas depicting what appears to be a tenant farmer and his wife features a man holding a baby—an image that immediately calls to mind the picture of Troy Maxson standing helplessly alone in his own family's front yard while cradling his infant daughter shortly after the death of his mistress and the baby's mother. Guided by his concern that images of black men still suffered much distortion at the hands of white hegemony, Wilson found in the work of Bearden an artistic release or road map to both shape and guide his response to this misleading generalization. Thus, Bearden's deceptively simple work took the playwright deep into the recesses of his mind where he contemplated the anatomy of responsibility. As Harry Elam observes, "Wilson sought to subvert the dominant culture's representations of African American men as irresponsible, absentee fathers," and—with the example of his own irresponsible German father as an opposite model from which to work—responded by creating Troy Maxson, "a larger-than-life figure who feels an overwhelming sense of duty and responsibility to his family. In fact, it is around his concepts of duty and responsibility that the character of Troy is problematized."[7] Bearden's collage, then, provided Wilson with the spiritual, emotional, and creative impetus to write a play that challenged hegemonic constructions of black masculinity.

August Wilson's ideas about the responsible black man also correspond directly to lessons he learned from his African American stepfather David Bedford, who died in 1969. Though Wilson did not know it at the time, Bedford was fond of him and showed that fondness largely by intervening in the young man's personal affairs. Bedford strongly disapproved of Wilson's decision to quit high school football in the early 1960s, and that disapproval grew into a long-standing feud between the two. Caught up in the revolutionary fervor so prevalent among young black men during the politically and socially turbulent 1960s, Wilson flatly rejected Bedford's authoritarian position over him and went further to dismiss his stepfather's entire generation as compromisers and accommodationists. It was only in hindsight that Wilson learned what was really at the root of Bedford's strict control. While overhearing someone reminisce about Bedford's past, he realized why this man had been so unyielding. His admiration for this black man (albeit posthumous) increased significantly. As critic Samuel French notes,

> Bedford, it turned out, had been a high school football star in the 1930s, and had hoped a sports scholarship would lead to a career in medicine. But no Pittsburgh college would give a black player a grant and Bedford was too poor to pay his own way. To get the

money, he decided to rob a store, and during the theft he killed a man. For the 23 years before he met Wilson's mother, Bedford had been in prison. By the time he was free, only a job in the city Sewer Department beckoned.[8]

The revolutionary politics that had so indoctrinated young August Wilson at this time eventually would be compromised by the decade's concurrent cultural nationalist movement. Although Wilson embraced anti-establishment sentiments, his competing allegiance to cultural nationalist causes forced him to soften his position to the point of venerating the African American past and by extension, paying homage to the same older generation he had earlier denounced.

Fences, then, is in large part, a tribute to David Bedford, but it also represents Wilson's coming of age. Clearly Bedford's influence upon Wilson figures prominently in the play; however, parallel lines between fiction and fact have been blurred and/or problematized in several instances. Cory desperately wants to play football, for example, while a defiant young Frederick August Kittel (August Wilson's birth name) refused to do so. At the same time, in biographically similar fashion, Troy Maxson serves jail time for homicide, as did Bedford, and upon his release, he also becomes a family man. Wilson's fond retrospective regard for Bedford guided him in constructing *Fences* as a lasting tribute to him. He admitted,

> I found myself trying to figure out the intent of these lives around me . . . Trying to uncover the nobility and the dignity that I might not have seen. I was ignorant of their contributions. Part of the reason I wrote *Fences* was to illuminate that generation, which shielded its children from all of the indignities they went through.[9]

But the power of *Fences* is also evidenced in its ability to bring the past to bear on the present—to provide relevant historical contexts that demonstrate the usefulness of the African American past as a frame of reference for negotiating present circumstances and looking to the future. For this same reason, *Fences* is often referred to as a generational play. As such, the play captures the stories of three generations of Maxson men and points to the interconnectedness of their lives. Their tripartite historical narrative becomes especially evident in the play's retrospective on Troy Maxson's father. Although brought to life only in Troy's painful memories of his early life, the senior Maxson patriarch has clearly left his mark upon his son as well as upon his grandson's character. Troy recalls bitterly, "Sometimes I wish I hadn't known my daddy. He ain't cared nothing about no kids. A kid to him wasn't nothing. All he wanted was for you to learn how to walk so he could start you to working. When it come time for eating . . . he ate first. If there was anything left over, that's what you got" (1.4.50). This brief bit of depressing nostalgia provides a key to understanding Troy's ideas on love and commitment. As Harry Elam explains, "The repetition of behavior patterns by father and son underscores Wilson's conviction that history plays an important role in determining contemporary identity. Only by literally confronting the embodiment of the past, one's father or 'forefathers,' can one gain entrance into the future or ascend into adulthood."[10] Consumed by his frustration at being passed over for major-league ball and poisoned by irreverence for his ancestry, Troy seems destined for a tragic end.

The blood links that bind the Maxson males in *Fences* extend back to a generation of African American fathers who, for various reasons, rejected the responsibilities of fatherhood. They were programmed instead for backbreaking labor and conditioned to endure brutish treatment and minimal human contact. Perhaps due to conditioned detachment occasioned by the ravages of slavery and the subsequent Reconstruction upon African American nuclear families, Troy's father and African American men like him could not offer lasting allegiance to a single family unit. His cruelty to Troy's mother causes her to abandon him and her children. Likewise, the lustful, animalistic behavior that he displays before his son and Troy's young female companion lead to deep psychological wounds and sheer hatred between the two. We see glimpses of Wilson's stepfather David Bedford in the domineering but misunderstood Troy Maxson. We also equate tendencies peculiar to Troy's sharecropper father with the remoteness and emotional detachment Troy displays. Further, we note parallels between the rebellious young Cory Maxson and his tyrannical father.

Whereas numerous antecedents exist for the male portrayals in *Fences*, the bedrock of many of Rose Maxson's characteristics may be traced to a single source: Daisy Wilson, August Wilson's biological mother. Left alone to raise five children in post–World War II America, Daisy found work as a janitor while her German baker husband withdrew more and more from his responsibilities. As the oldest, August took odd jobs to assist his mother with upkeep of the household, and in the process, he became a man and internalized many of his African American mother's values. Moreover, Daisy Wilson's influence upon her son spread beyond the maternal realm into the political arena. As a strong African American woman with ties to North Carolina and, by extension, Africa, she was a major influence in shaping Wilson's cultural nationalist agenda. But in *Fences*, the source of Rose Maxson's compassion, faithfulness, selflessness, and her indomitable strength is Daisy Wilson. In a candid moment, Wilson admitted, "My mother's a very strong, principled woman. My female characters like Rose come in large part from my mother."[11]

Although the definitive version of *Fences* takes its shape from the numerous factors that inspired Wilson's creativity and his political agenda, along the way he encountered some significant resistance to these impulses. For example, at one point during the pre–Broadway production phase of *Fences* in 1984, the artistic integrity of Wilson's work came under attack. In particular, the play's producer, Carole Shorenstein—who had invested some $85,000 to bring the play to New York—urged the complete removal of Troy's brain-damaged brother, Gabriel. In addition to her difficulty understanding his motivation and significance in the play, she feared that his anticlimactic attempt to blow the horn, to engage in a light shuffle, and to utter the final words, "That's the way that go" (2.5.101) would offend sophisticated Broadway audiences. Her apprehensions were heightened because of evidence that the play's ending had drawn laughter and essentially baffled previous audiences.

Wilson was clearly aware of Shorenstein's substantial financial investment in *Fences* as well as the legal limitations of his artistic privilege as playwright. However, arguing on the grounds of artistic integrity, Wilson and then-director Lloyd Richards refused to write Gabriel out of the script. Apparently Wilson invested significant meaning in Gabriel—meaning that escaped Shorenstein's fiscal shrewdness. As such, he regarded Gabriel's role as inexpendable to the play; Richards, who shared his artistic vision, was just as adamant about his worth. Gabriel's role is not only warranted, but also conveys crucial meaning that undergirds Wilson's Afrocentric-inspired agenda. Troy's mentally impaired brother personifies Africa but in a more modern context. In other words, according to Harry Elam, Gabriel is "an exhibit of a syncretic cosmology, the presence of African tradition within New World religious practice."[12] Elam also argues that "Gabriel invokes racial memory, an African inheritance. His actions again reinforce the impact of the past on the present as the family's African heritage provides a benediction for their African American present."[13] Following several tense political maneuvers initiated by Shorenstein, in March of 1984, *Fences* opened to superlative reviews at the 46th Street Theatre. Gabriel's role had not been touched.[14]

Critical assessments of performance pieces may follow two different trajectories: one is based exclusively upon how the work is translated to the stage; the other rests exclusively upon how its artistry enhances the written text. It is not uncommon, then, for such work to fall short in aspects of performance and do exceptionally well as a published text. However, *Fences* is a clear exception; the play excelled in both categories. In terms of performance, August Wilson's *Fences* exceeded expectations of producers and critics alike. Regarded as "the first serious play in many a season on Broadway," it swept numerous awards categories for its staged presentation. It also broke all manner of records as the first play in thirty years to capture all of the major theatrical awards—including the Pulitzer Prize for Drama and awards from the New York Drama Critics Circle, Outer Critics Circle, Drama Desk, and American Theatre Critics Association for Best Play. As an artistically complex and psychologically riveting text, *Fences*—with all of its accolades from connoisseurs of performance—earns as much respect from text-based critics. When the Pulitzer Committee conferred upon *Fences* in 1987 the coveted Pulitzer Prize, it also set the play as a high water mark for critical achievement. The results of the committee's usual sober judgment also raised the bar for subsequent critical assessments of *Fences*.

Since earning the coveted Pulitzer, *Fences* has received much critical attention beyond the typical performance review. The focus of that attention ranges from the linguistic lyricism of his characters' speech to the marvelous complexity of the play's protagonist. By and large, this growing body of critical commentary about *Fences* evolves from the given premise that the play is both a performance and textual masterpiece. This awareness shapes the caliber as well as the tone of post-Broadway scholarship on *Fences*.

If one looks past the play's commercial appeal and focus attention beyond the veritable shelves of awards it has received, what becomes increasingly clear is that the full extent of *Fences*'s power cannot be measured in such terms. First and foremost, the power of the play lies in its ability to lift the ordinary man to noble heights—to articulate his joy and his pain, his success and his failures in ways that compel compassion and prompt moments of recognition. In large part the marvelous complexity that describes Wilson's rendition of Troy Maxson makes this possible.

The power of *Fences* is also attributable to its characters' magnificent use of language—both as a means of conveying the private turmoil as well as a way of reflecting their zest for life. In the span of one act, Troy's speech may be bawdy, lyrical, jubilant, or blues ridden. In seamless fashion, Troy captures the imagery of each of these moods in words and phrases that belie the voice of the onetime poet turned playwright. Troy is not alone in his exquisite linguistic capabilities. Rose, too, exercises a growing command of language as she blossoms amidst the turmoil around her. Her skills at communicating evolve from one-liner responses to her loquacious husband to full-blown speeches infused by vivid images that define the extent of her faithfulness to him. One critic concludes, "Wilson has one of the finest ears for language in American theater. Using characters that speak with rolling, fluid rhythms, Wilson accurately and purposefully records black speech and life. *Fences* is full of rich idioms, funny lines and arresting images."[15]

Coming to terms with the power of August Wilson's *Fences* must also take into account the play's uncanny ability to generate electricity during its two major conflicts. There is much artistry in the way Wilson shapes— indeed grooms—the ultimate confrontations between Troy and Rose as well as between Troy and Cory. Just as crafty is the manner in which Wilson gradually unfolds each of these conflicts and maximizes meaning in their explosive fallout. For example, Wilson has perfected the use of timing to the extent that he can magnify and hold in the spotlight some of *Fences*'s most searing moments. During what is perhaps the most climactic moment in the play, Troy struggles to find words to inform Rose of his marital indiscretions: "I'm trying to find a way to tell you . . . I'm gonna be a daddy. I'm gonna be somebody's daddy" (2.1.66). But as soon as he musters up the nerve to do so, Gabriel interrupts the scene carrying a rose to present to his sister-in-law; "Hey, Rose . . . I got a flower for you. That's a rose. Same rose like you is" (2.2.66). The explosive anger that has been temporarily abated out of deference to Gabriel hovers over the set just long enough for the impact of Troy's affair to be more fully realized. Also during this temporarily suspended battle, the convergence of Troy, Rose, and Gabriel in the same scene calls attention to just how opposite the characters of Rose and Gabriel are to that of Troy. While Rose and Gabriel suggest fidelity, self-sacrifice, and honor, Troy conjures up images of selfishness, deception, and opportunism. Because of Wilson's attention to aspects of timing, the impact of this scene, and several other conflicts that surface in *Fences*, is undeniable.

More evidence of the play's artistry may be seen in two relatively lesser conflicts that function much like undercurrents in *Fences*. Troy also has less than ideal relationships with his older son Lyons and with his brother Gabriel. Not nearly as acerbic, however, as the gaping divide that develops between Troy and Cory, these somewhat problematic relationships provide more evidence to support a critique of Troy's overbearing character. For example, Gabriel's imagined rift with his brother and Troy's labored though suspect attempts to dismiss it provide strategic commentary upon Troy's notions of fair play and sensitivity. Troy's older son Lyons is also the source of lighthearted conflict within *Fences*. Lyons allows Troy to revel in overt displays of responsibility; he participates in a frequent ritual of showing up on his father's payday to borrow money. Wilson adapts strategies that minimize the potential for sparks in Troy's dealings with Gabriel and Lyons. By so doing, he avoids the same no-holds-barred showdown that becomes the defining moment between Troy and Cory's strained and seemingly irreparable relationship. Instead of being fraught with friction, Troy's relationship with Lyons and Gabriel is infinitely more tolerable.

Conflict emerges in *Fences* not just as a result of Wilson's skilled manipulation of characters, dialogue, and action. A more subtle form of conflict is also at work in the play's very premise. That is, according to Wilson, Troy's exclusion from playing major-league baseball and the subsequent turmoil that this fate visits upon his family are symptomatic of a much larger issue for African Americans in general. For example, the tragedy that results from Troy's virtual shutout from major-league baseball also personifies Wilson's beliefs about various areas of limited access for African Americans. He contends that sports and music historically have been the only avenues by which African Americans could advance in any appreciable way. Given that, he contends, tragedy results when racism permeates and blocks either of the two areas. The most poignant conflicts, therefore, are those that hinge upon this contention. Works such as *Ma Rainey's Black Bottom* (1985), *Fences* (1987), *Seven Guitars* (1996), and an earlier play by Wilson called *Homecoming* (1976) are based upon conflicts that emerge when the limited trajectories of sports and music are blocked.

In a discussion that preceded the Broadway production of Wilson's *Ma Rainey's Black Bottom*, Director Lloyd Richards characterized such dire circumstances as "deprivation of possibility"—a condition that he defines as the most tragic of all conflicts African Americans may face.[16] In some ways this "deprivation of possibility" is comparable to the tragic flaws that cause self-destruction in a host of Greek prototypes. Oblivious to a dire fate that awaits them, such characters set out to achieve dreams that will never be fulfilled.

But in other ways, this "deprivation of possibility" is an exclusively African American phenomenon that pertains only to the African American experience, the likes of which Wilson is compelled to re-imagine in his cycle of plays. Alice Walker articulates this sense of preemptive annulment of dreams or a virtual poisoning of the well of human aspirations in her landmark essay "In Search of Our Mothers' Gardens" (1972). Here, she eloquently expresses similar deprivation in the lives of early African American women who have little or no outlet or encouragement for their artistic expression. She writes,

> For these grandmothers and mothers of ours were not Saints, but Artists; driven to a numb and bleeding madness by the springs of creativity in them for which there was no release. They were Creators, who lived lives of spiritual waste, because they were so rich in spirituality—which is the basis of Art—that the strain of enduring their unused and unwanted talent drove them insane.[17]

Although Walker targets African American female creativity in her essay, her premise also addresses Troy Maxson's condition as well as the conditions of countless African American men and women before, during, and after his time, who, for want of merely a chance, gave up, perished, or died. The "strain of enduring unused and unwanted talent" is singularly responsible for the misery that Troy Maxson inflicts upon himself and indirectly passes onto his wife and family. For Troy, baseball was not just a sport or pastime. It was indeed equivalent to an art form, one that he so highly esteemed that it dictated his moral code and served as a yardstick by which he measured his life.

Yet singling out the culprit most responsible for depriving garbageman Troy Maxson of a baseball career is both difficult and—now that he is in his late 50s—essentially futile. Therein lies a major source of *Fences*'s simmering and contentious conflict. In 1957 Troy is the dinosaur of major-league baseball. Through no fault of his own, he was born too early to play the game, and now the ravages of time have taken their toll on his body. In a search to find ways to vent his frustration, he can find no real, tangible adversarial targets against which to crack his constantly poised bat. And so, he must create a world that will allow him to unleash his anger in some physical way. In the real world, Cory becomes this sort of substitute target for him. However, in the spiritual realm, Death personified suffices as Troy's archenemy. This phantomlike entity is at the center of Troy Maxson's imagined (yet necessary) confrontation with the Grim Reaper. And so, in this makeshift scheme of things, Troy can only achieve some semblance of honor by creating sparring partners, against whom he wagers courageous battles to ward off the label "victim."

NOTES

1. Joan Herrington, *I Ain't Sorry for Nothin' I Done: August Wilson's Process of Playwriting* (New York: Limelight, 1998), 63.

2. Heather Henderson, "Building Fences: An Interview with Mary Alice and James Earl Jones," *Theater Journal* 16 (summer/fall 1985): 68.

3. Dennis Watlington, "Hurdling Fences," *Vanity Fair*, April 1989, 110.

4. Ibid.

5. Kim Powers, "An Interview with August Wilson," *Theater Journal* 16 (fall/winter 1984): 52.

6. Herrington, *I Ain't Sorry*, 65.

7. Harry Elam, "August Wilson," in *African American Writers*, 2d ed., vol 2, ed. Valerie Smith (New York: Scribner's, 2001), 847.

8. Samuel French, "A Voice from the Streets: August Wilson's Plays Portray the Sound and Feel of Black Poverty," *New York Times*, 15 March 1987, 49.

9. Ibid.

10. Elam, "August Wilson," 847.

11. Bill Moyers, *A World of Ideas* (New York: Doubleday, 1989), 175.

12. Elam, "August Wilson," 848.

13. Ibid.

14. For more details concerning the controversy over changing the ending of *Fences*, see Richard Christiansen, "Artist of the Year: August Wilson's Plays Reveal What It Means to Be Black in This Country," *Chicago Tribune*, 27 December 1987, sec. 3, F8–F10, and Michael Kuchwara, "Convictions of 'Fences' Producer Prove Lucrative," *New Haven Register*, 27 March 1988, sec. D14.

15. David Lida, "Fences—A Review," *Women's Wear Daily*, 27 March 1987, 8.

16. Ishmael Reed, "In Search of August Wilson," *Theater* 16 (1984): 93.

17. Alice Walker, *In Search of Our Mothers' Gardens* (New Brunswick, NJ: Rutgers University Press, 1994).

4 Contexts

The foundation of August Wilson's dramatic agenda stems largely from his early fascination with history. *Fences* is one of many by-products of this fascination. As a precocious seventh-grade student attending Catholic school in Pittsburgh, Wilson looked past English and mathematics and found his kind of heroes in the history lessons served up by his teacher, Sister Mary Eldephonse. History, ala Sister Eldephonse, was but one long, exciting narrative peopled by the likes of Charles Martel and Attila the Hun. Presented as such, Wilson soon began "to look beyond the colorful characters to the cause and meaning of events and how they connected and contributed to the shaping of other events."[1]

Wilson's intense curiosity for identifying causal relationships in history, a fascination that grew out of his Catholic school experience, would eventually become the premise for his project to "rewrite the history" of twentieth-century African Americans. At some point in the early 1980s after Wilson had completed his second play, he identified a causal pattern that would later become the convenient glue to bind together ten distinctly different plays set in ten respective decades. He recalls, "I wrote a play called *Jitney* set in '71 and a play called *Fullerton Street* that I set in '41. Then I wrote *Ma Rainey's Black Bottom*, which I set in '27, and it was after I did that I said, 'I've written three plays in three different decades, so why don't I just continue to do that?'"[2]

When Wilson wrote *Fences* in 1983, he did so fully aware of its place within his newly conceptualized history cycle of plays. His ten-play approach to rewriting history, he reasoned, would allow him to reconstruct a historical narrative composed of plays "laid end to end to comprise a dramatic tracing of the black American odyssey through the twentieth century."[3] Thus, Wilson discovered early on that, as a playwright, he could essentially fill in the gaps in African American history left in documented accounts by others for whom sensitivity to the culture was not a factor. Lloyd Richards, who directed *Fences* at the Yale Repertory Theatre and on Broadway, shared this view:

> He [Wilson] has put them in a position where we can get to know them through their attempts to deal with the issues of their time as they affect their everyday lives. And in their struggle to live, to survive, to thrive, to respect themselves, one begins to perceive these people in their time; you see the history flowing to the time and flowing from it as it affects the lives and the decisions of those characters.[4]

Fences is a strategically positioned link in Wilson's causal chain of African American history. Set in 1957, the play is chronologically midway in the twentieth century, thus inviting a pivotal view of historical circumstances for African Americans prior to the turn of this century while, at the same time, turning attention toward more hopeful events of the 1960s. The parameters of *Fences's* history lessons extend as far back as post-Emancipation and as far forward as the dawn of the civil rights era.

Within the 100-year span referenced in the play—from the late 1800s to the brink of 1960s—are several historical moments that profoundly impacted African American experience: the Great Migration, the Harlem Renaissance, the Great Depression, and World War II, for example. But much like Troy's mistress Alberta, who remains half in the shadows for the entire play, despite her inextricable importance to its conflict, many of these important events referenced by the play remain part of the backdrop. That is, Wilson treats these landmark events as understood history (i.e., contexts) and, rather than rehearsing details of each, concentrates instead upon fleshing out his characters and tightening the conflict.

Situating *Fences* at the midway mark of the twentieth century, then, provides a unique perspective on the entire African American experience from the painful record of the antebellum past for African Americans to the postwar present. Holding these two eras up to closer scrutiny, then, allows more sober judgment of the status of African Americans in the impending civil rights and Vietnam War eras of the 1960s. Wilson observes, "My work benefits from looking back because we can look and see . . . the actor, the character going down a road that, given the benefit of a fifty-year historical perspective, we can see whether that is the correct road or not because we've learned. We know how all this turned out. So history is certainly important in my work."[5]

To some degree *Fences* establishes an indirect causal link between three generations of Maxson men, and, at the same time, brings to the forefront the historical circumstances responsible for shaping each of them. The colorful narratives handed down by Troy and Bono to a younger generation of African American men to whom they offer counsel reflect the dismal circumstances of their own childhood. But it is clear that they dredge up their depressing experiences to deter these young men from following a similar course. Both Troy and Bono knew fathers who shirked their duties and cared little for instilling in them any lasting values. Both recalled growing to manhood while enduring extreme poverty, racism, and lack of guidance. As a result, they both bear indelible impressions as adult men—impressions that function as revealing commentary upon how the dire circumstances of slavery, emancipation, and the Reconstruction era in African American history continue to impact generations of African Americans two or three times removed.

Troy's blues-informed nostalgia about his past invites a backward gaze at the historical contexts that gave rise to his emotionally sterile father. As Troy brings back into focus memories of his biological father, what also comes along are the painful reminders of this man's indifference toward him and his mother, his violent nature, and his cruel, self-serving demeanor. Moreover, the resurrected reality of Troy's father invites an examination of conditions of the post–Civil War environment that created such a despicable character. As Troy reminisces, "The only thing my daddy cared about was getting them bales of cotton in to Mr. Lubin. That's the only thing that mattered to him. Sometimes I used to wonder why he was living. Wonder why the devil hadn't come and got him" (1.3.51).

Troy's father was among hundreds of newly freed slaves brainwashed into accepting principles of another oppressed form of labor—one that, in no small way, was modeled after the peculiar institution of slavery still fresh in their minds. When large masses of African American men were manumitted in the late 1800s, they left thousands of acres of untended cotton and tobacco fields, which threatened the financial ruin of many white plantation owners. In a desperate measure, southern white

landowners devised the system of sharecropping whereby they could continue growing and harvesting their cash crops and thus maintain their
economic status. For a significant period of time, the system worked well
for white landowners, but eventually the predominantly African American male work force came to realize the cruel limitations of this dishon-
est, self-serving agreement. In his landmark work, *Souls of Black Folks*
(1903), W.E.B. DuBois describes the particular plight of sharecroppers
who knew the physical and psychological abuse experienced by the likes
of Troy Maxson's father. He writes,

> Every year finds him deeper in debt. . . . The poor land groans with
> its birth-pains, and brings forth scarcely a hundred pounds of cotton
> to the acre, where fifty years ago it yielded eight times as much. Of
> this meager yield the tenant pays from a quarter to a third in rent,
> and most of the rest in interest on food and supplies bought on
> credit. Twenty years yonder a sunken-cheeked, old black man has
> labored under that system, and now, turned day-laborer, is support-
> ing his wife and boarding himself on his wages of a dollar and a half
> a week, received only part of the year.[6]

Black men of the generation that encompassed Troy's father were forced
to eke out a living in this same dehumanizing and emasculating agrarian
South where "every crop took him further into debt."[7]

While critical and historical accounts of the antebellum era dub it "the
nadir of the black experience," August Wilson personifies the social and
cultural havoc that this historical juncture wreaked upon the African
American psyche some fifty years beyond this historical moment. As he
does to an even greater extent in *Joe Turner's Come and Gone*, Wilson
explores the scarred emotional landscape left in the wake of this low
point in African American history. In the person of Troy Maxson,
post–Civil War history lingers in *Fences*, and the sins of Troy's father are,
indeed, visited upon him. Troy's history has accustomed him to hard work
and sacrifice. It also assists him in framing his own definition of love,
fidelity, loyalty, and responsibility to his immediate family. But Troy's history also serves as impetus for conscious wrongdoing. In each of the egotistical maneuvers he makes against Cory, Lyons, Gabriel, and, of course,
Rose, one can identify a historical antecedent by contemplating the ramifications of his turbulent relationship with his father, his past criminal
activity, and most damaging, his preclusion from playing major-league
baseball.

And so Troy lumbers into the twentieth century carrying historical baggage that pins upon him the label "Social Pariah" of the 1950s. He has no concept of the new womanist tenor of his wife's conversion, nor is he phased by educational opportunities that easing legislation has opened up for his son. He thumbs his nose not only at educational institutions but also at the institution of marriage, seeing no harm in appeasing his sexual lust outside his marriage. Nor does he see the harm of using his brother's war wound compensation and, with no obvious remorse, eventually committing him to a mental hospital for life. "I can't taste nothing no more" (2.4.89) becomes a declaration of Troy's emotional and spiritual autonomy much like the blasphemous assertion made by *Joe Turner's Come and Gone* nomad Herald Loomis: "I don't need nobody to bleed for me. I can bleed for myself!" (5.2.93).[8] Troy's survival at this point in the play is based upon complete oblivion to the very causal links that have cast him the villain that he is. Remorse, forgiveness, and fear of retaliation or abandonment are not part of his self-constructed survival kit. Instead Troy governs himself, no less, according to what "feels right" to him.

Fences also raises a series of stark contrasts between a time when having sufficient amounts of food on the table was a child's biggest concern to a time when having access to a television set was in vogue; from a time when educating African Americans was not a priority on the nation's agenda to a time when an athletic scholarship could easily provide an African American with an all-expense-paid college education; and from a time when the chores of young African American men involved walking behind mules for most of the day to a time when a part-time job at the local A&P provided money for extracurricular activities such as dating. Cory Maxson, whom we may assume to be seventeen or so, comes of age in a decade that, for African Americans, was marked by less-urgent concerns about poverty, illiteracy, and preoccupation with sheer day-to-day survival. In a number of ways, the 1950s was an important decade for African Americans—both in terms of key political events unfolding at that time and in terms of even greater advances for the race in the 1960s and 1970s.

Lorraine Hansberry's *A Raisin in the Sun* (1959)—set "sometime between World War II and the present,"[9] is informed by these same stirrings of positive change associated with this juncture in African American history. Much like what Wilson does in *Fences,* her characters are pointed to the future as she infuses her work with ingredients that foreshadowed a number of national and international political issues that, interestingly, had not yet come to fruition: Pan-Africanism, womanism, issues in housing, abortion rights, religion, education, and employment for African Americans. *Fences* offers similar futuristic projections for African Americans, but its author works from a decidedly different space.

It is worthy to consider here the distinct differences in the historical realities that each playwright experienced and how those separate realities impacted the general outcome of each play. Whereas Hansberry was herself a part of the immediate reality of her play's time frame, Wilson is removed by several decades. Hence, the respective ground on which these two playwrights stood (1950s and 1980s) affords them different perspectives from which to examine the African American condition. Hansberry's speculative construction of an attainable future that looms beyond *Raisin* invites African American audiences to envision possible end results of current struggle and sacrifice. Although she skillfully crafted the conflict in *Raisin* during the same historical context depicted in the play, Hansberry did so without the kind of retrospective gaze on history that August Wilson employs. Her eerily credible projections, therefore, in *Raisin* are more so the result of her keen intuition about the course of history. No doubt, the gifted, proactive, well-traveled, and well-versed intellectual that she was allowed her to make some reasonably conceivable inductive leaps into the future. This appears to be especially the case in her portrayals of Beneatha, Asagai, and, to some extent, Walter Lee in the play's treatment of developing consciousness among African American women, growing Pan-Africanist concerns in America, and shifting images of African American men as revolutionaries.

If the forward march of history in *Raisin* stirs the winds of political change, how, then, does Wilson's seeming foreshadowing of a future that has already happened impact those who experience *Fences*? How does the play maintain its level of interest among today's audiences or readers when they are privileged by a near forty-year advantage beyond its 1965 ending? For example, Wilson's readers as well as his audiences are likely to know that one of the many examples of the positive fallout from hard-fought civil rights legislation of the 1960s and 1970s was the institution of Black Studies programs along with increased enrollment of African Americans in many of the nation's leading universities. They also know that African Americans not only went on to play in the major leagues but also to break Babe Ruth's home run record several times over (most recently by Barry Bonds of the San Francisco Giants). Yet, at the same time, they are aware of statistics that show that extramarital affairs and divorce rates among African Americans increased significantly with women's liberation movements of the 1960s and 1970s and that the nuclear family unit that Rose Maxson so cherished in the 1950s is now threatened due to a number of social changes that she would, no doubt, find unconscionable.

The tactic of renegotiating history is an important part of August Wilson's narrative process. A careful reinvestigation and reconfiguration of African American history is Wilson's means of achieving these ends. Thus, in *Fences*, the reader's experienced history becomes something other than rehashed history. It becomes a landscape that lends itself to a different level of investigation—one that minimizes attention to historical markers and particularities and focuses instead upon the playing field of cause and effect. As such, history is regarded as a given set of circumstances from which one may find clues in contemplating the play's lessons.

Efforts to achieve further insight on such new historicist issues raised by *Fences* will undoubtedly lead one to contemplate August Wilson's affinity with Argentine essayist and short-story writer Jorge Luis Borges. Although the two men hail from different cultures and nationalities and write within different genres, they share strategies for creating new meaning by defamiliarizing history's chronological narrative. As Joan Herrington observes,

> Both men write of man's need to fulfill his destiny and understand his place within a historical continuum. . . . Borges and Wilson are more concerned with how things happen than with what actually happens. Wilson was specifically influenced by Borges' technique of revealing the ending of his stories in the first lines, which forces the reader to focus on the process and not the outcome.[10]

Concerns for the *how* rather than for the *what* in *Fences* deflect attention away from the temporal ground on which August Wilson stands. That the play points to a fictional future that is the same as the reader's past stirs that attention instead toward a closer investigation of the interconnectedness among causal factors that contributed to the devastating decisions Troy Maxson makes.

As Wilson puts history to work for him in *Fences*, he is apparently not obliged to call upon each significant moment in the African American past to recount the Maxson family's story. Along the play's chronological course from post–Civil War times to the brink of the 1960s, Wilson selectively alludes to several key historical moments. Yet, just as selectively, he bypasses events that others may regard as milestones in the record of

African American achievements and setbacks. Noticeably absent from *Fences*'s historical chain is the black arts movement of the 1920s known as the Harlem Renaissance, an era considered by many to be the high water mark in African American intellectual achievement. Often described in upwardly mobile terms, such as "New Negro Renaissance," this phase of cultural consciousness was intentionally promoted as the definitive commentary on the status of the black masses during 1920s America. Yet despite the hype that surrounded this short-lived phase, many saw it as a very limited and misconceived movement that sprang from a cadre of intellectuals bent on affirming that the Negro's intellectual capacity was equivalent to that of European writers and artists and that he was capable of producing so-called high art on their terms.

Upon examining Wilson's ideas on perceived factions among African Americans, it is not too difficult to understand why the Harlem Renaissance is not referenced in *Fences*. Wilson is offended by perceptions of elitism among its promoters and their failure to set forth more accurate representations of African American life in the 1920s. Moreover, according to Wilson, the exclusionary politics of the movement omitted the very people about whom he writes: the forsaken sons and daughters of slaves and ex-slaves, not members of the literati. An example of such anti–Harlem Renaissance sentiment surfaced during a recent address at which Wilson respectfully took W.E.B. DuBois to task for creating what he calls an "artificial superiority" in his conception of a so-called Talented Tenth.[11] Wilson explains,

> The concept of a "talented tenth" creates an artificial superiority. It is a fallacy and a dangerous idea that only serves to divide us further. . . . All blacks in America . . . originated from the same place: the slave plantations of the South. We all share a common past, and despite how some us might think and how it might look, we all share a common present and will share a common future.[12]

Wilson's position situates him among playwrights of the 1920s (Willis Richardson and Randolph Edmonds, Montgomery Gregory, and Alain Locke, for example) who debated similar issues concerning the proper portrayal of African Americans on stage. DuBois's contemporary Alain Locke "maintained that the major failing of the writers [of the Harlem Renaissance] was their lack of depth or understanding and realization of 'what was truly Negro.'"[13] The discriminating choices Wilson makes in constructing the fictional (yet painstakingly real) history of Troy Maxson reveal his commentary upon what was, in his estimation, truly representative of the African American experience.

As Wilson constructs the history of African Americans in twentieth-century America, he does so cognizant of the extent to which past experiences among this group of people are interwoven with aspects of their culture. While redressing history determines the direction and shape of Wilson's project, he gives equal attention to contextualizing African Americans' cultural realities. As he came to understand the place of culture in his developing aesthetic position, he also realized,

> I was as interested in the culture as [I was] in the history. . . . Since I was not an historian but a writer of fiction, I saw as my task the invention of characters. These personal histories would not only represent the culture but illuminate the historical context both of the period in which the play is set and the continuum of black life in America that stretches back to the early 17th century.[14]

From the pervasive presence of the blues aesthetic and the overarching influence of Christian and African religious traditions to a host of familiar African American rituals, Wilson is committed to depicting African Americans realistically by conveying their culture realistically. He explained in an interview with the author,

> I try to actually keep all of the elements of the culture alive in the work, and myth is certainly a part of it. Mythology, history, social organizations—all of these kinds of things—economics—all of these things that are part of the culture, I make sure—I purposefully go through and make sure each element of that is in some way represented—some more so than others in the plays, which I think gives them a fullness and a completeness—that this is an entire world.[15]

The blues tradition is perhaps the most constant and most influential cultural signifier to appear in some shape or form in each of Wilson's dramatic installments. Wilson regards the blues as the receptacle for "the cultural responses of blacks in America to the situation that they find themselves in. Contained in the blues is a philosophical system at work. You get the ideas and attitudes of the people as part of the oral tradition. This is a way of passing along information."[16]

The role of the blues in *Fences* is no less pronounced. It plays a significant role in gauging the failures and relative triumphs in the life of Troy

Maxson. It becomes a way to fathom both the depths of his depression and the apex of his optimism. The blues measures the emotional bankruptcy of this African American man who has been completely deprived of possibility and conveys the negative fallout from the impenetrable fences that not only encircle him and his family but also that inhibit the masses of African Americans who sought refuge in northern cities before and after World War II.

The blues becomes Troy's way of responding to a world that has so thoroughly rejected him. A career in professional baseball eludes him. Unfortunately, the self-destructive means he adopts to cope with this rejection alienates his wife, son, and brother. At his lowest point, only the blues can keep him company, and only the blues can fill up the emptiness in his life. During one of Troy's lowest emotional points in the play, he resorts to actually singing the blues. This lyrical lament comes in the external form of a tribute to an old dog named Blue. However, outwardly the ditty is equivalent to a human howl of extreme loneliness and melancholy:

> Old Blue died and I dig his grave
> Let him down with a golden chain
> Every night when I hear old Blue bark
> I know Blue treed a possum in Noah's Art.
> Hear it ring! Hear it ring! (2.4.84)

Wilson's portrayal of what appears to be the nadir of Troy's life is conveyed through the emotional release afforded by the blues. In much the same way, it conveys the profound disappointment of a race of people upon their arrival up North only to be shunned from a European-dominated work force.

No aspect of African American culture exists in isolation in *Fences*. Indeed, just as Wilson laid events in African American history end-to-end to better analyze the causal relationships between them, he demonstrates how certain aspects of the culture metamorphosed and survived the Middle Passage as well as the South-to-North trek of African Americans after official decrees of their freedom. As scholar/critic Henry Louis Gates reminds us,

> These Africans nevertheless carried with them to the Western hemisphere aspects of their cultures that were meaningful, that could not be obliterated, and that they chose, by acts of will not to forget their music ... their myths, their expressive institutional

structures, their metaphysical systems of order, and their forms of performance.[17]

This continuum of African American cultural practices in America is sustained in the implicit dialectic that Wilson sets up in *Fences* between African spiritualism and Christianity. Historically these two cultures have clashed for a number of reasons, chief among which is the belief that Christianity bore the mark of white oppression and that "Christianity engendered in black slaves a passive resignation toward their fate."[18]

Echoing August Wilson's contention that "God does not hear the prayers of blacks,"[19] Troy Maxson does not seek refuge in the saving grace of Christianity and the black church. At his lowest point, he does not seek help from the Lord, nor does he feel the need to repent for his sins. Instead, according to Kim Pereira, Troy assumes the characteristics of his African cultural descendant, Eshu. That is, he is "imbued with a sense of indestructibility."[20] He adds,

Such an attitude is the prerogative of the self-empowered trickster whose goals are survival and success, whatever the consequences. The so-called realities of the social world around him matter little, for he dances to an internal rhythm, answering a call for self-authentication that springs from a cultural, even cosmological, dimension.[21]

Troy seems oblivious to African American Christian tradition as he reinvents himself out of alternative models from a competing African tradition.

Despite its de-emphasis, Christianity remains a part of the fabric of *Fences* just as it remains very much a part of African American culture. Today, African American culture embraces a hybrid or reinvented version of Christianity. As Wilson explains, "Blacks have taken Christianity and bent it to serve their African-ness."[22] This cross-fertilized spirituality among African Americans heeds the basic tenets of Christianity yet contextualizes these beliefs within an Africanist cosmology. It is not coincidental, therefore, that Wilson identifies as his optimum mission in *Fences*, as well as in each of the other plays that make up his cycle, a campaign to bring proper balance to the traditional binary opposite aspects of African spiritualism and Christianity. He contends that, for various reasons, African Americans have relegated African spiritualism to a lower rung status while Christianity enjoys more widespread acceptance among African Americans. While he makes no concessions to Christianity, he believes that African Americans can only exist in America as Africans and that until they realize this imperative, they are doomed to repeat the mistakes of their past.

In *Fences* and in the body of August Wilson's work, the playwright continues to challenge the misconstrued binaries between African spiritualism and Christianity. As one of Wilson's so-called spectacle characters,[23] Gabriel Maxson, Troy's mentally wounded brother, becomes the purveyor of what Wilson contends is the preferred order. His actions, comments, and gestures not only draw attention to the inhumane treatment he and other African American veterans received following active duty in World War II, but they also introduce an Africanist cosmology that moves from the play's backdrop to become a very powerful presence by the end of the play. During the final funeral scene after Gabriel's horn fails to issue forth a ritual blast to honor his dead brother (who, according to African belief, has not died but has crossed over to another realm), Gabriel substitutes "a dance of atavistic signature and ritual" (2.5.101). In performing this dance, as one critic surmises, "Gabriel invokes a racial memory, an African inheritance. His actions again reinforce the impact of the past on the present as the family's African heritage provides a benediction for their African American present."[24] Gabriel becomes the conduit for initiating the healing process that the Maxsons face. Clearly, as the play leads its audiences to believe, re-establishing ties with Africa will play a large role in that process.

Noticeably, Troy's final send-off appears offstage. In effect, the play's exclusion of the goings on inside the church during his funeral service stifles any audible ritualistic displays associated with a Christian burial: hymns, testimonials, eulogies, prayers, scriptural passages, and animated displays of grief. Instead, the play only privileges scenes that lead up to and immediately follow Troy's funeral. Christianity and its associated rituals seem to be eclipsed in *Fences* by Africa's lure. These conscious choices on Wilson's part ever so discretely affirm a position he frequently advances:

> We are Africans who have been in America since the seventeenth century. We are Americans. But first of all, we are Africans. . . . We have different philosophical ideas and attitudes, different values, different ideas about style and linguistics, different aesthetics.[25]

Hence, *Fences* provides ample space for contemplating an African alternative.

In a much less pronounced way, Rose Maxson provides a visible representation of Christianity's apparently limited influence upon this African American family. As she begrudgingly accepts the consequences of Troy's breach of their marriage vows, she finds comfort and stability in the church. In the brief hymn that she sings as she hangs the day's laundry, she asks Jesus to function in much the same way as the fortress she has asked her husband to build:

> Jesus, be a fence all around me every day,
> Jesus, I want you to protect me as I travel on my way. (1.2.21)

Even though Troy thinks little of Rose's noticeably increased activities outside of their home and within the church ("All them preachers looking for somebody to fatten their pockets" [2.4.83]), this religious institution is but one of few at that time able to offer women support during domestic crises. Yet Troy holds a very pragmatic view of the church as an institution infiltrated by criminals masquerading as men of the cloth. He concedes to the fine line separating the likes of those, like him, who hold no god before them and those who profess Christianity.

Although the Christian Church becomes a place of refuge for Rose during a tumultuous period in her marriage, symbolically the institution is fraught with lingering negative historical baggage. For African Americans, Christianity and the so-called Christian Church carry with them vestiges of white domination that dates back to slavery. As Kim Pereira explains, "By forcing its God on blacks, the white church could control their spirits. This process attempted, in part, to change the African into an imitation white man, a carbon copy of the European model; it was a process that robbed him of his individuality, dehumanized him, and turned him into chattel."[26] Thus, Rose's church signifies one of many systemic tools of mental oppression—a tool used centuries ago among slave owners as a means of countering rebellion and ensuring passivity. Given this pervasive and enduring impression of the so-called white man's Christianity, it becomes all the more understandable why Troy Maxson does not go down on his knees to pray for forgiveness from the Christian God and why August Wilson continues to foreground African spiritualism as the more culturally appropriate response to the world.

A significant outgrowth of the Afro-Christian fusion in contemporary African American culture is an acceptance of a parallel spiritual universe. Hence, much credence is given to supernatural and paranormal phenomena, such as ghosts, magic, and superstition. Indeed, as Wilson affirms,

"[R]elating to the spirit world is very much a part of African and Afro-American culture."[27] Troy brings Death to life and, by doing so, creates a formidable sparring partner. As he recalls the imaginary battle he waged with the Grim Reaper, during a bout with pneumonia, he accords the spirit a degree of respect, knowing that in a matter of time, the spirit will return to claim victory over him.

> Death ain't nothing to play with. And I know he's gonna get me. I know I got to join his army . . . his camp followers. But as long as I keep my strength and see him coming . . . as long as I keep up my vigilance . . . he's gonna have to fight to get me. I ain't going easy. (1.1.12)

In much the same romanticized way, Troy conjures up the spirit of his first creditor as he recalls for Bono the difficulty he faced trying to furnish his empty new home. Despite steady employment, local merchants refused him credit. His big break came when, according to Troy, the Devil himself appeared at this door peddling credit along with a high interest, seemingly interminable loan. This phantomlike being is a composite of the white man, the Devil, and Troy's boundless exaggeration. Troy embellishes his talk by granting the nameless vendor mysterious, foreboding qualities and by regarding the driver who delivers his furniture the next day as an agent of evil. The stuff of folklore, Troy's two tall tales romanticize the spirit world and, at the same time, make for light entertainment. Yet they also purposefully blur the lines between physical and spiritual realms while promoting a healthy regard for the latter.

Of course, Gabriel epitomizes the African response to ghosts, magic, and superstition in *Fences*. Himself somewhat of a clairvoyant, he possesses super-sensory capabilities that more easily put him in touch with African ancestral spirits. Although his mental capacity has obviously been altered by his war injury, that alteration ironically lifts a veil from his eyes to allow him unguarded access to the African spiritual realm. At the end of *Fences*, Gabriel's performative gestures suggest that he responds to some extraterrestrial stimuli that initiates in him an atavistic dance and that ultimately opens wide the gates of Heaven—quite presumably for Troy to enter. Each of the above instances demonstrates the interconnectedness of the spirit world with the daily lives of African Americans such as the Maxsons. Often regarded in less ominous and more familiar terms, the spirits occupy a respectable position within African American culture.

With seamless effort but with meticulous attention to details, August Wilson re-creates in *Fences* the culturally specific world of African Americans in the late 1950s America. Beyond capturing the Afro-Christian spiritual essence of their lives or giving attention to the blues dynamic, he highlights the prevalence of a still vitally important oral tradition—a tradition that has its roots in the West African griot whose charge was to maintain and disseminate as accurately as was possible the oral history of his people. *Fences* is set in a time that predates America's love affair with the television set and when lingering Jim Crow laws allowed movie houses to become sites of racial animosity. The radio, not the newspaper, was the most immediate link to the outside world for African Americans and a way to follow major accomplishments of the select few African American sports legends who brought honor, purpose, and a sense of empowerment to them in their daily struggle for survival in America. Because the majority of African Americans at that time did not have access to such technological gadgets and were not as prone to reading, they placed even greater emphases upon telling their stories accurately. For many who were illiterate, oral history kept alive by various narrative forms was their only means of knowing their history and their culture. In such an environment, talk becomes a commodity and the art of storytelling and reminiscing become not only a means of free entertainment, but also an act of communal bonding.

Troy Maxson is the consummate symbol of this narrative tradition in *Fences*. A direct descendant of the African storyteller, Troy possesses a flair for constructing colorful, engaging narratives. His tendencies toward stretching the truth and toward reversing misfortune also place him within the African trickster tradition. So adept is he at spinning tall tales that Bono jokingly makes him a relative of Joel Chandler Harris's Uncle Remus (1.1.13). His stories are laced with supernatural feats and heroic acts that are so powerful that one temporarily ignores the truth factor and accepts the fantastical world his words construct—a world in which he invariably triumphs. True to form, Troy can talk more "trash" and out-brag, out-lie, and out-exaggerate any in the field. Talk reveals the competitive nature of his character as he frames his account of the widening rift between Cory and him and explains to Rose his infidelity using baseball terminology: "Do you understand after eighteen years I wanted to steal second" (1.2.70). Talk fills the space where a portion of Troy's ego remains deflated from being barred from an all-white playing field. Talk overshadows his vulnerabilities and masks his insecurities.

Economic factors also figure in defining the culture of African Americans. The various related problems of labor, finance, high interest, taxation, and so forth are highlighted in an unfair, racist work environment, such as the one Troy faces daily. Indeed, worries over finances rival his worries over the racism and injustice he faces. At every turn, the play reinforces the correlation between responsibility and money (or the lack thereof). Troy's repeated references to his $76.42 weekly paycheck, his decision to convert Gabriel's money into a down payment for the home they now occupy, and his insistence that Cory maintain a job at the local A&P all demonstrate how issues involving finance impact the Maxson household.

Economics also wed Troy's generation to that of his sharecropper father. As prevalent as money issues are in *Fences*, Troy's economic circumstances pale against those that drastically inhibited his economically doomed father: " 'Get them bales of cotton in to Mr. Lubin' and find out he owe him money" (1.4.51). Most importantly, Troy experiences the sense of self-worth that comes with ownership of property. Even though the means by which he acquires his real estate appear unscrupulous, he measures his worth in terms of seemingly cherished responsibilities of upkeep and monthly payments.

Troy Maxson and his family are but one paycheck away from poverty—an awareness of this makes his weekly ritual of relinquishing his earnings all the more poignant. This noble gesture epitomizes the responsibility he preaches about for much of the play and establishes his economic priorities. But $76.42 per week cannot finance the college education that Cory wants. Nor can it provide the life that Rose so richly deserves. Still, under the prevailing circumstances of economic limitations and racism against African Americans, it is the best that he can do.

Food is just as much a cultural signifier for African Americans of this decade as their economics. Often during economically bad times, food affords a measure of comfort and sustains cultural continuity. What people eat, how they prepare it, and their rituals of consuming it provide telling features of their culture. Wilson admits, "I try to approach people with an anthropological eye. That's why I make constant references to food. If you study culture, you want to know what people eat."[28]

In *Fences*, the introduction of food serves in several capacities. Foremost, the offering of food is a communal ritual that has antecedents in African tribal customs. It is a way of honoring one's guest and of extending to them an unqualified welcome to the home. On a number of occasions, Rose presses food upon Bono or her stepson Lyons, who is a frequent visitor to her home—especially on Troy's payday. Baked chicken, short ribs, meat loaf, lima beans, and biscuits are regular features of her menu, and fresh coffee usually simmers in the background. Rose is Earth Mother and matriarch, providing sustenance along with comfort and good counsel.

But food also functions as a dramatic device in *Fences*. In several instances, attention is diverted to food just in time to diffuse potentially explosive scenes. At other times, the introduction of food appears ridiculous and irrelevant when overshadowed by major conflict. Wilson's juxtaposition of such unequal dramatic elements highlights even more the severity of the conflict at hand. For example, as Troy is about to confess his clandestine affair to his wife, she interrupts him with the announcement that his lima beans–and–corn bread lunch is ready:

TROY: Rose . . . got something to tell you.
ROSE: Well, come on . . . wait till I get this food on the table.
(2.1.65)

At another juncture Rose is on the brink of a verbal explosion but is interrupted at the very onset by her innocently naive brother-in-law Gabriel. Even so, she admirably restrains her anger against her husband long enough so that Gabriel can take her up on an offer of watermelon and, therefore, spares the emotional fireworks that she holds temporarily at bay. In both of these instances, food stalls the inevitable while increasing suspense and tightening the conflict. The slight delays caused by such diversions prepare audiences and readers for the confrontations that are sure to follow.

One director summarizes best Wilson's regard for food as integral to capturing the cultural reality of African Americans. She explains, "So many of the recollections he [Wilson] invokes in his plays deal with food, and the feelings surrounding its creation and consumption. Grits, coffee and collard greens have epic meaning in his writing."[29] Food in *Fences* is part of the very texture of the play. What the Maxsons and their associates eat bears as much cultural significance as what they earn and how they earn it, on one hand, and how or where they spend it on the other.

Without question, the Great Black Migration from southern locales, such as Alabama, Arkansas, Georgia, and Mississippi to northern enclaves, such as Detroit, Pittsburgh, New York, and Chicago represents the largest shift in the African American population in history. Along with this massive relocation came the melding of southern customs, rituals, and beliefs with northern ways of living. But the Great Migration came with another shock to legions of southerners duped by employment propaganda that was vigorously promoted by the then-popular *Chicago Defender*. As one study notes,

> Reality never matches the dream of the Great Migration. Black workers were recruited for the lowest-level jobs—dirty work shunned by the native white population. They worked in vulnerable positions from which they were laid off at the first sign of economic downturn and moved into positions from which there was no upward mobility.[30]

In 1918 a fourteen-year-old Troy Maxson "hitched a ride up with some of them fellows that was heading this way" (1.4.54). He did so with as much optimism as the next man. Having recently gone to blows with a father who had earned his disgust, Troy joined the ranks of many young African American men lured by the much-touted rumor of better opportunities up North. But for Troy the North was but a gilded version of the South he had just left. Soon he came to realize that, unlike European immigrants who were infinitely more welcomed and who more easily found work, "the descendants of African slaves were offered no such welcome of participation."[31]

In an effort to cope with the reality of life in the North, many migrants—especially those who chose to remain or had no choice in the matter—found it necessary to rethink certain moral and ethical values that they brought with them from the Bible Belt of the South. The result of such shuffling of principles was an increased tolerance among them for criminal activity and an overall decline in morality. Consequently, the black church lost a good share of its once loyal southern congregation to juke joints and pool halls. The faster paced, more-crowded lifestyles of the urban North won many converts from among the so-called clodhoppers and field hands.

Troy provides a clearer example of how the dynamics of survival in the urban North impacted upon newly migrated African Americans. Like many, he comes with an already ingrained moral code and work ethic. He is eager for honest work, but, finding none, he begins to compromise his principles as the reality of northern racism and discrimination settles in. In a matter of a few years, Troy goes from being eager to contribute to the workforce to joining the growing prison population as a convicted murderer. His sins take him from stealing food to stealing money and subsequently killing the first man who resists him. Because of the prevalence of such hard-luck crimes, northern prison cells became home to many once well-intentioned African American men. One study notes, "Many were arrested for such minor offenses as gambling, being drunk and disorderly, or violating minor city ordinances. Some cases would probably have been dismissed with a fine, but migrants had no money."[32]

The migration north and the streetwise education it required for survival had even greater sociological ramifications for African American men. As Troy exemplifies, many learned quickly that the key to their longevity and to any reasonable level of security was their ability to adapt to the white man's rules. Unfortunately, that frequently meant deferring their dreams, suppressing their masculinity, and appeasing whites that held power over them. As seen by African American men, such as Troy, whites were notorious for not only making the rules but also for changing them to their advantage. Northern whites, he soon discovered, were no different. The practice of exclusion, in particular, led to numerous blatantly obvious double standards. According to one study, "The very best people—bankers, realtors, editors, merchants, and community leaders—led the black exclusion movement."[33] Another reports that in Indianapolis landlords got $25 a month for flimsy one-story frame row houses that would have rented to whites for $18.[34] In her study on the Great Black Migration, Carole Marks concludes, "Chicago surveys in 1909 and 1919 showed blacks paying 100% more."[35]

But playing by the white man's rules is not exactly what Troy Maxson has in mind when he comes north. As he continues to wrestle free from shackles imposed upon his father's generation, he adopts an assertive—even aggressive—posture to penetrate fences erected by the white man's rules. Intolerance, agitation, and resistance characterize Troy's decidedly different approach to his oppressors. Undaunted by either his illiteracy or his skin color and without claim to a legitimate driver's license to operate a garbage truck, Troy becomes an advocate for fair labor practices on behalf of his African American coworkers. He demands an explanation from his immediate supervisor, Mr. Rand:

"Why you got the white mens driving and the colored lifting?" Told him, "what's the matter, don't I count? You think only white fellows got sense enough to drive a truck. That ain't no paper job! Hell, anybody can drive a truck. How come you got all whites driving and the colored lifting?" He told me "take it to the union." Well, hell, that's what I done. (1.1.2)

Troy's unwillingness to walk in his father's shoes and to acknowledge defeat stirs the warrior spirit within him to resist the white power structure at all cost.

Fences is a barometer for gauging sociological changes in the African American population during the 1950s, but, just as importantly, it mirrors August Wilson's repeated contention that African Americans must not sacrifice their African heritage to become Americans. According to the playwright, maladies such as incarceration, family dissolution, premature death, and, in Troy's case, deferred dreams are their just rewards for attempting to do so. Wilson counsels:

> As African-Americans, we should demand to participate in society as Africans. That's the way out of the vicious cycle of poverty and neglect that exists in . . . America, where you have a huge percentage of blacks living in the equivalent of South African townships, in housing projects. No one is inviting these people to participate in society.[36]

And so, the implicit curse upon Troy, the entire Maxson family, and, by extension, all African Americans who ignore their African connections compels them to failure and to self-destruction. The vengeful wrath of Mother Africa is wrought in Troy's regretful circumstances as a would-be major-leaguer; the dissolution of his marriage; his alienation from his son Cory; his strained friendship with Bono; the death of his mistress; the motherless plight of his infant daughter; his brother Gabriel's mentally impaired state; Rose's disgust at herself, her husband, and her marriage; and Lyons's confusion about how to be a man. In Wilson's dramatic view, neither love, fidelity, loyalty, nor sustained peace come to those who turn their backs on Africa. That they left the South en masse and relinquished valuable land in the process has been dubbed by Wilson to be their Original Sin. However, that they came north and relinquished ties with Africa, according to the playwright, is tragic.

Fences is well situated within several literary traditions, yet it is difficult (and perhaps unnecessary) to assign credit in any particular order to the numerous influences that have impacted the work. Largely because Wilson has, over the years, granted scores of extensive interviews in which he details what goes into the making of his plays, a clear record of his creative process exists. Among other things, these interviews reveal that the varied contexts for *Fences* are as varied as Wilson's own boyhood experiences with his stepfather, African American literary and artistic works, European hegemonic thought, and the African continuum.

Partially in an effort to refine his developing skills and to prove to others and to himself that his then still-questioned talents as a playwright were flexible, Wilson molded the story line of *Fences* after the popular well-made play paradigm. As such, *Fences* adopts a widely accepted European construction whose beginnings may be traced back to nineteenth-century French drama in the works of Eugene Scribe and Victorien Sardou. In several recognizable ways, the play follows classic characteristics of the genre:

(1) a plot based on a withheld secret that, being revealed at the climax, produces a favorable reversal for the hero; (2) a steadily mounting suspense depending on rising action, exactly timed entrances, mistaken identity, misplaced documents, and a battle of wits between hero and villain; (3) a climax culminating in an obligatory scene (scene a faire) in which the withheld secret is revealed and the reversal of the hero's fortunes achieved; and (4) a logical denouement.[37]

The conventions of the well-made play proved especially appropriate for *Fences*, as it allowed Wilson to shape a three-dimensional protagonist whose carefully delineated story of his life raises him above the level of common man and places him comfortably among the likes of Hamlet or other men of means. Moreover, the dynamics of the well-made play provide room for a comprehensive introduction to Troy Maxson, who noticeably grows in stature with each revelation on his background—so much so that Rose, Cory, Lyons, Raynelle, Gabriel, Bono, and Alberta all orbit around his massive presence, illuminating different aspects of his domineering personality. Once Troy's centrality to the play is established, a more clearly discernible causal chain emerges, linking certain underlying causes of his fatalism to the overshadowing effect of his self-centered universe.

In addition to acknowledging that his work owes a debt to pioneers of European drama, Wilson also privileges the influences handed down by warriors of his own African ancestry—uncompromising fighters who stood for "the affirmation of the value of one's being, an affirmation of his worth in the face of society's urgent and sometimes profound denial."[38] Among the ranks of such warriors were Nat Turner, Denmark Vesey, Elijah Muhammad, Marcus Garvey, and Wilson's own grandfather. These are the men whom Wilson idolizes and whose composites come through clearly in his more modern warrior Troy Maxson. Much like the would-be major-leaguer, each has resisted some form of oppression. The ramifications of the unethical forms of resistance these warriors sometimes employ, in Wilson's estimation, have little bearing on his regard for them.

Yet despite Wilson's tip of his hat to his European, American, and African American predecessors, *Fences* has been cited as being somewhat in violation of that influence. The play has more than once been the subject of critical speculation that it bears more than an uncanny resemblance to Arthur Miller's postwar domestic drama, *Death of a Salesman* (1949). Of course, such speculation does not credit the playwright for his intertextual ingenuity. Rather, it calls into question what is considered his unlicensed appropriation of elements peculiar to Miller's play. This charge becomes all the more interesting in light of Wilson's 1996 speech at Princeton where he delivers an unequivocal denunciation of the practice known as color-blind casting. To expand on this issue, he summons *Death of a Salesman* as a generic prototype: He explains,

> To mount an all-black production of a *Death of a Salesman* or any other play conceived for white actors as an investigation of the human condition through the specifics of white culture is to deny us our own humanity, our own history, and the need to make our own investigations from the cultural ground on which we stand as black Americans.[39]

In this context, Miller's work seems antithetical to Wilson's aesthetic principles. It seems to follow logically, therefore, that *Death of a Salesman* would not have been considered earlier as a model for Wilson's *Fences*. Add to this Wilson's repeated insistence that he has not engaged the canon of American or African American dramatists and the issue becomes even more of a conundrum—one that only Wilson is qualified to address.

But the paradox remains. Although Wilson qualifies the level of influence Miller has had on his work, both *Fences* and *Death of a Salesman* nevertheless are shaped—whether consciously or coincidentally—from similar molds. Diverting the essentially unproductive discourse on possible kinship between the two plays, therefore, can show more constructively how the works complement each other. A nonbinary examination of comparable aspects, such as the two troubled fathers; the two sons in their charge; their loving, supportive wives; their infidelity to these wives; their deferred dreams; and their tenuous relationships with death lend themselves to useful comparisons. The most pressing question that begs itself, then, is what does a simultaneous examination of these plays reveal about how Troy Maxson and Willie Loman deal with their respective dilemmas. Does such a comparison demonstrate that one culture is any more immune from society's backlash? Does such a comparison demonstrate the shared humanity of these two men's struggles or move audiences to feel their pain? The answers to these and other questions that parallel aspects of the two plays can lead to a better understanding of the commonalties that bind diverse cultures.

Just as it is useful to find meaning in certain external similarities between the two plays, it may also be productive to discuss *Fences* in terms of the intertextual commentary it offers on *Death of a Salesman.* That commentary, as Mark Rocha argues, yields a view of *Fences* as "a deliberate point-to-point signifying parody" of this postwar Jewish-American play. Rocha considers Wilson to be "facing" or challenging outright Western tradition in *Fences* and, at the same time, subverting any ideas of victimization with the unceremonious phrase "in your face."[40] Henry Louis Gates defines this defiant phrase as "a standard signifyin(g) retort, meaning that by which you intended to confine (or define) me I shall return to you squarely in your face."[41]

Read in tandem with *Death of a Salesman, Fences* becomes more than the black-faced counterpart of Miller's drama. Conversely, Wilson's 1950s play can be understood as an effort to place the African American experience on the same ground as that occupied by the more dominant culture. The potential for a balanced and complementary investigation of Anglo American and African American experiences puts to the test Wilson's nagging conclusion that "[w]hite America looks at black America in this glancing manner. They pass right by the Troy Maxsons of the world and never stop to look at them."[42] But *Fences* makes a strong case for elevating the African American experience to a grand scale and for erasing the so-called color line long enough to make Troy Maxson's misfortune and pain more than simply one black man's predicament.

Wilson acknowledges forthright and often the role that African American culture, a select few African American artists, and close family members have played in shaping *Fences.* For example, he has publicly cited the impact of collagist Romare Bearden's *Continuities*, the blues impulse, and the tense relations that existed between stepfather David Bedford and him during his youth. Yet most consistently, he has embraced the philosophy of noted African American essayist, novelist, and playwright James Baldwin, whose phrase "field of manners and rituals of intercourse" gives purpose to one of Wilson's most conscious missions in *Fences*: "to illuminate the culture so that you are able to see 'the field of manners and rituals of intercourse that can sustain a man once he's left his father's house.' "[43] Baldwin's thinking on African American cultural matters, which Wilson has conveniently reduced to one of his favorite phrases, provides Wilson with an opportunity to draw a direct line to Africa in *Fences* by unapologetically celebrating cultural differences that African Americans possess apart from those of the dominant white society. Like all of Wilson's plays, *Fences* speaks to the kind of cultural specificity that Baldwin endorses. It also prompts consideration of Troy's actions, attitude, and beliefs within the African context of his father's house.

Baldwin believed that the African American writer's highest calling is to sustain the culture by passing along to present and future generations of African Americans crucial codes of thought and behavior. Wilson interprets this directive as his obligation to affirm that the play's characters—Troy, in particular—are African. Hence, Troy becomes Wilson's translation of the neo-African man living in America but whose sensibilities are grounded in Africa. Painting Troy African, then, means successfully demonstrating that his rituals and his manners are not of America, but residual cultural traits that survived his ancestors' Middle Passage from Africa. Rituals such as telling stories, facing death, and providing for the household, as well as systems of belief pertaining to being a good husband, parent, and friend take their cues from systems of belief whose origins may be traced to Africa. Critics Harry Elam and Kim Pereira take this new historical approach to heart in their respective summations of Troy as "an African griot or folk raconteur"[44] and "a cultural descendant of Eshu [the Yoruba trickster deity]."[45] Similarly, Paul Carter Harrison adopts an Africanist frame of reference to describe Troy's character:

> Troy has no respect for the limitations imposed on him by a hostile world and thus avoids engaging in cynical devaluation of self-esteem that might reduce him to a victim. Neither does he repress the immutable hostilities of the world. Instead, in the spirit of the Yoruba trickster, Eshu . . . Troy will erect a fence to set the boundaries of the universe, a barrier that serves the dual function of keeping the profane at bay and containing divine order within his immediate province.[46]

It stands to reason, therefore, that in order to more fully understand Troy's character, one must first become acquainted with certain African cultural practices that shape him and then remain faithful to them in assessing his significance within the entire context of *Fences*. An African contextual reading of *Fences*—a reading that Wilson consciously elicits—opens up the work to a more culturally sensitive analysis.

Wilson does not openly acknowledge all of the literary sources that inform *Fences*. Indeed, as is often the case with many works of literature, this universal drama opens itself to numerous intertextual readings beyond those facilitated by its author. Notwithstanding influences that Wilson admits, some defy identifiable connections whereas others may bring about forced comparisons for the sake of discussion or in the interest of qualifying his success. For example, *Washington Post* theater critic David Richards observed that "[t]here are moments in *Fences* that bring to mind the elemental power of Eugene O'Neill,"[47] and author Peter Wolfe proclaims that "*Fences* belongs on the top table. It's an ironclad, no-arguments classic, ranking alongside such American stage masterpieces of the post-Vietnam era as David Rabe's *Hurlyburly* (1984), David Henry Hwang's *M. Butterfly* (1988), and Terrence McNally's *Master Class* (1995)."[48]

Not only has it become customary to situate *Fences* alongside works of other accomplished dramatists of the twentieth century, but continuing efforts to find appropriate yardsticks to measure the play's level of artistry and dramatic power redirect the gaze of contemporary critics back to classic Shakespearean and Greek drama. Regarded in these classic contexts, the irreversible fate of garbageman Troy Maxson calls to mind similar conflicts in Shakespeare's prototypical tragic plays where would-be heroes—like protagonists of Greek drama—perish seemingly at the whim of the gods. Still, despite Wilson's contention that he has not read Shakespeare or other classic dramatic works, the tendency to trace Troy's brooding, solitary nature, his fits of passion, and his bouts of melancholy back to Shakespeare's reluctant warrior Hamlet is common. Likewise, Troy's repeated negotiations with Death for a new lease on his life may lead to a discussion of *Fences*'s adaptation of Faustian legend just as Wilson's magnification of Troy's chronically tragic life invites comparisons to the biblical Job of the Old Testament.

Wilson pays homage to white dramatists, such as William Shakespeare, Henrik Ibsen, and Eugene O'Neill, because, as he admits, he feels empowered by their example as pioneers who faced and overcame the same demons that continue to plague him as he sits alone with his pen and writing pad. But the respect that Wilson grants these literary forefathers is not to be construed as an admission that they have influenced his work, for the aesthetics that govern each installment of his ten-play cycle are grounded in the cultural politics that emerged from his involvement in the Black Power movement of the 1960s. As he notes in his 1996 speech titled "The Ground On Which I Stand," "the kiln in which I was fired"[49] was the Black Power movement and Malcolm X. Elsewhere he proclaims, "I could not have accomplished any of this if the black playwrights working in the sixties had not laid the groundwork. . . . I have an enormous respect for the their talents and work and I place myself in that long line of the tradition of African-American letters that has nurtured us all."[50]

August Wilson lists as influences several fellow African American artists and activists who were part of the same political landscape that he occupied in the sixties: Malcolm X, Amiri Baraka, Philip Hayes Dean, Richard Wesley, Lonne Elder II, Sonia Sanchez, and Barbara Ann Teer. To some extent, each shared his mission to "raise consciousness and politicize the black community."[51] Although collectively each contributed to Wilson's cultural nationalist ideology, two, in particular, had noticeable impact upon *Fences*: Amiri Baraka (a.k.a. LeRoi Jones) and Philip Hayes Dean.

In addition to their status as fellow warriors of the movement, Wilson was intimately familiar with the bulk of Amiri Baraka's revolutionary plays, having staged several from the collection *Four Revolutionary Plays* (1969) while involved with Pittsburgh's Halfway Art Gallery from 1965 to 1968. In the wake of several awkward attempts at imitating Baraka's style, Wilson was convinced more than ever that he should find his own voice rather than imitate another. In the process, he found it necessary to reject the influence of Baraka's violent, abrasive, anti-white messages in favor of "a more internal examination of African American life rather than the 'pushing outward' of overt political propaganda."[52] Wilson reminisces,

> My own youth is fired in the kiln of black nationalism as exemplified by Amiri Baraka in the sixties. It posited black Americans as coming from a long line of honorable people with a cultural and political history, a people of manners with a strong moral personality that had to be reclaimed by strengthening the elements of culture that made it unique and by developing institutions for preserving and promoting it. The ideas of self-determination, self-

respect, and self-defense which it espoused are still very much a part of my life as I sit down to write.[53]

Wilson discretely distanced himself from Baraka's Manichaean agitprop but sustained particular interest in Baraka's black nationalist ideas that advocated self-determination, self-respect, and self-defense among peoples of African descent. He does so while continuing to affirm his camaraderie with the core of revolutionary artists who supported the Black Arts movement. Perhaps this kinship is most obvious in Wilson as he continues to call himself a "race man" and reminds us that "the kiln in which I was fired" was the "Black Power Movement of the '60s."[54]

Baraka's influence upon Wilson is most evident in Troy Maxson, the antithesis of Baraka's prescription for the so-called revolutionary hero. Much more restrained than Baraka's angry protagonists, Troy does not curse or threaten violence against his white supervisors down at the refuse plant. Neither does he cower before them or quietly accept his lot. Instead, Troy resists. He confronts management and systematically challenges the status quo practice of assigning the physically more demanding work details to African Americans while calling into question the practice of awarding white coworkers with "plum" jobs. By his actions, Troy changes the dynamics of his workplace, thereby distinguishing himself as a self-determined and self-respecting individual—one who exercises self-defense in refusing to accept the label "victim" at all cost.

In 1987 Wilson admitted to journalist Bill Moyers, "Other than Baraka, the first black playwright I found who wrote anything that even approached what was, to my ear, realistic dialogue for black folks was Philip Hayes Dean."[55] This realization followed a short stint at Pittsburgh's Black Horizons Theatre where Wilson directed Dean's tense domestic drama *The Owl Killer* (1974). His particular interest in Dean's ability to convey "realistic dialogue for black folks" was indicative of his own running battle to reflect similar verisimilitude in his characters' speech. For much of the 1970s, he wrestled with demons that had convinced him that the speech of fellow urban-based African Americans was not worthy of artistic consideration. But Dean's example, combined with Wilson's relocation away from Pittsburgh locals to Saint Paul, Minnesota, brought about a significant change in his perspective.

Fences, therefore, can be regarded as a shining example of Wilson's graduation from stilted and excessively figurative conversations of African Americans to the kind of talk one might easily overhear on any street corner or in any barbershop, restaurant, or kitchen where they commune. Troy Maxson is the consummate speechmaker, and—thanks to Wilson's much-improved ear for dialogue—at one moment he can rival Hamlet's profound musings and, at another, he can amuse his audience with a bawdy joke or delightfully ridiculous and humorous narrative. Critics have been uniform in their praise of Wilson for having "one of the finest ears for language in American theater. Using characters who speak with rolling, fluid rhythms, Wilson accurately and purposefully records black speech and life. *Fences* is full of rich idioms, funny lines and arresting images."[56] Actor James Earl Jones, who defined the role of Troy Maxson in the 1987 Broadway performance of the play, also weighs in on Wilson's mastery of dialogue: "But August's language has a certain root—I've heard other people speak with the same kind of inarticulateness. You find it in other cultures—the uneducated Irish too sometimes speak with great floweriness, they use language very richly—and I think August is catching this sort of speech."[57]

But realistic dialogue was not the only aspect of Dean's play that had an apparent influence on *Fences*. Striking similarities also exist in the plots of the two works. Much like *Fences* and *Jitney* (Wilson's 1970s play), *The Owl Killer* resonates with the same father-son friction that disintegrated the real-life August Wilson–David Bedford relationship. Emma and Noah Hamilton, a hardworking black couple residing in a small midwestern city called Moloch, have raised their two children to adulthood, yet the sinful behavior of both their daughter, Stella Mae, and their son, Lamar, shame them. Stella Mae is a harlot, bearing children by several different men and stealing another woman's husband. Lamar murders a man and, for much of the play, runs from the law. In blues-infused speeches much like the typical highly figurative rhetoric of *Fences*'s Troy and *Jitney*'s Becker, their father, Noah Hamilton, references the same responsibility that he was forced to curb for the sake of supporting his family:

> For thirty years that hot oven has been sucking' th' blood outta me. And y'all layin' up on your behind parts ridin' me. Eatin' up my grub an' sleepin' out my bedclothes. Yes, I hated all y'all sittin' 'round while I had to go an' meet the man everyday. How'd you think I felt, knowin' y'all hated to see me comin'? All y'all ever wanted from me was what I was slavin' to get ahold of. That's all you ever wanted from me—a place to lay your head and somethin' to put in your stomach. Use' to wish th' house would burn down with all y'all in it so I wouldn't have to feed your behinds. Yes, I took that cracker's

shit, I had to. Couldn't do no better. 'Cause if I had knock him on his butt you wouldn't have nothin' to eat an' neither would them chaps.[58]

Aside from their three disappointing sons, what makes these three men kindred spirits is a healthy regard for the work ethic; that is, they consider the daily ritual of going to work, earning a paycheck, and handing it over to their wives for the support of their families to be their consummate duties as fathers, husbands, and providers. Although overworked, underpaid, degraded, and discriminated against, they remain responsible African American men.

The politics of resistance and affirmation lie at the core of *Fences* and indeed informs Wilson's entire mission to chronicle the African American experience in the twentieth century. He makes no pretense otherwise: "All art is political," he boldly asserts. "It serves a purpose. All of my plays are political but I try not to make them didactic or polemical. Theatre doesn't have to be agitprop. I hope that my art serves the masses of blacks in America who are in desperate need of a solid sure identity."[59] As if heeding this political mandate, *Fences* bristles against a white power structure that deems the African American experience moot.

As was the case with Wilson's contemporary Amiri Baraka, South African playwright Athol Fugard's politics held his attention more so than his plays. Given that, it becomes quite conceivable that Fugard's Marxist commentary on apartheid victims and their oppressors inspired Wilson to adopt a similar approach for eerily similar circumstances between whites and blacks here in the United States. No doubt Wilson had politics and resistance on his mind when in 1976 he sat up and took note of several works by Fugard, which were performed at the Pittsburgh Public Theater then. "Something happened,"[60] he admitted upon seeing *Sizwe Bansi Is Dead* (1972), one of several of Fugard plays that attracted him.[61] That "something," one may surmise, is a sudden recognition that the politics of apartheid in South Africa addressed in these plays was strikingly analogous to various not-so-different forms of oppression against African Americans in the United States. In other words, as Joanne Gordon observes in a discussion of remarkable parallels that exist between the African American Wilson and the white South African Fugard,

Just as Fugard wants his fellow South Africans to acknowledge how their entire lives are being distorted by an obscene set of archaic laws, Wilson needs his fellow African Americans to recognize and embrace their African selves. Like Wilson, Fugard gives the voiceless masses of South Africa a mouth and in the delineation of the special nature of their pain, he provides the powerless disenfranchised of South Africa with a sense of self and pride.[62]

In setting his plays against the backdrop of racial apartheid, Fugard examines a racially charged landscape that appears to have been resurrected in Wilson's later work. While *Ma Rainey's Black Bottom, Joe Turner's Come and Gone, The Piano Lesson, Two Trains Running, Seven Guitars, Jitney,* and *King Hedley II* have decidedly different stories to tell, each features characters who exemplify what Wilson refers to as the warrior spirit or the unqualified potential to just say "No" to victimization and oppression.

Fences is the consummate product of a number of competing influences upon a still struggling young playwright. Not only does the play evolve out of Wilson's desire to prove himself in a highly competitive and critical profession, but it may also be seen as an extension of his personal life—in particular, a testament to an attentive and concerned stepfather. In no particular order of influence, *Fences* also responds to Wilson's impressions of artwork, the blues, Africa, and various African American literary giants whose aesthetics, politics, and rhetorical styles complemented his mission.

Still, access to a plethora of behind-the-scenes facts about Wilson as they relate to the creation of *Fences* can certainly enhance one's reading and comprehension of the play. Critic Mark Rocha observes that such privileged information makes possible "an extraordinary opportunity to attain a truly interdisciplinary perspective. Reading Wilson requires that we learn about the blues and American music, about Bearden and modern art, about Baraka and Black Nationalism, and about Borges and the postmodern."[63]

Any investigation into the myriad ingredients that make up Wilson's contemporary classic *Fences* must be accompanied with a sobering warning: One who becomes preoccupied with the creative process at the expense of understanding the message contained within the definitive, organic work will invariably miss Wilson's message. Granted its universal themes, *Fences* is, first and foremost, about African people living in an American culture. The very eclectic nature of all that goes into its making affirms this truth even more so. August Wilson, much like Romare Bearden, has made a career out of demonstrating that African American culture is simultaneously eclectic and communal. Their life's work has been to make wonderful sense out of the scattered parts.

NOTES

1. August Wilson, "Characters behind History Teach Wilson about Plays," *New York Times*, 12 April 1992, sec. H5.

2. Sandra Shannon, *The Dramatic Vision of August Wilson* (Washington, D.C.: Howard University Press, 1995), 203.

3. Wilson, "Characters behind History," sec. H5.

4. August Wilson, "The Historical Perspective: An Interview with August Wilson," interview by Richard Pettengill, in *August Wilson: A Casebook*, ed. Marilyn Elkins (New York: Garland, 1994), 203.

5. Shannon, *Dramatic Vision*, 202.

6. W.E.B. DuBois, *The Souls of Black Folks*, in *Three Negro Classics* (New York: Avon, 1965), 296–97.

7. August Wilson, "Introduction," *Fences* (New York: Plume, 1986), vii.

8. August Wilson, *Joe Turner's Come and Gone* (New York: Plume, 1988), 93.

9. Lorraine Hansberry, *A Raisin in the Sun* (New York: Signet, 1959), 22.

10. Joan Herrington, *I Ain't Sorry for Nothin I Done: August Wilson's Process of Playwriting* (New York: Limelight, 1998), 4.

11. The "talented tenth" was W.E.B. DuBois's label for what he envisioned to be a small group of well-educated African Americans who would accept the mission of elevating the entire African American race. Articulating the principles of one of his best-known concepts, DuBois published the essay "The Talented Tenth" in the anthology *The Negro Problem* in 1903, the same year *The Souls of the Black Folk* appeared. DuBois contended that no nation was ever civilized by its uneducated masses and concluded, "The Negro race, like all other races, is going to be saved by its exceptional men." The talented tenth profile encompassed mostly male college-educated urban northerners descended from relative privilege or affluence. Including artists, doctors, lawyers, undertakers, preachers, teachers, businessmen, and politicians, the talented tenth advocated a controversial class-based dynamic of racial progress, which regarded the uplifting of the African American lower classes as its burden and duty.

12. August Wilson, *The Ground On Which I Stand* (New York: Theatre Communications Group, 2001), 39–40.

13. *Call and Response: The Riverside Anthology of the African American Literary Tradition*, ed. Patricia Liggins Hill (Boston: Houghton Mifflin, 1998), 791.

14. Wilson, "Characters behind History," sec. H5.

15. Shannon, *Dramatic Vision*, 202–3.

16. Bill Moyers, *A World of Ideas* (New York: Doubleday, 1989), 168.

17. Henry Louis Gates, *The Signifying Monkey: A Theory of African-American Literary Criticism* (New York: Oxford University Press, 1988), 3–4.

18. Kim Pereira, *August Wilson and the African American Odyssey* (Chicago: Illinois University Press, 1995), 79.

19. Ishmael Reed, "In Search of August Wilson," *Connoisseur*, March 1987, 95.

20. Pereira, *August Wilson*, 37.

21. Ibid., 38.

22. August Wilson, "An Interview with August Wilson," interview by David Savran, in *In Their Own Words: Contemporary American Playwrights* (New York: Theatre Communications Group, 1988), 302.

23. Wilson's spectacle character, somewhat similar to Shakespeare's fool, is one whose status as the "Other" grants him or her paranormal powers to transcend the literal, the earthly, the ugly and to know a higher order of truth and goodness. Such a character may be mildly retarded or mentally imbalanced and exist on the fringes of society. His or her role, as its label suggests, is to command attention and to force both acknowledgment and understanding of issues that are sooner ignored (cf., Hambone [*Two Trains Running*], Gabriel [*Fences*], and Hedley [*Seven Guitars*]).

24. Harry Elam, "August Wilson," in *African American Writers*, 2d ed., vol. 2, ed. Valerie Smith (New York: Scribner's, 2001), 848.

25. Moyers, *World of Ideas*, 172.

26. Pereira, *August Wilson*, 31.

27. Savran, 302.

28. Ibid.

29. Denise Gantt, "Letter from Denise A. Gantt," *The Next Stage at Center Stage* (Playbill for *Seven Guitars*) 3 (1996–1997): 1.

30. Carole Marks, *Farewell—We're Good and Gone: The Great Black Migration* (Bloomington: Indiana University Press, 1989), 3.

31. *Fences*, "The Play," xvii.

32. Ibid., 147.

33. Lerone Bennett, *Confrontation: Black and White* (Chicago: Johnson Publishing, 1965), 117.

34. Ray Stannard Baker, *Following the Color Line* (1908; reprint New York: Harper & Row, 1964), 113.

35. Marks, *Farewell*, 145.

36. Savran, 299.

37. "Well-Made Play," in *A Handbook to Literature*, 6th ed., ed. C. Hugh Holman and William Harmon (New York: Macmillan, 1992), 499.

38. Wilson, *Ground On Which I Stand*, 11.

39. Ibid., 30–31.

40. Mark Rocha, "August Wilson and the Four B's," in *August Wilson: A Casebook* (New York: Garland, 1994), 4–5.

41. Gates, *Signifying Monkey*, 66.

42. Dennis Watlington, "Hurdling Fences," *Vanity Fair*, April 1989, 110.

43. Savran, 302.

44. Elam, "August Wilson," 847.

45. Pereira, *August Wilson*, 37.

46. Paul Carter Harrison, "August Wilson's Blues Poetics," in *August Wilson: Three Plays* (Pittsburgh: Pittsburgh University Press, 1991), 303.

47. David Richards, "The Powerful Confines of *Fences*," *Washington Post*, 27 April 1990, D4.

48. Peter Wolfe, *August Wilson* (New York: Twayne, 1999), 75.

49. Wilson, *Ground On Which I Stand*, 12–13.

50. August Wilson, preface to *August Wilson: Three Plays* (Pittsburgh: Pittsburgh University Press, 1991), xii.

51. Alex Pointsett, "August Wilson: Hottest New Playwright," *Ebony*, 24 November 1987, 74.

52. *Dictionary of Literary Biography*, vol. 228: Twentieth-Century American Dramatists Series, 2d ed., ed. Christopher J. Wheatley (New York: Gale, 2000), 291.

53. Wilson, *Three Plays*, ix.

54. Wilson, *Ground On Which I Stand*, 12.

55. Savran, 292.

56. David Lida, "Fences—A Review," *Women's Wear Daily*, 27 March 1987, 8.

57. Heather Henderson, "Building Fences: An Interview with Mary Alice and James Earl Jones," *Theater Journal* 16 (summer/fall 1985): 68.

58. Philip Hayes Dean, *The Owl Killer*, in *The Best Short Plays: 1974*, ed. Stanley Richards (Radnor, PA: Chilton, 1974), 90.

59. Savran, 304.

60. Ibid., 292.

61. In addition to seeing *Sizwe Bansi Is Dead*, Wilson admits having seen Athol Fugard's *Blood Knot*, *Master Harold and the Boys*, and *Boesman and Lena*.

62. Joanne Gordon, "Wilson and Fugard: Politics and Art," in *August Wilson: A Casebook*, ed. Marilyn Elkins (New York: Garland, 1994), 20.

63. Rocha, "August Wilson," 15.

5   Ideas

Literary references in *Fences* range from works that a defiant and truant young Frederick August Kittel (Wilson's birth name) read while holed up in the so-called Negro Section of the Pittsburgh Library to the plays of white South African Athol Fugard, which he experienced while the two worked with Lloyd Richards at the Yale Repertory Theatre in New Haven, Connecticut. The play is also informed by autobiographical echoes from Wilson's life that attest to poor chemistry between the playwright and his stepfather and hints of his subsequent immersion into the politics of cultural nationalism. Yet of even greater fundamental relevance to *Fences* are several of the playwright's core beliefs that he culled from the tenets of the Black Arts movement of the mid-1960s. From the thrust of this widespread cultural nationalist campaign, he fashioned the culturally edifying mission of his own art. For the most part, Wilson's fundamental artistic concerns have evolved from discoveries he made during his earlier private efforts to claim his racial identity as an African American and to foreground his Africanness in a society that privileges whiteness. But his dramatic vision also springs from a sense of the universal struggles that all oppressed people encounter, as they demand participation in a hegemonic society.

Wilson is not only concerned that African Americans are allowed full participation in American society; he is also adamant that they are allowed to participate as Africans. That means that they should not have to choose between relinquishing the distinct signature of their African-based culture in order to enjoy their rights as Americans. They should be able to retain their rituals, their systems of belief, and their distinct ways of life while at the same time enjoy the privilege of American citizenship. He essentially rejects the "melting pot" analogy so often attributed to America as one of the country's greatest assets and sees it as a philosophy bent on systematic cultural annihilation. He argues, "Those who would deny black Americans their culture would also deny them their history and the inherent values that are a part of all human life."[1]

Wilson does not single out white Americans as sole agents of cultural annihilation. According to him, African Americans share in this injustice, although sometimes as unwitting participants in the process. He argues that by failing to celebrate cultural differences and by not demanding full participation in America as Africans, they are no better than bigots who assert that "black Americans do not have a culture."[2] He explains in an interview,

> I find it criminal that after hundreds of years in bondage, we do not celebrate our Emancipation Proclamation, that we do not have a thing like the Passover, where we sit down and remind ourselves that we are African people, that we were slaves. We try to run away, to hide that part of our past. If we did something like that, then we would know who we are, and we wouldn't have the problem that we have. Part of the problem is that we don't know who we are, and we're not willing to recognize the value of claiming that, even if there's a stigma attached to it.[3]

As an extension of this line of reasoning, Wilson has adopted the following position as an African American playwright who identifies as his mission rewriting the history of African Americans in plays he strategically locates in the twentieth century: "What I want is that you walk away from my play, whether you're black or white, with the idea that these are Africans as opposed to black folks in America."[4] In numerous ways, therefore, the playwright insists in his dramaturgy that African Americans continue to embrace their African cultural traditions while living in America. Similar sentiments echo in the much-ballyhooed cultural nationalist remarks he made in 1996 and find their way into plays that "give expression to the spirit that has been long shaped and fashioned by our history."[5] That spirit, which may be identified as Africa, is at work in *Fences* as well as it is in *Joe Turner's Come and Gone*, *The Piano Lesson*, and *Seven Guitars*.

Wilson's arguments for retaining cultural distinction in America are not confined to his interviews and public addresses. They also work their way into the fabric of his plays in both implicit and explicit ways. From naming the gods and calling on the ancestors to dancing the African juba and performing bloodletting rituals with pigeons, signifiers of African American culture are integral to the lives of his characters. But the African retentions that inform Wilson's plays are not limited to the physical world. Indeed, many of the Africanist concepts espoused in his work also draw attention to a metaphysical world that defies sensory perception. While writing as such, Wilson mirrors observations that "Africanisms in African-American culture . . . exist as conceptual approaches—unique ways of doing things and making things happen—rather than specific cultural elements"[6] and that "[m]eaning is not prosaically represented in words alone but . . . finds 'objective materialization' in movement, gesture, and sound."[7]

Wilson admits that the African presence in *Fences*, though functioning in less-conspicuous ways, is not as pronounced as it is in plays such as *The Piano Lesson* and *Joe Turner's Come and Gone*. Rather than insisting that the characters in *Fences* be accepted as Africans, he insists that African American parents and grandparents born in America also be accorded the status of cultural bearers. He argues, "You should start by making connections to your parents and your grandparents and working backwards. We're not in Africa anymore, and we're not going back to Africa. You have to understand your parents and understand your grandparents. I like to say I'm standing in my grandfather's shoes."[8] In *Fences*, Wilson privileges the often-overlooked codes for living contained in the wise counsel of the more immediate generations of African American ancestors. Hence, *Fences* celebrates intergenerational connections between Africans in America.

Fences provides an interesting example of how both physical and metaphysical manifestations of certain African retentions converge to flavor contemporary African American culture. The Africa that Wilson resurrects in this play reveals itself by varying degrees and in both implicit and explicit forms. Often these forms cannot be comprehended if Western logic prevails as the only standard. These African connections emerge in unspoken codes that shape the daily rituals of these characters and infuse the play on a number of levels. By examining *Fences* within an African cosmology rather than by relying solely upon Western paradigms of analysis, the play yields a much more telling portrayal of how African Americans negotiate the ambivalence of their "double consciousness" in

America. That African cosmology becomes an essential part of the play's subtextual narrative—a narrative that contrasts America's divisive racism with Africa's capacity to heal, empower, and reunite.

Troy Maxson draws attention to the double consciousness of his status as an African and as an American. The inevitable tensions that arise as he attempts to negotiate his way in both worlds underscores W.E.B. DuBois's familiar concept and calls attention to his unique and problematic status of "two-ness,—an American, a Negro; two souls, two thoughts, two unreconciled strivings; two warring ideals in one dark body, whose dogged strength alone keeps it from being torn asunder."[9] On one hand, Troy is forced to abide by rules set by exclusively white-controlled entities (major-league baseball, the garbage profession, his mortgage company, furniture creditors, college recruiting agents, the prison system, the store manager, the law, etc.) while, on the other, he tries to pass on to his son values of his culture that involve reclaiming the spirit of the African warrior. Some of Troy's controversial and seemingly contradictory decisions may very well be attributed to an internalized battle he apparently wages between his "blood memory" (atavistic retentions passed from Africans to Americans) and his sensibilities as a black man in America. Although Troy wrestles these demons and appears to have succumbed to them, by the end of the play, African sensibilities prevail. We are led to believe by the play's concluding scene of atonement and reconciliation that Troy has succeeded in passing on to his son valuable lessons in perseverance and responsibility that are the legacy of his own father.

Troy Maxson's portrayal as a study in contradictions may also belie his kinship to an influential African prototype, Esu Elegbara. Because he apparently governs himself outside boundaries imposed by Jim Crow laws, marital vows, Christian Commandments, and fences, he invites comparisons to this African trickster deity whom Henry Louis Gates describes as, "the guardian of the crossroads" and as a master of "indeterminacy, open-endedness, ambiguity, sexuality, chance, uncertainty, disruption and reconciliation, betrayal and loyalty, closure and disclosure, encasement and rupture."[10] If measured according to characteristics associated with such an enigmatic cultural antecedent, Troy's errors in judgment and his complete reversals and his behind-the-scenes maneuvers become noteworthy attributes rather than cause for his damnation.

However, at least one member of a Chicago audience did not buy into this Africanist defense of Troy's mischief. Wilson vividly recalls the reactions of an African American woman who thought it was hypocritical for

Troy's brother to announce Troy's arrival in heaven by blowing his horn to alert Saint Peter to fling open the Pearly Gates for him:

> I'll never forget one performance of Fences in Chicago I was at, the theater was very, very quiet because Gabriel was getting ready to blow his horn, and this black woman is sitting about five seats back from me, and she says just loud enough so the whole theater could hear: "ey don' need you blowin' that horn; he goin' straight to hell."[11]

For her, the performance obviously provided a clear-cut case for Troy's indictment as a scoundrel rather than as an African deity. No doubt also for her, an Africanist reading would do little to sway her judgment of a man, the likes of whom she may have very well known all too well.

What this African American woman objected to at the end of Fences has been the focus of considerable discussions that raise both practical and aesthetic concerns. Some, like the play's 1987 Broadway producer, Carole Shorenstein, regarded Gabriel's concluding gesture as superfluous and potentially confusing—so much so that she feared audiences would boycott performances to the extent that her generous financial investment would be in jeopardy. In addition, certain largely white audiences considered this last scene when Gabriel does "[a] dance of atavistic signature and ritual" (2.5.101) entirely laughable. Of course, the play's detractors regarded this ill-timed laughter as an indication of some flaw in its overall structure. That flaw turned out to be Gabriel.

Although eventually relegated to the margins of the play, Troy's brother plays a crucial role, one that both Wilson and his director, Lloyd Richards, were willing to "go to bat" for in 1987 in order to retain. Both obviously understood that Gabriel is more than a mentally challenged misfit of the Maxson household and that he merits more than the obligatory recognition accorded him in the label "Troy's brother." Paradoxically, the key to understanding Gabriel's significance to Fences lies in his seeming insignificance—a reverse strategy that Wilson utilizes to some extent in Bynum (Joe Turner's Come and Gone) in Hedley (Seven Guitars) and in Hambone (Two Trains Running). He refers to these misunderstood individuals as "spectacle characters," and, as this name suggests, he expects that they will agitate emotions and force recognition of an otherwise suppressed truth. Through Gabriel, Wilson forces us to sit up and take note of tactics employed by the white American hegemony to continue to relegate African Americans to the status of Other and to bar them from full participation in the American Dream. Even more telling in Gabriel's subtle example is the cruel indifference that America shows toward him when it fails to provide him sustained support for an injury that irreversibly alters his life.

By casting Gabriel as a brain-damaged and slightly confused member of society—much as Shakespeare does in his construction of the fool—Wilson pricks the consciousness of his audiences and demands that they focus their gaze upon how, in the wake of World War II, America discarded its African American soldiers as so much refuse—what Toledo, the posturing intellectual of Wilson's *Ma Rainey's Black Bottom*, calls "leftovers from history."[12]

Yet despite the devastating blow to his head that seems to impair Gabriel's understanding, he is left with enough of his memory to comprehend that he must work for a living, that he must strive to be self-supporting, and that he must respect and honor his family. As Gabriel strives to live according to these cultural codes that miraculously survive the trauma of war and surgical implantation, his plight appears analogous to the history of Africans in America. After surviving the trauma of the Middle Passage, slavery, cultural erasure, and cultural imposition, "Africans nevertheless carried within them to the Western hemisphere aspects of their cultures that were meaningful, that could not be obliterated, and that they chose, by acts of will, not to forget."[13] Regarded as such, Gabriel becomes a necessarily visible conduit to the African past, one who stands outside of the strictures of the Western well-made play but at the same time aligns himself with an African cosmology. Inasmuch as this reading of Gabriel's significance clearly advances Wilson's Africanist agenda, there is little wonder why the playwright and his director who shared his vision stood their ground against an earlier campaign to drop Gabriel from the script.

The importance of Gabriel to *Fences* lies chiefly in his role as a visible link to the past or as a personification of an African retention that stirs up the blood memories of contemporary African Americans who have severed ties with their past. The fact that a head injury has rendered this grown man childlike makes him all the more significant to Wilson's construction of Africa. Although Gabriel's wounds may at first appear tragic, they also create in him a kind of veiled perception—a seventh sense, if you will—through which he can filter the racism and animosity that exist around him. Privileged by this veil, Gabriel enjoys a direct line of communication with the spiritual world. He is drawn within this circle to the extent that he may even interact with them: "Did you know when I was in heaven . . . every morning me and St. Peter would sit down by the gate and eat some big fat biscuits? Oh, yeah! We had us a good time" (1.2.26). This relationship that Gabriel enjoys is also one to which spectators are not privileged. Some obviously regard Gabriel's difficulty at rendering sound from his horn at the end of the play to be a cue for laughter. Yet viewed from within the circle of African spirituality, Gabriel's silent gestures may very well be silent only to the onlooker. Indeed, his attempts at speech and his trance-like dance movements belie a closed communication between him and the spiritual world that only he, in this hypersensitive state as African conduit, is capable of receiving.

Audiences that perceive Gabriel in a strictly literal, Western sense would understandably reject the notion that he occupies a position of honor in the play and would find Wilson's pronouncement that he is African equally problematic. Certainly, the community's efforts to bar Gabriel from public interaction, coupled with his own brother's decision to hand him over to a mental institution, offer support for such reactions to him. But as Harry Elam notes, "Gabriel's ritualistic and spiritual enactment is an exhibit of a syncretic cosmology, the presence of African tradition within New World religious practice. . . . Gabriel invokes racial memory, an African inheritance."[14]

An interesting correlation exists between Wilson's plays of the twentieth century. On one hand, Africa's influence is understandably more pronounced in those plays that are chronologically closer to the period that marked the height of slave trafficking from Africa and the onset of slave labor in America. On the other, in those works that are situated in decades from mid to late twentieth century, the clarity of Africa's voice—although still somewhat audible—seems not as focused. For example, plays such as *Joe Turner's Come and Gone* (set in 1911) and *The Piano Lesson* (set in 1936) seem more heavily informed by African-inspired dramatic devices. Vestiges of slavery exist on the plays' surface levels in a number of recognizable markers, such as Loomis's nightmare of the Middle Passage and the Charles family's carved piano.

The varying degrees of African influence may be attributed to factors that range from certain distancing techniques that the playwright uses in reconstructing both a collective and private past to the culturally numbing potential of technology and the exponential popularity of postmodernist thought. Hence, the Africa that Wilson constructs on stage for contemporary audiences—both African American and white—is quite different from the Africa that exists for them as a geographically and historically distant continent. Therefore, the obviously more contemporary settings of plays such as *Fences* (set in 1957), *Two Trains Running* (set in 1969), *Jitney* (set in 1971), and *King Hedley II* (set in 1985) bear the morally bankrupt trappings of modernity yet offer a subliminal African backdrop as potential relief. These plays still involve the stories of Africans in America, but the presence of Africa takes on decidedly different forms within more contemporary historical contexts. In *Fences*, issues such as paying mortgage, buying furniture, challenging employment practices, financing a college education, and buying a television set must be weighed against more positive ethics and morals that Mother Africa provides.

But even amid the hubbub of daily living, the characters in *Fences* are still plugged into a larger African cosmology. In order to identify the Africanisms at work in the play and to comprehend their function, it is necessary to expand our understanding of African concepts beyond the physical realm to include, for example, African myths, African metaphysical systems of order, and African concepts such as ambiguity, imbalance, and resistance to closure that have survived in African Americans. Such perspectives echo an important observation made by Joseph Holloway in *Africanisms in American Culture*: "Africanisms in African-American culture, therefore, exist as conceptual approaches—unique ways of doing things and making things happen—rather than as specific cultural elements."[15]

Such a view not only makes possible an entirely different interpretation of Troy Maxson's questionable choices, but it also has the potential to significantly alter the play's cathartic end. Much has been made about the very unconventional ending of *Fences*, especially about significant events following Troy's death: Gabriel's failure to render his brother a musical send-off and the Maxson family's ultimate reconciliation on the day of his funeral. Critic Alice Mills notes that "*Fences*, for example, has both a traditional Western ending in death (death of Troy) and an African one (his son prepares to follow a similar path)."[16] While the play embraces Western notions of finality in its attention to Troy's death and the accompanying familiar rituals of last rites, it also provides a window for Africanist metaphysical ideas that regard death as simply a necessary event to mark passage into another realm. It follows, then that cathartic closure is denied in *Fences* and becomes subverted to an even greater degree when Cory accepts his role as his father's son and steps forward to carry on his legacy. Thus, Troy's death, as seen through an Africanist lens, brings into focus cultural linkage, continuity, and hope that the next generation will set right what the previous generation has left undone. His expiration becomes a catalyst for reuniting the very family that he has torn apart. Troy's death represents the termination of life, finality, and closure—aspects that run counter to Wilson's Africanist aesthetic, which seems adverse to finite endings. Paul Carter Harrison describes the play's culminating moments as "a soundless ritual gesture which is at once grotesque and triumphant in its revelry of Troy's transformation into the spirit which promises a new day."[17] It is, therefore, fitting that celebration rather than melancholy should mark his transition.

Mills argues further that both African and European approaches are intertwined in *Fences*.[18] As an example, she points to the ambiguous nature of the fence image as this boundary-making structure has both interior and exterior qualities. It protects as well as excludes. While Rose's aspiration is to erect a fortress to encircle and protect her family, she does so also as a measure to forbid negative agents to penetrate the haven she so lovingly maintains for her family. Moreover, as an extension of this African metaphor, "Troy does not face a trial of initiation until he crossed the fence and left behind the protection of his family for the world of difficult choices. And that world is none other than the world of crossroads, the realm of Ananse-Esu-Elebara."[19]

Wilson endows Troy Maxson with a degree of verbal agility that further underscores his role as an important link within the African continuum. Of course, in the pre-television setting of the play, talk is essential as a form of communion and entertainment, but, for Troy, it also serves to sustain his larger-than-life image. In addition to his trickster-like dualities, Troy's eloquence places him squarely within the well-wrought oral tradition of his African ancestors. As he spins several vivid tales that emerge from his very active imagination, he keeps alive an oral tradition that spans the Atlantic Ocean and predates African slaves in America. Examples of Troy's verbal dexterity emerge when Cory asks him "How come you ain't never liked me?" (1.3.37) or "Why don't you buy a TV?" (1.3.31). Under fire to respond, within seconds, Troy transforms the everyday talk of his blue-collar environment into poetic diction—language that is arguably on par with that of any of Shakespeare's orators, but a language that is nonetheless grounded in a rich African tradition. "You my flesh and blood. Not cause I like you! Cause it's my duty to take care of you. I owe a responsibility to you!" (1.3.38), he tells Cory. He is even more eloquent before his wife as he justifies his affair with Alberta:

Rose, I done tried all my life to live decent . . . to live a clean . . . hard . . . useful life. I tried to be a good husband to you. In every way

I knew how. Maybe I come into the world backwards, I don't know. But . . . you born with two strikes on you before you come to the plate. You got to guard it closely . . . always looking for the curve-ball on the inside corner. You can't afford to let none get past you. You can't afford a call strike. If you going down . . . you going down swinging. (2.1.68)

Troy's verbal agility points to still other African antecedents. When, for example, he weaves exaggerated accounts of his physical strength, his endurance—and, of course, his responsibility—he steps into the shoes of the African storyteller whose enthralling words and vivid images of gods, humanized and deified animals, and agents of the spiritual realm invariably transfixed their audiences. Not limited to entertainment or pastime, however, these storytellers also used their deceptively simple art form to impart cultural values among the slave community and to allay their fears of the natural world around them. Lest one should wonder about the mysteries of death, Troy personifies the Grim Reaper and takes him on as a formidable sparring partner. Lest one should wonder about the mysteries of purchasing by credit, Troy conjures up a sensational narrative wherein the Devil (a.k.a. a "white fellow") provides him with three rooms of furniture, a book of payment coupons and a mandate to "send ten dollars, first of every month to the address in the book" (1.1.15). In true story-teller form, Troy brings a sense of immediacy to each of these exaggerated impromptu adventures, citing exact lines of his characters and recalling minute details of their actions. If it were not for Rose's usual last words, "Troy lying" (1.1.15), his audience just might be tempted to believe at least some parts of his story.

A byproduct of the oral culture that Troy represents is his dogged determination to be accurate. Indeed, Troy's insistence to "get it right" while recalling certain episodes from his past or while sparring with Bono or Lyons over baseball statistics or baseball players situates him well within the West African tradition of the griot or the village historian. Understandably, accuracy was of primary importance within African villages when one took on the supreme role of cultural bearer. In the absence of written records, the griot prided himself (or herself) in the ability to commit to memory aspects of the past and the capacity to recall at will the historical narratives of their people. Still, one might wonder what does it matter that Troy gets right the name of Yankee right fielder Selkirk or that he cites exact batting averages even as he airs his disgust at being kept out of the game. Intermingled with Troy's hyperboles, his braggadocio, and his fantastical stories of supernatural feats is an obvious regard for accuracy, especially when citing events of his lived history. He is not alone in his penchant toward accuracy; both Cory and Raynelle take up this mantle not long after their father joins his ancestors in death. In their flawed attempts to get right the lyrics to a dirge that Troy often chanted, they honor this aspect of his legacy:

RAYNELLE: Did you know Blue?
CORY: Blue? Who's Blue?
RAYNELLE: Papa's dog what he sing about all the time.
CORY: (Singing.) Hear it ring! Hear it ring!
  I had a dog his name was Blue
  You know Blue was mighty true
  You know Blue was a good old dog
  Blue treed a possum in a hollow log
  You know from that he was a good old dog.
  Hear it ring! Hear it ring!
(Raynelle joins in singing.)

(2.5.99)

Interestingly, Cory claims complete ignorance of the canine that is the endearing subject of his father's melancholy lyrics. However, after more prompting from his sister, the dog and the song suddenly come into clear focus. In an act that symbolizes not only the newfound solidarity between the siblings but also their commitment to carry on their father's cultural legacy, Cory and Raynelle conjoin their voices in rendering a strikingly detailed version of Troy's song. It is significant that this binding gesture is immediately followed by a pivotal cue from Cory. After a sudden consciousness obviously prompted by the song, he indirectly affirms that he will indeed attend his father's funeral: "You go on in the house and change them shoes like Mama told you so we can go to Papa's funeral" (2.5.100). Thus, in subtle ways, Wilson's ambiguous ending takes into account a Western tradition that begs closure. At the same time, however, as Mills suggests, Africa's influence resounds equally—if not more so—in the play's strong indication that Cory "prepares to follow a similar path."[20]

The Africa that informs *Fences* announces itself in other rituals and images that often may be prone to oversight. One such residual lies in the play's culinary references. Food functions as a dramatic device in *Fences* and, when offered at certain points in the play, punctuates the action and prompts certain emotional responses from its characters. As the short ribs, lima beans, and pigs' feet simmer in Rose's and Lucille's kitchens, the women showcase not only their perfection of culinary art, which they most likely inherited from their African American mothers and grand-mothers, but they also underscore the important role that food plays among these descendants of Africa in calming the domestic environment and promoting communal bonds. Rose asks Gabriel to go fix himself a sandwich, as she is about to tear into Troy for his recent confession of infi-delity. In the midst of calling Troy to his lunch, she learns that he has impregnated his mistress. In such instances, food functions as a pressure valve, creating diversions that are significant enough to at least allow calmer heads to prevail.

Food also becomes the focus of the testosterone-driven friendly rivalry between Bono and Troy, both of whom assert that their wives are excel-lent cooks. But perhaps most importantly, food is that gift that Rose so lovingly prepares for her family. Like the fence, it becomes an image that is intimately related to her capabilities as nurturer and her identity as a 1950s wife and mother. Wilson keeps his commitment to infuse his plays with recognizable images of African American culture by highlighting its integral role in facilitating communal and familial intercommunication and harmony. Aside from its dramatic function in *Fences*, as well as in each of the plays that make up Wilson's history cycle, images of food, its preparation, its communal tendencies, and its potential to soothe and to bond have their origins in an African context. As Joseph Holloway notes, "Africanisms were shared and adopted by the various African ethnic groups of the field slave community, and they gradually developed into African-American cooking (soul-food)."[21]

Wilson's aesthetic position as a dramatist is one that challenges the tra-ditional definition of the term "ancestor"—a definition that limits rever-ence to deceased and temporally very distant African elders—and upgrades the term to encompass as well not-so-remote African American elders. These are the generations of folks, he contends who "suffered indignities they did not like to talk about with their children"[22] and who frequently turned the other cheek to workplace harassment and degrada-tion in order to maintain their ability to provide for their families. These are the generations whose advice he urges contemporary African Ameri-cans to place as much stock in as the age-old wisdom of their African ancestors.

In 1987, Wilson sat for a revealing interview with Theatre Communi-cations Group host David Savran, during which he outlined the premise of his beliefs about the need to sustain intergenerational connections among both young and old African Americans. This belief manifests as a major theme in *Fences*:

> First of all, we're like our parents. The things we are taught early in life, how to respond to the world, our sense of morality—everything, we get from them. Now you can take that legacy and do with it anything you want to do. It's in your hands. Cory is Troy's son. How can he be Troy's son without sharing Troy's values? I was trying to get at why Troy made the choices he made, how they have influenced his values and how he attempts to pass those along to his son. Each generation gives the succeeding generation what they think they need. One question in the play is "Are the tools we are given sufficient to compete in a world that is different from the one our parents knew?" I think they are—it's just that we have to do different things with the tools. That's all Troy has to give.[23]

Wilson's comments provide a much more liberal and more enlightening context for reassessing the crude actions of both Troy and his father. The fact that Troy endures the ugly politics of his own workplace in order to keep the steady paycheck must be evaluated alongside his infidelity and devious tactics against Cory, Rose, and Gabriel. Judged also within this new framework, Troy's father merits less scorn for his decision not to give in to the "walking blues" and remain with his family even as he endured backbreaking labor while employed by his merciless white proprietor, Mr. Lubin.

Despite his poor relationship with his father, Troy appears to have taken stock of at least some redeemable features in his character. Most obviously, he inherits a strong work ethic and a serious regard for responsibility to his family. Although Troy's father does much to disgust his son (drives his mother away with his cruelty, sexually assaults Troy's girl, punches him unconscious when confronted, and denies food to his children), Troy is still able to boast "he felt a responsibility toward us. Maybe he ain't treated us the way I felt he should have . . . but without that responsibility, he could have walked off and left us . . . made his own way" (1.4.51).

Just as Troy is able to do, Cory eventually brings himself to accept and put to use certain life lessons that his father somehow manages to impart. Although Cory at first does not see anything worthy of emulation in Troy, when he faces the profound final ritual marking his father's death and when he is subjected to Rose's compassionate appeal for a truce in their longtime feud, he indicates a change of heart. In the wake of his mother's emotional speech, he urges his young sister Raynelle to "go on in the house and change them shoes like Mama told you so we can go to Papa's funeral" (2.5.100). Through subtle and indirect means, Cory indicates his acceptance of the generational torch passed on to him by Troy. At this redemptive moment in the play's action, he truly becomes his father's son and the hope for his family's future.

Although both Troy and Cory become embroiled in bitter physical and emotional wrestling matches with their fathers, each carries with him some praiseworthy aspects of his father's legacy. Despite the inevitable sparring rituals that come with the onset of puberty, time allows them to transcend the ugly reality of their differences and ultimately gain a healthier perspective on their fathers' actions. As is the case in *Jitney* (in which there is another one of Wilson's father-son contests), these revelations occur posthumously, recalling the bittersweet moments when Wilson himself finally came to understand his stepfather's motives. Along with the postmortem catharsis following the death of such difficult and often misunderstood fathers come reconciliation, redemption, and closure. But on a larger scale, the death of the African American father in these instances illuminates an all-important transition for sustaining the African American continuum of cultural experience. At the critical historical moment when the father's life lessons—and indeed the cultural lifeline of the African American race—are passed along to the son, the cultural lifeline of the African American race is preserved for another generation.

The tragic dimensions of *Fences* loom even larger when one considers the overwhelming obstacles African American fathers like Troy and his dad encounter as they attempt to pass on valuable paternal wisdom to their sons. While contending with a racist America that essentially emasculates them in full view of their families, they must find ways to maintain some semblance of dignity and credibility in their eyes. Otherwise, the younger generation would be quick to dismiss their advice as hypocrisy and deem them senile. Of course, Troy complicates his situation even further and greatly diminishes the impact of his example before Cory by engaging in an extramarital affair that shames Cory's mother and by intercepting Gabriel's government compensation to buy a house and later taking steps that prevent Gabriel from occupying it.

Troy Maxson's tragic stature may be attributed in large part to what has been termed "deprivation of possibility."[24] Coined by Wilson's director/

mentor Lloyd Richards during rehearsals for *Ma Rainey's Black Bottom*, the phrase suggests interesting comparisons to the divine forces that seal the fates of many a Greek tragic figure. That is, fight as much as they like, forces over which they have no control have already predetermined the destiny of their lives. And so, equipped with the knowledge that Troy "just come along too early" (1.1.9) to participate in integrated baseball, we watch him rail against his fate but at the same time negotiate ways to ward off the label "victim" and avoid self-destruction.

The theme "deprivation of possibility" very much aligns *Fences* with the classic ideals of tragedy. Like Macbeth, whose circumstances at birth negate his attempts to secure the throne or like Oedipus, whose incestuous fate was predetermined as an infant, Troy wages a losing battle against the irreversible fate of timing; he is born too soon. At 57, he is deprived of even the chance to realize his dream of playing professional baseball. It is tragic enough to be barred from participating in the sport on this level, but the fact that Troy is disqualified because of the ridiculous technicality of his age situates the play among conventional tragedies.

Another major theme that runs like a single thread through each of Wilson's history cycle plays involves, in his estimation, a costly error committed by earlier generations of African Americans once manumitted from slavery. That huge mistake, as he describes it, occurred when, for various reasons, newly freed slaves relinquished their rights to southern land ownership in favor of migration north. Further, he believes that the various types of misfortune and tragedies that befell them during this post-Reconstruction era as they struggled to make new lives in places such as Chicago, Illinois; Pittsburgh, Pennsylvania; and Cleveland, Ohio, must be interpreted as indications that their efforts ran counter to a more natural, more ordained order:

> We were land-based agrarian people from Africa. We were uprooted from Africa, and we spent 200 years developing our culture as black Americans. And then we left the South. We uprooted ourselves and attempted to transplant this culture to the pavements of the industrialized North. And it was a transplant that did not take. I think if we had stayed in the South, we would have been a stronger people. And because the connection between the South of the 20's, 30's and 40's has been broken, it's very difficult to understand who we are.[25]

If one accepts the profound implications of Wilson's assertion, then the next logical premise in his argument would be that because of the impaired judgments of thousands of African Americans who were guilty of abandoning their properties, they have forfeited their right to any substantial degree of success in a hostile northern environment.

Wilson takes his theory a step further in his plays. The so-called original sin of abandonment exacts its toll on his characters in the form of deferred dreams, dead babies, a dead mistress, troubled marriages, homicide, unexplained scars, accidental deaths, mental impairment, professional stagnation, alcoholism, scattered families, and the dreaded walking blues. *Fences* endures its share of this sort of cosmic retribution. Troy Maxson's story is part of a larger historical narrative that chronicles the city's refusal of the southern Negro into its economy. In such a hostile environment, African Americans, such as Troy, encountered their first major obstacle to the rumored good life. Wilson notes in the "Play" section of *Fences*, "The city rejected them and they fled and settled along the riverbanks and under bridges in shallow, ramshackle houses made of sticks and tar paper." The rules of the game had suddenly changed, and for many, compromises had to be made just to survive.

Hardest hit by the North's aversion to black labor were those whose skills were limited to agrarian and equestrian work. These workers, cut from the same mold as Troy, knew well the art of plowing a straight row while viewing the backside of a mule all day or working in the fields or tending the master's stable. Unfortunately, the skills they had to offer were no longer in demand in urban environments where industrial might ruled. Wilson also weighs in on this issue:

> We came to the North, and we're still victims of discrimination and oppression in the North. The real reason that the people left was a search for jobs, because the agriculture, cotton agriculture in particular, could no longer support us. But the move to the cities has not been a good move. Today . . . we still don't have jobs. The last time blacks in America were working was during the Second World War, when there was a need for labor, and it did not matter what color you were.[26]

Fences concedes further to the mistake of selling land and moving north. Retribution for this sin shows up most notably in the fate of its characters. Wilson communicates in *Fences* that this is a "transplant that does not take" by underscoring what has been lost in the process of relocation: "the connection between the South of the 20's, 30's and 40's has been broken. It's very difficult to understand who you are."[27] In the wake of the disruption in the continuum of cultural experience, fragmentation, alienation, and separation reign.

For Troy Maxson, the so-called transplant that did not take sets into motion a pattern of mistakes. Not only is he among the hundreds of migrants who made their way North during the early 1900s, but also, because of continued mistakes, he finds himself amidst a burgeoning prison population as a result of killing a man in an attempted robbery gone bad. Mistakes continue to plague him as he is drawn into an affair that thoroughly disrupts his family and leaves behind an innocent symbol of his sinful ways. He compounds his errors in his use of underhanded tactics to derail Cory's football aspirations and to commit his brother to a mental institution. He seems unwilling and unable to fathom the magnitude of the impact that his clandestine actions bring.

Coming out of a slave tradition that essentially decimated the African American family unit, Rose is keenly sensitive to acts that continue the splintering. Not only does Rose deplore Troy's affair for the irreparable harm it brings to their marriage, but she is also miffed because the introduction of Troy's child to the Maxson clan spoils her ideal image of the nuclear family. She tells Troy, "I ain't never wanted no half nothing in my family. My whole family is half. Everybody got different fathers and mothers . . . my two sisters and my brother. Can't hardly tell who's who. Can't never sit down and talk about Papa and Mama. It's your papa and your mama and my papa and my mama" (2.1.68). But Rose's wish for an uncomplicated family construct is the stuff of fantasy, for when she marries Troy, he has already fathered a son in a previous marriage. Thus, like each of the characters in *Fences*, Rose pays a price for the mistake of moving north. No matter what ideals she clings to, they cannot be realized according to Wilson's theory about the fate of those who defect from the South.

Troy's oldest son also pays a price. Although good-natured and sensitive, Lyons cannot seem to achieve any sort of stability in his life. From his loosely defined relationship with Bonnie to his lackadaisical attitude toward steady work, he seems thoroughly detached from a cultural legacy that promotes responsibility and family. Instead of steady work, he settles for borrowing from his girlfriend and father and—most disturbing—feels no sense that his actions are aberrant to the norms of his culture: "Me and Bonnie been split up about four years now. About the time Papa retired. I guess she just got tired of all them changes I was putting her through" (2.5.93). One may attribute Lyons's hit-and-miss attitude toward life not just to Troy's absence during his early life. Lyons's indecisiveness and noncommittal may also be due to the broken cultural connections in his father's past; apparently he inherits the sins of his father.

Perhaps it is Gabriel, however, who pays the greatest price for the egregious error his people commit. Moving north has brought him little more than derision, isolation, and ultimately permanent institutionalization at the hands of his own brother. The play's naturalistic backdrop of the urban North renders Gabriel particularly vulnerable against not only societal forces outside of his immediate family but this same alien environment dissolves traditional bonds within the family. In *Fences*, we witness the destruction of fraternal ties, and in its place, we see opportunism and clinical objectivity.

Gabriel's condition earns him no special consideration in a world shaken by the effects of cultural disconnection—a world where only payola allows this gentle man to walk the streets and a world where his own brother diverts his modest injury compensation into payment toward a family dwelling. Through it all, Rose remains constant in meting out compassion, food, and genuine concern for her mentally challenged brother-in-law.

Repercussions are also evident in the relationship between Troy and his younger son. Granted, there is a certain amount of inevitability in the showdown that erupts between Troy and Cory, due in part to the biological rite of passage that every young man must experience as he outgrows his father's shadow; the sparring signals his normal phase of growth toward manhood. But male hormones aside, the ever widening chasm that separates Cory from Troy can be regarded as another fence erected to ensure that negative consequences befall those who have turned their backs on their manifest destiny in the South. This being the case, neither Troy nor Cory will ever know peace. Because they bear some of the brunt of this major past mistake, they are destined to remain at odds.

According to Wilson's theory of cosmic retribution, no one is immune, including Troy's lifelong friend Bono. Their longtime friendship significantly weakens under the strain of Troy's affair. Bono is one of the first to take note of Troy's wandering eyes and moves quickly to dissuade him from seeing more of Alberta and causing unbearable anguish for Rose. But Troy ignores the wise advice of his friend and plunges even further into the relationship. Subsequent to Troy's affair, Bono visits him less and moves to the periphery, leaving Troy to wallow alone in his own despair. We last see Bono as a well-wisher at Troy's funeral.

Friendship among African American men has been a constant factor in Wilson's plays. He regards the love and camaraderie that exist among them as magical, especially in light of the fact that these relationships offer them a venue for enacting rituals that both restore and bolster their masculinity. What goes on among these fraternal orders of African American men whom Wilson puts together in barbershops, in restaurants, in pubs, in boarding houses, or on front porch stoops is an often unspoken commiseration. Ironically, in such environments commiseration among African American men does not entail conceding to the blues. Instead, it assumes the unlikely form of raucous humor and loud, uncensored talk. What those outside these circles may deem useless and offensive braggadocio, others within the circle regard as therapeutic sessions in negotiating America from an African American male's perspective. Part of Troy and Bono's Friday night routine includes rituals involving heavy drinking and talk of sexual prowess. But Troy's racy references to sexual intercourse with his wife, which he has no qualms sharing with Bono, are just as much indications of the depths of their friendship as they are public affirmations of Troy's masculinity: "Don't you come by my house Monday morning talking about time to go to work . . . 'cause I'm still gonna be strokin!" (1.1.20). Rose appears to understand Troy's need to spout off about his virility and in good spirits joins in the merriment.

Having acknowledged the role that male friendships play within African American culture, the rift between Troy and Bono becomes all the more tragic. Their once abiding relationship deteriorates from one involving outward professions of love for one another to avoidance and eventually complete disconnection. As Bono withdraws, Troy becomes an island drifting further away until separation from his cultural base is complete. The sting of death seems anticlimactic, then, when one considers the price he has already paid for his sins to his family and to his race.

The dominant image of the fence offers even more support for Wilson's pervasive theme of the big mistake. As the play's namesake, "fences" yields a variety of interpretations that allow a better understanding of the need that African Americans have to establish protective boundaries. At the same time, the fence metaphor illuminates the need that African Americans have to dismantle them. This duality of the fence image has resulted in a number of critical interpretations from both perspectives. Michael Awkward asserts that the play

is peopled with characters who attempt to erect domestic and social boundaries—literal and figurative fences, if you will—as means of marking both domestic space itself and its inhabitants as "property and possession" in order to shield them from the corruptive and/or murderous forces of the outside world while at the same time protecting the marking subject from the threat of abandonment.[28]

Alan Nadel sees the play's reference to the fence as the symbolic Mason-Dixon Line or a measure of the country's geographical and racial polarization:

> The fence that divided these sites was the Mason-Dixon line. For the slave, that line represented the fence on the other side of which his or her humanity ceased to be figurative. . . . The Mason-Dixon line, no longer literal, became the universal metaphoric fence that marked the properties of race as criteria for inhuman treatment.[29]

Elsewhere it is noted that the fence "raises issues ranging from economic and professional deprivation to emotional and moral isolation. The fence, which may either inhibit or protect, is both a positive and negative image to various members of the Maxson family."[30]

In keeping with the tragic implications of *Fences* and in keeping with its consistent theme of atonement for past crimes against the land, the fence image becomes an emblem of self-imposed incarceration. It is not coincidental, therefore, that Rose is the only one who sees good in the construction. Conversely, her opinion seems overshadowed by resistance and complaints from both husband and son, who regard it as unnatural and unnecessary. To them the tasks of erecting the fence signals much more than busy work. On the simplest of levels, the project becomes a tangible symbol of all that stands in the way of Cory's independence. For Troy it represents added restrictions placed upon one whose very nature is to ignore restrictions and rules that put him in check. But most pertinent is the fact that the fence is an embodiment of limitations placed upon the Maxson family. As such, it becomes another manifestation of the mistake that continues to revisit them. In many ways the fence imposes the same barriers as the concept Lloyd Richards labels as deprivation of possibility, which first characterized the fate of slaves and subsequently extended to the ancestors of slaves who left the South.

One of the many troubling issues on which Wilson bases his dramatic revision of African American history is "that there are no avenues open for them to participate in society, where they might prove whatever is inside them."[31] Sports and music, he observes, have provided only fleeting opportunities to a select few African Americans fortunate enough to break through the many restrictions imposed by society. To highlight the tragic consequences of being denied access to either of these two venues, Wilson invites us to entertain what happens to the individual under such circumstances. In *Ma Rainey's Black Bottom*, for example, trumpet player Levee is denied access to his music because he is shortchanged by white promoters who downplay his talent while they capitalize financially upon his genius. Similarly, Floyd Barton of *Seven Guitars* (1995) has written a hit record, and, as Harry Elam points out, he "believes that his future success depends on a new record deal with Mr. T.L. Hall, a white producer and agent."[32] But this record deal never materializes, and unfortunately, Floyd is murdered in Pittsburgh before realizing his dream of relocating to Chicago to make it big in the music industry.

In *Fences* sports takes on a role similar to that of music. Playing the game of baseball is Troy Maxson's raison d'etre, yet because he is on in years when access to the major-league game is finally granted to African Americans, he is denied the privileges of any such access. He must watch from the sidelines while Jackie Robinson and other younger African American talents—perhaps not quite as good as he—play the game. From the margins, then, Troy is limited to using his verbal gifts to brag about his batting potential and to rejuvenate, to some extent, his severely deflated masculine ego. Herein lies the premise of the play. Troy's every act and his every word are driven by his reaction to this tragedy of denial—this deprivation of possibility.

Like the men in *Fences*, Rose Maxson has to put her dreams in storage. In lieu of unbridled ambition, she settles for domesticity, motherhood, and marriage to Troy. Somewhat of an anomaly, Rose complicates the mold for the 1950s African American woman by exercising profoundly motivated choices. Most importantly, she *chooses* to subordinate her will to that of her husband and, by doing so, in theory, she fences herself off from the possibility of an alternative lifestyle that would leave room for her own personal growth and achievement. Rose's assertion of her own will is like that of many of the strong-willed African American women in Wilson's plays "who assert feminist positions, but who, either through their own volition or as a result of external social pressure, ultimately conform to traditional gender roles and historical expectations" while, at the same time, they "attempt to establish relationships with men on their own terms."[33] She discloses some of these choices when she musters the energy to castigate Troy: "I gave eighteen years of my life to stand in the same spot with you. Don't you think I ever wanted other things? Don't you think I had dreams and hopes? What about my life? What about me?

Don't you think it ever crossed my mind to want to know other men?" (2.1.70).

To be sure, African American women in the 1950s, such as Rose, had few options upon reaching adulthood. Seldom did these choices extend beyond marriage, motherhood, and domesticity. Money spent toward their education was considered an unwise investment, especially because few jobs awaited them that required more than an ability to clean, cook, and cater to the service demands of a white world. Moreover, the prevailing climate of anti-intellectualism against women suggested that education "spoiled" women and prevented them from being good wives and homemakers to potential husbands.

Wilson's emphasis upon the exclusion of African Americans from realizing the American Dream applies just as much to African American women as it does to their men: "No avenues [were] open for them to participate in society, where they might prove whatever is inside them."[34] Such deprivation of black women's self expression recalls similar concerns expressed by Alice Walker in her essay "In Search of Our Mothers' Gardens," in which she imagines what life must have been like when avenues of artistic expression are denied: "driven to numb and bleeding madness by the springs of creativity in them for which there was no release."[35] But Rose does not yearn for a release from her domestic duties in order to become the new woman. In fact, contrary to what her name suggests, she appears to have essentially put on hold the natural process of blooming or evolving, consciously choosing not to expand her boundaries outside the box of her husband's definition. She willfully takes herself out of circulation in the larger sphere of society where she would face certain race and gender discrimination. Instead she opts to promote harmony in the smaller, more controlled sphere of her home.

Through the sheer exercise of her will, Rose transcends the deprivation of possibility that so plagues the men in *Fences*. The phrase just does not suit her, for Rose clearly complicates this label by choosing her lot in life in an era when African American women were, as society decreed, without voice. Most challenging to the concept of victimization is her decision to accept and raise as her own Troy and Alberta's baby daughter Raynelle. She causes quite a stir among audiences and readers alike when she steps forward to claim the motherless infant her husband has fathered outside their marriage. Although she qualifies her decision by letting her husband Troy know that their marriage, in effect, no longer exists, the relative ease with which she becomes this child's substitute mother speaks to her innate nurturing capabilities: "From right now . . . this child got a mother. But you a womanless man" (2.3.79).

A closer look at circumstances reveals that Rose further complicates the "deprivation of possibility" label by enlisting her own means of empowerment. Much of this relative power comes from her ability to make choices. She exercises the freedom of choice in a major way as she knowingly and willfully subordinates her aspirations in the marital arrangement to those of her husband. Later, she chooses to raise her husband's love child while, at the same time, she redefines the relationship by eradicating the sexual intimacy that was so much a part of their union; they begin to sleep apart. Interestingly, her choice does not include divorce.

Rose Maxson finds a way to circumvent exploitation and oppression while retaining her sense of wholeness and satisfying her desire to nurture. When she agrees to raise the infant Raynelle, her single altruistic gesture of maternal compassion reverses the fate that had predetermined that she could not have the babies she so desperately desired. She explains to Cory her coveted victory over such fate—a victory that came in the form of a motherless child humbly handed over to her by an unfaithful husband: "I took on to Raynelle like she was all them babies I had wanted and never had" (2.5.98). Rose effectively eludes the label "victim" that is associated with deprivation through the force of her will. By exerting the power of choice, she affirms selfhood at the same time that she expresses the African American woman's cultural capacity for nurturing.

Rigid gender prescriptions in American society in the 1950s exacted a large price from African American women and made it quite difficult for women, such as Rose, to veer from them. Fortunately for many, the church provided a site for contending with such limitations. This institution, which is historically grounded in African American cultural tradition, affords them an alternative haven—a room of their own, so to speak—and a possible site of resistance. While dutifully performing household rituals in her domestic environment, Rose Maxson basks in the soothing refrains of a favorite Christian hymn: "Jesus, be a fence all around me every day Jesus, I want you to protect me as I travel on my way" (1.2.21). Despite her seeming bliss at this moment, Rose foreshadows in the images of this hymnal the domestic chaos that will soon follow. Although she has consciously shut herself off from the world outside her home, her words still suggest an uneasy awareness that demons lurk about her gate. Unfortunately, the fence that she calls for in this hymn as well as the one she menaces Troy to finish will not prove effective in staving off this evil.

Rose's demons take on various identities, yet Alberta, the big-legged and big-hipped "Florida gal," who lures her husband away is not the single focus of her misery. What also emerges out of the ashes of her failed marriage is her awareness that she, too, played a part in its disintegration. By not shedding light on dimensions of her identity above and beyond those of being Troy's wife or Cory's mother, she curtails the blooming process and yields too much to codified roles for African American women of the 1950s. Moreover, in her desire to erect a fence, she does not allow for a gate where she can escape that which limits her in establishing her own identity: "I got a life too," she tells Troy. "I gave eighteen years of my life to stand in the same spot with you. Don't you think I ever wanted other things? Don't you think I had dreams and hopes?" (2.1.70).

As Rose's marriage disintegrates, and her family slips away from her, she adopts the church as a kind of surrogate family and protective barrier. She wraps the church around her like a garment and continues the twin processes of withdrawing from her husband and constructing an identity of her own. As Telia Anderson observes in her essay titled "Calling on the Spirit," "a black woman's most powerful weapon against the devastating effects of patriarchy both within and outside of the church is her internal connection with the divine."[36] Rose Maxson has such a connection from which she apparently gains emotional strength as she contends with the upheaval caused by her marital crisis.

Some critics have noted that Rose's exodus to the church merely affirms conventional notions of African American women rather than suffice as an act of resistance. In doing so, they expose the open-ended discourse that *Fences* invites about the implicit patriarchal idealism that is often associated with male constructions of female roles. Ironically, the church becomes part of that construction in the play. For example, Harry Elam argues that "[t]he avenues into which Rose channels her new freedom ... affirm rather than assault traditional gender limitations and hegemonic legitimacy. She finds solace in the church and the mothering of her adopted daughter, Raynell." Thus, as he concludes, "Rose, despite her spiritual independence, continues to conform to the traditional expectations and limitations placed on women."[37] Black feminist scholar bel hooks makes a similar assertion:

> *Fences* poignantly portrays complex and negative contradictions within black masculinity in a white supremacist context. However,

patriarchy is not critiqued, and even though tragic expressions of conventional masculinity are evoked, sexist values are re-inscribed via the black woman's redemption message as the play ends.[38]

More than once Wilson has extended the politics of his art beyond the fictitious world he creates in his plays. From the relatively small-scale aesthetic battle that erupted over Gabriel's significance to *Fences* to the national debate inspired by his catalytic speech to the American theater community ("The Ground On Which I Stand"), Wilson has essentially erased the line between artist and activist. As he has become increasingly inclined to verbally articulate certain egregious inequities in the arts industry, so too has he used his plays as a platform for revealing the latent and damaging effects of racism against the African American community. Clearly, then, it has proven difficult for him to dissociate his concerns about African American theater from the concerns of his life as a black man living in America. His art and his politics are inseparable.

To date, *Fences* remains at the epicenter of an ongoing battle over an aesthetic fence that Wilson has built around the play. At issue since 1987 has been his insistence that Paramount Pictures, who purchased movie rights to the play, hire a black director for the project instead of another who, in Wilson's words, "does not share the specifics of a culture."[39] While his position generated much rhetoric from both supporters and detractors (some of whom were African American directors unwilling to limit their range and their marketability), Wilson remains adamant and eloquent in articulating his vision for the play: "I want somebody talented, who understands the play and sees the possibilities of the film, who would approach my work with the same amount of passion and measure of respect with which I approach it, and who shares the same cultural sensibilities of the characters."[40]

Truth be told, the resulting stalemate surrounding attempts to mount a movie version of *Fences* conceivably could have also plagued any similar effort to co-opt for the screen any of Wilson's plays of the twentieth century. Because *Joe Turner's Come and Gone*, *Ma Rainey's Black Bottom*, and *The Piano Lesson* are just as much indicators of Wilson's aesthetic vision as *Fences*, it stands to reason that the playwright—when faced with giving up any degree of ownership to his work—would express similar anxieties over the possibility that persons seeking to transfer his work to another medium may not be particularly sensitive to African American culture. These plays, too, could result in something unrecognizable.

Fences seems particularly well suited in its role as the center of this highly publicized controversy. The play's emphasis on boundaries, borders, and margins on one hand and on declarations of ownership, dispossession, and expulsion on the other may be viewed as extended commentary upon Wilson's own politics of retaining cultural ownership of his work—the very same politics embedded in his publicly proclaimed aesthetic position that calls for uninhibited cultural expression and absolute cultural autonomy. He concluded, "Therein lies the crux of the matter as it relates to Paramount Pictures and the film *Fences*—whether we as blacks are going to have control over our own culture and its products."[41] Critic Michael Awkward concedes to the favored status for *Fences*, labeling it one of the "the flag-bearers for Afro-American self-determination and self-identity."[42]

On one side of Wilson's fence is the African American director who, by virtue of his race, is inherently more qualified for the task of interpreting African American life to stage and screen. On the other side of Wilson's fence are directors of other races who, despite proven reputations for excellence in their field, can never fit the bill. An uncompromising essentialist, Wilson baffles his adversaries by insisting that the performance of blackness should be entrusted to African American directors only. He finds it impossible to believe that directors of other racial backgrounds can guide and interpret the essence of black life conveyed in his plays to the stage, especially when that blackness, for him, is intimately intertwined with his own identity.

Of course, Wilson's long and productive relationship with African American director/mentor Lloyd Richards set the bar at a very high level for staging Wilson's black aesthetics.[43] At the same time, however, their successful collaboration served to confirm Wilson's contention that only an African American director could do aesthetic justice to his work. It was Lloyd Richards who, in the early 1980s, discovered in Wilson a novice playwright whose stories of the African American experience rang true for him. Although the accomplishments of the director best noted for bringing Lorraine Hansberry's *A Raisin in the Sun* to Broadway in 1959 are astounding by any measure, it is his blackness and his ability to render blackness in performance that cemented the working relationship between August Wilson and him. Wilson very much approved of the way Richards guided him not only in pruning and focusing the initially unwieldy versions of *Joe Turner's Come and Gone*, *Ma Rainey's Black Bottom*, *The Piano Lesson*, *Two Trains Running*, and *Seven Guitars* but also in schooling him on more appropriate strategies for teasing out essential aspects of blackness in these plays. That is, Richards brought to bear on the plays more than the clinical eye of a seasoned director but an intimate understanding of the cultural specificity of Wilson's work. Wilson reveals,

> Because we [Wilson and Richards] share a commonality of experi-
> ence, I think we share a commonality of vision. I wouldn't have to
> be at rehearsal and Lloyd, knowing me and knowing the overall arc
> of my work, would know how I would want a scene to play or what
> the values of that scene would be.[44]

Paradoxically, the success of the Wilson/Richards model may have contributed indirectly to the still simmering director impasse between the playwright and Paramount. From the outset, Wilson knew that, in Richards, he had found someone who not only had amassed impeccable professional credentials but who also knew firsthand about the stories Wilson conveys in his plays. The extraordinary chemistry that defined their successful collaboration was due largely to their mutual awareness of the African American condition. Like Wilson, Richards—some thirty years his senior—had actually witnessed and been a part of them.

This shared vision that existed between director and playwright characterized a nearly ten-year collaboration that yielded a string of critically acclaimed productions. It was under Richards's guidance and shared cultural vision that Wilson honed *Fences* toward Pulitzer Prize status. The two got along marvelously. Whether engaged in heated discussion over the fate of a play, whether counseling Wilson's career moves, or whether honing a play for production, Richards and Wilson were frequently of the same accord.

Because Wilson is so adamant in his bid for a black director, compromise seems virtually impossible. Obviously perturbed by counterarguments that challenged what some of his dissenters perceived as reverse discrimination, Wilson offered a drastic, across-the-board solution: "Let's make a rule: Blacks don't direct Italian films. Italians don't direct Jewish films. Jews don't direct black American films"—a solution, which, when translated, amounts to "let it be every man for himself."[45] As of this writing, however, Wilson appears to have won the bout with Paramount Pictures to hire a black director.[46]

Fences also qualifies as an appropriate centerpiece for the ensuing "I-Want-A-Black-Director" cause célèbre because of certain thematic parallels between the fiction of the play and the reality of the director controversy. Although born at a time when African Americans had little control over forces that determined their fate, Troy Maxson, to some extent, mirrors the same warrior spirit that Wilson invokes in his campaign to secure an African American to interpret his work for the big screen. Troy, like his creator, does everything within his power to reject those who would control him and his forms of expression. Moreover, he exudes the same passion in his crude efforts to steer Cory clear of potentially stifling control of white institutions. And though drawing similarities between Troy Maxson and August Wilson may seem far-fetched, in many ways the two seem fully aware of the need to resist hegemonic forces that have the potential of erasing and negating their manhood, their culture, and their humanity.

Wilson's own fencelike obstinacy against hegemonic forces of the movie-making industry has implications far beyond the color-blind vision revealed in Eddie Murphy's curious proclamation, "I don't want to hire nobody just 'cause they black."[47] This statement became the center of a highly publicized aesthetic brawl in the early 1990s that pitted Wilson against more liberal-minded theater practitioners for whom the race of *Fences*'s director should not be an issue. Paramount Pictures was poised to purchase film rights to the play, and Murphy, acting as their agent, invited August Wilson to contemplate who might direct the project. Yet Murphy's disturbing assertion changed the tone of the discussion; Wilson was offended by its various negative implications.

Wilson's position actually provides a powerful backdrop for the warrior-like resistance that Troy Maxson displays on a daily basis as he faces insurmountable odds for survival while at the same time he demands just treatment. In addition to being an act of defiance against Paramount on matters of aesthetic principle, Wilson's artistic battle is also reflected in Troy Maxson's willingness to go against an all-white workforce knowing full well that doing so would place his job (and his family) in jeopardy. The issue of resisting control over one's person or over one's art—whether it be in the workplace or on the set, defines Wilson's character as an artist.

Fences not only inspires debate, but it also inspires ideas about the human condition. The play invites a level of understanding that surpasses the particular experiences of the Maxson family and goes on to convey a kind of earthy wisdom for both the individual and for that same individual as a link in a family structure. All of this is brought to the fore within full view of the economic and racial fallout that African Americans experienced during postwar America. In his 1987 review of *Fences*'s Broadway performance, reviewer Clive Barnes best articulates the play's formula for greatness: "What is particularly pungent about Wilson's play is how the story and the characters are plugged into their particular historic relevance ranging from the lessons of prison to the metaphors of baseball. It is this that makes the play resonate with all its subtle vibrations of truth and actuality."[48]

NOTES

1. August Wilson, *The Ground On Which I Stand* (New York: Theatre Communications Group, 2001), 15.

2. Ibid.

3. Bill Moyers, *A World of Ideas: Conversations with Thoughtful Men and Women about American Life Today and the Ideas Shaping Our Future* (New York: Doubleday, 1989), 176.

4. August Wilson, interview by David Savran, in *In Their Own Words: Contemporary American Playwrights* (New York: Theatre Communications Group, 1988), 302.

5. Wilson, *The Ground On Which I Stand*, 36.

6. *Africanisms in American Culture*, ed. Joseph Holloway (Bloomington: Indiana University Press, 1991), xvii.

7. John Conteh-Morgan, "African Traditional Drama and Issues in Theater Performance Criticism," *Comparative Drama* 28 (1994): 12.

8. Dennis Watlington, "Hurdling Fences," *Vanity Fair*, April 1989, 106.

9. W.E.B. DuBois, *The Souls of Black Folks* (New York: Fawcett, 1961), 17.

10. Henry Louis Gates, *The Signifying Monkey: A Theory of African-American Literary Criticism* (New York: Oxford University Press, 1988), 6.

11. August Wilson, interview by Roger Downey April 1988, in *Microsoft Encarta Africana*, Microsoft Corporation, 1999.

12. August Wilson, *Ma Rainey's Black Bottom* (New York: Plume, 1985), 57.

13. Gates, *Signifying Monkey*, 3–4.

14. Harry Elam, "August Wilson," in *African American Writers*, 2nd ed., vol. 2, ed. Valerie Smith (New York: Scribner's, 2001), 848.

15. *Africanisms in American Culture*, xvii.

16. Alice Mills, "The Walking Blues: An Anthropological Approach to the Theater of August Wilson," *Black Scholar* 25 (spring 1995): 33.

17. Paul Carter Harrison, "August Wilson's Blues Poetics," in *August Wilson: Three Plays* (Pittsburgh: Pittsburgh University Press, 1991), 305.

18. Mills, "The Walking Blues," 33–34.

19. Ibid., 34.

20. Ibid., 33.

21. *Africanisms in American Culture*, 17.

22. "August Wilson's Fences," in *Literature and Its Times: Profiles of 300 Notable Literary Works and the Historical Events that Influenced Them*, ed. Joyce Moss and George Wilson (New York: Gale, 1997), 149.

23. Savran, 299.

24. Ishmael Reed, "In Search of August Wilson," *Connoisseur*, March 1987, 93.

25. Mervyn Rothstein, "Round Five for the Theatrical Heavyweight," *New York Times*, 15 April 1990, 8.

26. Moyers, *World of Ideas*, 167.

27. Ibid., 8.

28. Michael Awkward, "The Crookeds with the Straights: *Fences*, Race, and the Politics of Adaptation," in *May All Your Fences Have Gates: Essays on the Drama of August Wilson*, ed. Alan Nadel (Iowa City: Iowa University Press, 1994), 215.

29. Alan Nadel, "Boundaries, Logistics, and Identity: The Property of Metaphor in *Fences* and *Joe Turner's Come and Gone*," in *May All Your Fences Have Gates: Essays on the Drama of August Wilson*, ed. Alan Nadel (Iowa City: Iowa University Press, 1994), 88.

30. Sandra Shannon, *The Dramatic Vision of August Wilson* (Washington, D.C.: Howard University Press, 1995), 108.

31. Moyers, *World of Ideas*, 172.

32. Harry Elam, "August Wilson," 854.

33. Harry Elam, "August Wilson's Women," in *May All Your Fences Have Gates: Essays on the Drama of August Wilson*, ed. Alan Nadel (Iowa City: Iowa University Press, 1994), 165.

34. Moyers, *World of Ideas*, 172.

35. Alice Walker, "In Search of Our Mothers' Gardens," in *Within the Circle: An Anthology of African American Literary Criticism from the Harlem Renaissance to the Present*, ed. Angelyn Mitchell (Durham, NC: Duke University Press, 1994), 402.

36. Telia U. Anderson, "Calling on the Spirit: The Performativity of Black Women's Faith in the Baptist Church Spiritual Traditions and Its Radical Possibilities for Resistance," in *African American Performance and Theater History: A Critical Reader*, ed. Harry Elam and David Krasner (New York: Oxford University Press, 2001), 115.

37. Elam, "August Wilson's Women," 179.

38. bel hooks, *Yearning: Race, Gender, and Cultural Politics* (Boston: South End, 1990), 86.

39. August Wilson, "I Want a Black Director," in *May All Your Fences Have Gates: Essays on the Drama of August Wilson*, ed. Alan Nadel (Iowa City: Iowa University Press, 1994), 201.

40. Ibid., 204.

41. Ibid., 203.

42. Awkward, "The Crookeds with the Straights," 215.

43. Beginning in the early 1980s, Lloyd Richards became Wilson's editor, business counselor, and confidante. He directed *Ma Rainey's Black Bottom* on Broad-

way in 1984 and returned to that stage in subsequent years with *Fences* in 1987, *The Piano Lesson* in 1990, *Two Trains Running* in 1992, and *Seven Guitars* in 1996.

44. David Barbour, "August Wilson's Here to Stay," *Theater Week*, 18–25 April 1988, 14.

45. Ibid., 204.

46. Unofficial word among the theater community is that Wilson's current director Marion McClinton will direct the screenplay of *Fences*.

47. Wilson, "Black Director," 200.

48. Clive Barnes, "Fiery 'Fences,' " *New York Post*, 27 March 1987.

6   Art

For August Wilson, the art of writing is inescapably political and personal. Sitting alone with only a notepad, pen, and one's thoughts or, as he often puts it, "facing one's demons" entails a complex act of self-discovery on one hand and a profound articulation of the black tradition on the other. Fortunately for those who wish to study the genius of his plays, August Wilson's art is no secret. Unlike many writers, he apparently has no qualms about revealing in great detail the genesis of his artistic inspiration as well as the aesthetic and political nature of his work. Just as willingly and just as frequently, he underscores what he wishes his work to accomplish; he is a writer with a mission. In countless interviews and public addresses about his plays and his politics, he continues to painstakingly explain not just the art of his writing, but the politics as well.

But what special course does Wilson follow that allows his dramatic art to flourish rather than self-destruct under the weight of his polemics? Having been "fired in the kiln of black cultural nationalism,"[1] he is well aware of the list of short-lived works by his fellow cultural advocates of the 1960s whose poems, plays, and fiction waned and disappeared exponentially as the "movement" waned and disappeared. He is also quite aware of sentiments expressed by conservatives such as *New Republic* critic Robert Brustein, who argues,

Those who believe in art as a political weapon, as a method of empowering the disadvantaged, may serve a vital social function—

but there is a cost. A passionate political purpose occasionally obliges these artists to sacrifice individual truth for the collective good. . . . Art at its finest is inclusive, but ideological art is exclusive.[2]

Undaunted by the plight of fellow artists of the 1960s and equally unmoved by the ultra-conservative position of Robert Brustein, Wilson continues to stay the course with his brand of artistic politics or political art. *Fences* is part of this trend.

Wilson's formal training in the art of writing plays serves him well as he balances didacticism with his artistry. In the summer of 1979, his intense experience in a crash course in playwriting at the Eugene O'Neill Theater Center in Waterford, Connecticut, forced him to discipline and expand his concept of dramatic art. There, he met seasoned theater professionals who convinced him that clever metaphors and passionate speeches did not a play make. He learned aspects of timing and logistics of staging, and the realities that actors and actresses faced in live performances. He discovered, "I have to sort out the questions that pertain to acting—questions that actors would ask even if they were doing Shakespeare."[3] *Fences*, written some three years after Wilson's stint at the O'Neill Center, bears the fruit of this intense experience.

As a performance piece, *Fences* is, from all indications, the most widely staged of Wilson's plays. In fact, the text has become a favorite among aspiring actors and actresses during professional auditions. The sheer poetry and passion embedded in its language and the gut-wrenching emotional scenes allow acting hopefuls to show off their dramatic range. In act 1, scene 5, for example, Troy's very animated recollections of mysterious credit arrangements that somehow emerge between him and a furniture retailer has potential to tease out the best in acting capabilities. For Thespians with similar aspirations for the stage, act 1, scene 3 of *Fences* is a favorite script. Here, Troy takes full advantage of the occasion to lecture Cory on the importance of making wise decisions as a responsible African American man, particularly one who takes seriously his commitment as head of his household. The moral of Troy's speech at this juncture in the play comes through clearly: When faced with the dilemma of purchasing a television set or patching a leaky roof, the responsible African American man, of course, chooses the latter. Similarly, for actresses wishing to tout their performance capabilities, act 2, scene 1 of *Fences* provides an appropriate scenario. Here, Rose sheds her cocoon of domestic complacency and transforms into a virtual spitfire as she reaches into the depths of her womanhood to find verbal expression equivalent to her disgust with Troy.

Much of Wilson's unassuming skill in writing *Fences* goes into creating an organically sound play that revolves around a single antiheroic character (Troy) who advances a single theme (responsibility). With this in mind, then, the strength of the three dramatically suitable scenes above does not simply lie in their potential to tease out a successful performance. Just as important is how these pivotal moments sustain the theme of responsibility that permeates the play and that draws even more attention to the fundamentally flawed nature of Troy's tragic character. Toward this end, the emotional landscape has been carefully cultivated in advance. When certain characters enter a scene, for example, they bring with them some unresolved controversy. The emotional baggage that dovetails from one scene to the next, in such instances, sets up an automatic frame of emotional reference for both audience and characters, often negating the need for verbal transitions. For example, act 2, scene 4 of *Fences* opens with Troy's misdeeds being virtually a matter of public record. In the previous scene, he has confessed his infidelity; he and Rose have sparred; and the rules of their marriage have been drastically reconfigured. Accounts of his sexual liaison with Alberta have been divulged, including news of the child the two have conceived. Thus the opening dialogue in this scene and the mood that looms over it are largely in reaction to what has already immediately transpired. In this manner, then, Wilson solidifies the organic unity of *Fences* by dovetailing emotional carryover from one scene to the next and by consistently embracing the theme of responsibility through its line. As such, the showcase performance quality of Troy's lessons in responsibility and in Rose's passionate soliloquy further attest to Wilson's concentrated attention to the art of composing a play—one that is equally effective as a performance piece and as text-based drama.

Timing is also very much of the essence in *Fences*. Two scenes demonstrate how this aspect of Wilson's art contributes to the very tightly controlled nature of this work. During what is perhaps one of the most highly charged scenes in the play, Rose Maxson prepares for an all-out verbal confrontation with her adulterous husband. He has not only just confessed to his relationship with another woman, but he also multiplies his marital transgressions by telling his wife of eighteen years that he has impregnated his mistress lover. As if this is not sufficiently gripping, Wilson prolongs the inevitable fireworks by timing Gabriel's untimely entrance as an obvious delay tactic that allows audiences to linger on this moment a bit longer. The very pregnant (no pun intended) silence that Rose interrupts by attempts to spare her brother-in-law from the ugly scene that is about to erupt temporarily staves off her unbearable anger:

ROSE: Gabe, go on in the house there. I got some watermelon in the frigidaire. Go on and get you a piece . . .
GABRIEL: Okay, Rose . . . gonna get me some watermelon. The kind with the stripes on it. (*GABRIEL exits into the house.*)

(2.1.67)

Once Gabriel clears the scene, Rose holds no punches as she verbally lashes Troy in retaliation for his infidelity.

The art of timing illuminates another tense dramatic moment in *Fences*. Several days in the wake of Troy's dual confessions of infidelity and impending fatherhood, he sits alone drinking, wallowing in his blues, and contemplating the much-altered status of his life. His mistress Alberta has died in childbirth; Rose has essentially annulled their marriage and has decided to focus her time and energy upon Raynelle and the church; Gabriel has been committed to an institution; Bono's visits are noticeably less; and Cory detests Troy because of what he has done to his mother and to him. By all accounts Troy is the epitome of the pariah. Yet at what seems the nadir of his existence, Cory approaches. Unquestionably, the scene that follows has been carefully timed:

CORY: I got to get by.
TROY: Say what? What you say? [. . .]
CORY: I ain't scared of you.
TROY: I ain't asked if you was scared of me. I asked you if you was fixing to walk over top of me in my own house? That's the question. You ain't gonna say excuse me? You just gonna walk over top of me?
CORY: If you wanna put it like that.

(2.4.84–5)

This encounter solidifies the dissolution of any remaining paternal ties between father and son. Respect has been irreversibly eroded. To Cory, Troy is an obstacle. To Troy, Cory is "just another nigger" (2.4.87).

Two other aspects of timing in *Fences* significantly contribute to the play's artistry. In the tradition of Tennessee Williams's *The Glass Menagerie* (1945) and Arthur Miller's *Death of a Salesman* (1949), *Fences* is a memory play. In other words, the narrative sequence of *Fences* is informed by both the playwright's remembered past and the recollections of the play's troubled protagonist Troy Maxson. The play proper spans eight years, yet when considering the extent to which memory informs *Fences*, its time frame increases to an additional six decades. As such, the play's larger narrative essentially begins with Reconstruction in United States history (1865–1915) and spans to the dawn of the civil rights era (1965).

Fences is strategically and pivotally situated in the 1950s—a decade that in retrospect, teeters on the brink of monumental civil rights legislation and a general improvement in the circumstances for African Americans. While this postwar play edges toward revolutionary change on the eve of the civil rights movement, its fifty-three-year-old protagonist can still recall his experiences as a sharecropper's son. Indeed, the play is deliberately situated in a time that invites both nostalgia and regret over the past and, at the same time, promises positive change.

From a structuralist perspective, Wilson's deliberate manipulation of time through the window of Troy's memory generates meaning. More than a matter of juxtaposing past, present, and future as signalled by three generations of Maxson men, *Fences*, as argued by Gunilla Kester and Harry Elam, invites dialectic discussions that underscore the profound impact that the past has on the present. Both view Troy's past as one that extends beyond the physical borders of the United States and that taps into an atavistic ancestral memory grounded in Africa. Kester writes,

> On the one hand, in contrast to a temporal sense of return, the spatialization of history strongly suggests that the distance as well as the need to approach Africa is equally vital for each new generation of African Americans. On the other, it contains a warning that, to become a dynamo of change, each such approach must involve a fresh revision of the metaphoric relationship between the black body and its history.[4]

Like Kester, Elam sees new meaning in the retrieval of history through memory in *Fences*. And, like Kester, Elam sees Africa as Troy's most dominant *lieux de memoire* (place of memory):

> While not unique, what is significant about Wilson's spatialization of time is its trajectory backwards into history. The journey points toward Africa and joins for me with the West African concept of

"Sankofa" in providing insight into the presence of the past in Wilson's work. In Swahili the term "Sankofa"—symbolized by the Sankofa bird, who as legend goes flies forward with his head turned backwards—means that one must understand the past in order to move present into the future.[5]

Wilson's compression of time in *Fences* allows history to become a much more obvious factor in determining the future. That is, by foregrounding mistakes as well as best practices from the past, Troy is able to make positive use of history to shape a better future.

Fences is simultaneously informed by Wilson's remembered past as well as a collective African American past to which he automatically lays claim as a member of this community. At the same time, *Fences* hinges upon vivid recollections of its protagonist, images of a past brought more clearly into focus through the lens of his memory. These experiences, which emerge in the form of nostalgia or nightmarish recollections, have much to do with Troy's philosophy on life and his general circumstances. Although Wilson's memory of his adolescence does provide a good deal of the framework for *Fences*, certain characters' remembrances of days gone by provide additional perspectives on his preoccupation with the past. Wilson allows memory in *Fences* to extend beyond his recognized moments from the past to include recollections of the characters he creates.

The definition of art must also acknowledge what goes into the process of its creation: the behind-the-scenes trials and errors and—as was the case with *Fences* up until and during its Broadway run—constant revisions. When one examines the persistent and methodical metamorphosis that the play underwent from a lumbering three-and-a-half-hour, unfocused script to a sharply polished Pulitzer Prize contender, one gains a renewed appreciation for the art of creating drama. In her study revealing the idiosyncrasies of Wilson's playwriting process, Joan Herrington examines the artistry that went into the making of the much-acclaimed definitive version of *Fences*. Having had firsthand access to August Wilson and having been allowed to examine successive drafts of *Fences*, the one-time dramaturg got a unique glimpse into intricate details of Wilson's art of revision.

The revision process for *Fences* hinged upon Wilson's insistence to advance a single theme in the play: the responsible African American man. The image of an African American man holding a baby in his arms that is featured in a collage by Romare Bearden (see *Continuities* 1969) became the catalyst that spurred Wilson to write against white America's prevailing assumptions that African American men are essentially irresponsible and ultimately shiftless: "White America pays no attention to the Troy Maxson's in this world. They see niggers as lazy and shiftless. Well, Troy is a man who is trying to fulfill tremendous responsibility."[6] This would not be the first time that Wilson's art was to take its cue from another artistic medium (see also *Joe Turner's Come and Gone* and *The Piano Lesson*). According to Wilson, the reason for his attraction to Bearden's work has much to do with the African American collagist's ability to capture in the patchwork images of *Continuities* what the African American playwright sought to convey in his dramatic text set in the 1950s.

The scenario of this apparently agrarian-inspired landscape evokes images of the Reconstruction era when the slavelike system of sharecropping turned Wilson's thoughts to the need to deconstruct the die-hard myth of the irresponsible and ultimately shiftless African American man that proliferated in that society. In pursuit of this goal, he fashioned each of the characters in *Fences* to underscore some aspect of the theme of responsibility. For example, Lyons, Troy's older son from a previous marriage, is antithetical to the notion of responsibility that Troy preaches throughout the play. Lyons's chief function in the play, then, is that of a foil character, as his avoidance of work at all cost and his dependency upon his working woman and his working father for support make Troy into a heroic figure by contrast. This is made quite obvious as his entrances and exits revolve around securing money from Troy. In fact, the frequency with which Lyons shows up, especially on Fridays (a.k.a. payday) turns the entire borrowing and lending game into a ritual. It also becomes a win-win situation for father and son: It gives Troy the opportunity to harp on being responsible and to expose the obvious shortcomings of his deadbeat son. It gives Lyons easy access to money on a weekly basis. Troy basks in his ability to hand over $10 of his hard-earned pay, but not without the additional pleasure that comes with shaming an essentially shameless son. Lyons, who appears to understand that his borrowing satisfies his father's fetish, gladly cooperates.

Similar energy is expended in focused attempts to foreground the theme of responsibility in the construction of Rose Maxson. In early drafts of the play, as Herrington points out, Rose "is much more a nagging wife."[7] However, Wilson did not want this nagging to have any connection to Troy's infidelity. Thus, in subsequent drafts, he removes much of the nagging and replaces it with tolerance, forgiveness, and understanding—qualities that clearly surface in her conversation with Cory just before they depart for Troy's funeral: "Your daddy wanted you to be everything that he wasn't . . . and at the same time he tried to make you into everything he was. I don't know if he was right or wrong . . . but I do know he meant to do more good than he meant to do harm" (2.5.97).

While it is Troy on whom the theme of the responsible black man rests, it is Rose on whom Wilson relies to punctuate it more clearly. For much of the play, her character stands half in the shadows, functioning exclusively within the domestic realm as Troy's helpmate, his lover, his cook, his center of gravity. As she fulfills the wifely and the domestic roles that society expects of black women of the 1950s, she fosters a climate wherein Troy can demonstrate at every opportunity just how responsible he can be. For Troy, reinforcing this theme becomes one of his favorite Friday night rituals. Handing over his weekly paycheck to Rose for household expenditures becomes a public ceremony in which he delights: "There it is. Seventy-six dollars and forty-two cents. You see this, Bono? Now, I ain't gonna get but six of that back" (1.1.19).

The extent of Wilson's art may also be appreciated by examining the roles of supporting characters; that is, those individuals who at first appear to be marginal to the play, but upon closer examination, prove essential to its conflict. Although, to a certain extent, each of the characters in *Fences* is peripheral to Troy, it is perhaps Raynelle and Alberta who seem most remote. Upon closer examination, however, both play key roles in highlighting antithetical examples of Troy's concept of responsibility. One causes the dissolution of Troy and Rose's marriage; the other forces reconciliation—albeit conditional. Alberta affirms Troy's walking blues or his tendency to stray from regimentation, commitment, and responsibility, and, unlike Rose, she demands nothing of him—not his loyalty, not his money, not even his time. Never physically appearing in the play and known only through conversations *about* her, Alberta becomes merely a manifestation of Troy's own flawed character. As such, she manages to escape judgment and persecution from both Rose as well as from the audience.

Troy and Alberta's love child Raynelle also plays an unassuming yet pivotal role in *Fences*. Harry Elam sees her as "a critical element in his [Wilson's] redemptive strategy" and posits that she "visually represents the inextricable connection between past and present. Not only is she a manifestation of Troy's past infidelities but also the signifier of his redemption."[8] However, at first as an infant and eventually as a child, she demands from both Rose and Troy an unprecedented degree of soul-searching. Doing so forces them to grapple with some profound issues involving their humanity. Deciding the child's fate—given the extremely difficult circumstances surrounding her birth—is perhaps one of the toughest arrangements that Troy and Rose have to make. Nevertheless both grow noticeably in the wake of their respective decisions to yield up the child to another woman and raise her husband's illegitimate daughter as her own.

Raynelle is a paradox. Although she is conceived in infidelity by a father who is approaching the waning years of his life, she represents hope. She offers that redemptive assurance that Wilson vows to impart at the close of each play that his African American characters are at least pointing in the right direction. This child who never knew her own biological mother, in turn, fills a maternal void in Rose, and in her childlike innocence, lures her brother back to the fold. In the midst of death, profound disappointment, and sadness, she unwittingly becomes an agent of healing. At the close of *Fences*, the Maxson family is intact and poised for unimaginably positive changes in their quality of living.

True to his early grounding as a poet, August Wilson conceives of his art in eloquent terms, likening what is for him a spiritual and deeply personal commitment to finding his song and to walking down an unfamiliar landscape. But he also sees in his calling a mandate to convey the imprint of black culture and to rewrite the history of African Americans. When asked to explain this empowering act, he resorts to visionary statements, such as "to write is to fix language, to get it down and fix it to a spot and have it have meaning and be fat with substance. It is in many ways a remaking of the self in which all of the parts have been realigned, redistributed, and reassembled into a new being of sense and harmony"[9] and "I write from the center, the core of myself. You've got that landscape and you've got to enter it, walk down the road and whatever happens, happens. And that's the best you're capable of coming to. The characters do it, and in them, I confront myself."[10] His compassion is matched by his eloquence.

Wilson's fascination with language—the sound and the sting of his words and the poetry he eventually discovered in the everyday conversations of black people—is perhaps one of his greatest gifts as a playwright. Earlier in his developing career, he actually labored to transfer that fascination from his ear to the written page. However, a fortuitous move to Minnesota in 1978 brought into sharper focus the language he haphazardly overheard on the streets and in the bars and restaurants of his native Hill District in Pittsburgh. This experience revealed to him that the conversations of these people, many of whom he had grown up with, were indeed worthy to be regarded as art. Nevertheless, it took the 1987 runaway success of *Fences*'s predecessor, *Ma Rainey's Black Bottom* to convince Wilson that his writing had evolved from the overblown, stilted speech that characterized his earlier efforts at writing fledgling plays, such as *Recycle* (1973) and *The Coldest Day of the Year* (1976). In what was apparently for Wilson a much-needed dose of confidence, reviewers heaped praise upon *Ma Rainey*, pointing to the playwright's exceptional skill at making his characters' speech familiar to the ears of many. As a result, audiences were more prone to know—and, therefore, understand—the predicaments of the individual member of Gertrude "Ma" Rainey's all–African American male band.

"Wilson has one of the finest ears for language in American theater. Using characters who speak with rolling, fluid rhythms, he accurately and purposefully records black speech and life. *Fences* is full of rich idioms, funny lines and arresting images."[11] So writes David Lida in his review of the Broadway premiere of *Fences*. Capitalizing upon a newfound confidence that *Ma Rainey* bestowed upon him, Wilson took his proven skill at putting words into his characters' mouths to another level.

The sheer artistry of language in *Fences* is evident on several levels, not just in the playwright's mission to set Troy Maxson apart from the mundane aspects of his environment. Wilson's carefully choreographed rhetorical, narrative, and performance maneuvers also call further attention to his mastery of the artistic craft of composing drama. Chief among the exemplary linguistic devices in *Fences* are realistic, recognizable markers of black vernacular. The uncut, unabridged presentation of cultural idioms and other idiosyncrasies peculiar to verbal communication among African American males during the late 1950s affirms Wilson's carefully trained ear. Troy and Bono, in particular, have adopted in the manner of their talk rhythmic cadences and tones that encompass a wide range of emotions from jubilation to despair. As is expected, these men drop all pretense of decorum in their verbal exchanges, yet even as they do so, they preserve the eloquence and power of their oral tradition.

The manner in which Wilson manipulates language in *Fences* to underscore Troy Maxson's humanity, his gusto for life, and his profound awareness of his own mortality does much to subvert stereotypical notions that might devalue the garbageman's blue-collar status. The play's protagonist speaks with rich, figurative eloquence even though his economic status places him clearly below the poverty level. The poet in Wilson transforms Troy into the common man's bard who fashions protective armor out of his words to ward against various forms of symbolic emasculation that threaten his humanity. At the same time, Wilson's careful crafting of Troy's many soliloquies, his retorts, his pontifications, and his blues laments enlarges Troy's character and noticeably transforms *Fences* into a clear example of the tragedy of the common man.

Troy Maxson's obvious gift for telling stories is also his uniquely round-about way of imparting life lessons to his sons. Still suffering from the left-over psychological effects of slave-master mentality that stifled the emotions of his father as well as his grandfather, Troy, perhaps unwittingly, adheres to the belief that any show of paternal warmth might be misconstrued as a flaw in his character. Somewhere also in his blood's memory is the idea that, in the face of imminent separation, self-preservation mandates a degree of emotional detachment. This stoic principle extends to both of his sons, whom he deals with essentially at arm's length and on strictly business terms. If there does exist a bond between Troy and Cory or between Troy and Lyons, it is one that he has carefully masked and suppressed beneath the exaggerated rhetoric that he has mastered. Somewhere within this space provided by storytelling, Troy accepts his role as father and tries to counsel his sons in terms that he knows best. "By teaching family responsibility to his sons through stories," Anna Blumenthal observes, "he enacts that responsibility which he teaches."[12]

Never having the benefit of a father to advise him on what being a man entails, Troy is left to his own means of constructing and becoming what is, in his estimation, the ideal African American man. Troy's version of black manhood would, understandably, reflect aspects of his own father's cruel indifference. But his construction of masculinity also bears the battered psyche of one who struck out on his own early from his father's house. Such an eclectic construct of black manhood must take into account Troy's street savvy as well as his self-righteous posture on responsibility. The tough lessons he learned from his father while in Alabama, his memories as husband and father, and his brush with crime while up North and subsequent incarceration shaped him into the unrelenting, rebellious, assertive, hardworking, sexually liberal, yet very responsible Troy whom we see for better or for worse in *Fences*.

So storytelling transcends its traditional role as entertainment in *Fences* to become a substitute for what might be, under different circumstances, fatherly advice. According to Blumenthal, "Troy's stories reflect his conscious narrative art."[13] While Troy's vivid accounts still cause laughter, capture the imagination, and engage his toughest critics, they also serve as a means of teaching by example. Blumenthal further asserts that "Wilson's dramatizing of Troy's struggle enhances our respect for Troy despite his failures in the play because in his stories, Troy enacts paternal and familial duty by teaching it in his narratives."[14] For example, the subtext beneath Troy's shameful recollections of his father's lust for his young girlfriend is a lesson couched in antithetical examples of fatherhood. Although Troy's understanding of father-son justice prepares him for the beating he thinks he deserves for neglecting the mule, it does not account for the shocking sexual liberties his father takes with the terrified girl. In this narrative, Troy communicates through his past experiences that his father was anything but a role model for him. This narrative also teaches that Troy's character, by contrast, far outshines that of his Neanderthal father. His decision to leave this environment of tyranny behind him and never to return speaks to his principles, his knowledge of what constitutes ethical and unethical, and his clear demarcation between barbarous and civil behavior. He wanted nothing more to do with the man who could rape his girlfriend just as easily as he could eat a whole chicken and leave his children his leftovers.

The art that characterizes Troy's keen sense for storytelling entails aspects of timing as well as knowledge of his audience's tolerance level. What gestures or rhetorical strategies might be used in the delivery to enhance credibility? How far can he stretch the narrative before his listener(s) dismisses it as a hoax? Is it more important to be heard or to be believed? Apparently Wilson knows the answers to such questions, for Troy is quite adept at sustaining the attention of his audience and at maintaining a delicate balance between the real and the supernatural elements: A coworker steals a watermelon and tries to get it past his boss by hiding it under his coat. Death becomes a wrestling partner when Troy lies sick with pneumonia. A mysterious stranger shows up at Troy's door and grants him credit to buy furniture. Cory learns why a television is not a responsible purchase. Old Blue never heeded a command; still he was a "good old dog." These and other such narrative jewels are testaments to Troy's oratorical artistry. Of course, Troy's art is a testament to Wilson's art, which, in his role of playwright, demonstrates his intimate understanding of the psychological and sociological importance of crafting and relating good stories within the African American community.

Wilson's dramatic art also revolves around opposites: life and death; separation and reunion; incarceration and emancipation; Christianity and African spiritualism; supernatural and natural. Frequently his audiences will find themselves laughing uproariously at one moment and, at another, experiencing profound sorrow. In *Fences*, for example, humor and tragedy coexist to the extent that the two human conditions actually complement each other to reflect realistically this man's—and any man's—triumphs and failures. At one point Troy can barely contain his amusement while recalling a humorously absurd incident from work involving a coworker charged with stealing a watermelon from his supervisor and attempting to conceal it under his coat. Within this same context, Troy later bitterly denounces discriminatory conditions on his job. As Qun Wang observes, "Humor is sometimes created in the blues with the use of 'comic hyperbole' . . . Yet at other times the sardonic tone of the lines highlights the speaker's tragic sense of life."[15] Langston Hughes defines this tendency among African Americans to erase the boundaries between tragedy and humor in *The Book of Negro Humor* where he writes, humor is "laughing at what you haven't got when you ought to have it" and humor is "what you wish in your secret heart were not funny, but it is, and you must laugh."[16] Humor is the medicine that keeps the tragicomic dimensions of Troy Maxson's life in their proper perspective.

That Troy and Bono appear to place so much stock in their verbal agility mirrors Wilson's early enlightenment about the profound beauty and artistry in black vernacular speech. Rich with sparkling metaphors and idiomatic wisdom, Troy's everyday talk stands to rival any of Shakespeare's carefully arranged lines. In justifying his attraction to Alberta, for example, he confesses, "But seems like this woman just stuck onto me where I can't shake her loose" (2.1.63). In issuing increasingly mounting warnings to his son Cory, he fashions a clever metaphor using the context that he knows best—the game of baseball: "I'm gonna tell you what your mistake was. See . . . you swung at the ball and didn't hit it. That's strike one. See, you in the batter's box now. You swung and you missed. That's strike one. Don't you strike out!" (2.4.58). In both instances, Troy's speech is immersed in figurative language that opens a window to his thinking and that captures his very particular emotions. In this fashion Troy can convey the recesses of his blues at one point and just as easily shift to celebrate a moment of triumph at another.

The calculated nature of Wilson's art in *Fences* is reflected in the cultural mission he openly expresses for his decade-by-decade chronicle of the African American experience in the twentieth century: "[T]o actually keep all of the elements of the culture alive in the work . . . I purposefully go through and make sure each element of that is in some way represented—some more so than others in the plays, which I think gives them a fullness and a completeness—that this is an entire world."[17] The ease with which African American folkloric expression permeates Troy

Maxson's casual conversations belies such a premeditated approach. In addition to Troy's skill in the use of figurative imagery, then, folklore also becomes part of his verbal arsenal.

In *Fences* the function of folklore goes beyond providing local color. Defined as "all of the unwritten traditional beliefs, legends, sayings, customs, etc. of a culture,"[18] folklore is, for Wilson, a major signifier and key contextual device. As Trudier Harris points out, "Wilson creates folklore . . . that is recognizable even in its surface unfamiliarity."[19] References to folklore add cultural flavor to Troy's exaggerated narratives, at the core of which often lie his keen awareness of his weaknesses and his strengths as an African American man in the 1950s. For Troy, the shortest narrative distance for getting at that truth is not a straight line. Rather it is a meandering, prolonged detour, complete with a loquacious display of verbal agility; he rarely communicates in strictly literal terms. In such instances, folklore allows Troy to move language from beyond the realm of the mundane, the commonplace, and the literal to that of the sublime, the fantastical, and the supernatural.

Folklore satisfies Troy's need for hyperbole and allows him to create a mythic world where he reigns supreme. At the same time, folklore provides the stuff of the blues and enables him to put a finger on the source of his melancholy. Drawing upon popular concepts about death, for example, that have been handed down from one generation of African Americans to the next, Troy is able to construct an image of himself as a formidable match for the Grim Reaper. At the same time, he fashions himself to be the penultimate example of masculinity—the undaunted, indefatigable warrior. When a three-day bout with pneumonia becomes a near-death experience for him, Troy refuses to play victim to Death's virtually unstoppable march. Determined to save face, Troy accords Death a convincing set of human characteristics and proceeds to tout his comparable physical and mental superiority over the embodied spirit: "Death ain't nothin. I done seen him. Done wrassled with him" (1.1.10), he tells Rose, who worries that he drinks too much. Once summoned to the realm of the living, Troy's arch foe engages him in lengthy mortal combat that ends in a standoff. To hear Troy tell it, Death finally yields, grabs his white robe, and stalks away after promising to give the battle-weary Troy an extension.

What is most intriguing about Troy's account of this harrowing experience is that its acceptance as reality does not depend upon the extent to which his immediate witnesses in the play suspend disbelief. In fact, neither Rose nor Bono put much stock in Troy's account of his rendezvous with Death. Rose discredits every aspect of her husband's story while Bono facetiously writes him off as a relative of Uncle Remus. Still, Troy seems energized by the apparent adrenaline rush that comes along with his attempt to perform Death into actual existence. Against the pleas of his wife to desist, he insists upon finishing his story.

Troy must know that Rose and Bono find his often-told story rather irksome, yet he persists out of what seems to be a self-therapeutic need to vent this particular experience—to remember. Unlike Herald Loomis, the psychologically and spiritually troubled protagonist of Wilson's *Joe Turner's Come and Gone* (1988) who has suppressed deep within his subconscious the African experience during the Middle Passage, Troy seems ever-willing and actually pressed to tell his story to anyone within ear range. Whereas Loomis finds relief only when Bynum, the resident conjure man, performs the role of spiritual healer and draws these experiences out of him, Troy needs no such therapy. Although, on the surface, the weight of these two African American men's experiences may seem incomparable, in actuality Troy's highly rhetorical—and, at times, amusing—performance deflects attention from issues that are, for him, just as profound and just as troubling as are Loomis's demons. Troy's much-rehearsed Death narrative, then, may very well be his unique way of grappling with the enormity of his own mortality while taking care not to jeopardize his cherished warrior image. Beneath the rhetoric and the posturing is the very conceivable implication that Troy Maxson is actually terrified of Death! The conflict of *Fences* insinuates as much. When Bono takes him to task about his selection of wood for Rose's fence, Troy bristles at even the remotest reference to his passing:

BONO: You don't need this wood [hardwood]. You can put it up with pine wood and it'll stand as long as you gonna be here looking at it.

TROY: How you know how long I'm gonna be here, nigger? Hell, I might just live forever. Live longer than old man Horsely.

(2.1.61)

Even though, to some extent, Troy performs for himself and becomes his own audience, he also presses his larger audiences to accept his reality. The extent to which Troy can create a credible image of Death in the minds of his immediate witnesses and the play's larger audience depends not just upon the garbageman's eloquence but also upon the credibility of his performance. Thus, to will Death into existence, Troy must bring all of his acting skills to bear to convince any listener that he has seen, talked to, wrestled with, and been touched by the Grim Reaper. Using verbal skills that rival the mime's convincing gestures, Troy is able to create reality through the sheer power of language. So convincing is he that, perhaps for a moment, audiences may suspend disbelief and accept Troy's exaggerated testimony as reality: "I looked up one day and Death was marching straight at me. Like Soldiers on Parade! The Army of Death was marching straight at me. The middle of July, 1941" (1.1.11).

Troy's efforts to will Death into existence via an exceptionally convincing performance also turn our attention to the role that the playwright plays in asserting this reality. Taking his cue from African American cultural perspectives on death and dying, Wilson creates a mythic image of Death that asserts its own reality. According to Trudier Harris,

> He [Wilson] does not establish the possibility of the existence of certain phenomena; he simply writes as if they are givens. We might say that his plays begin "in medias res." A world exists; Wilson invites viewers into it. Instead of going to meet the audience by trying to *prove* belief in supernatural phenomena, Wilson unapologetically invites the audience to come into his world, to rise to his level of belief.[20]

In African American culture, as in most cultures, death is accorded much respect. Its randomness; its inevitability; its impartiality to wealth, power, race, class, or religion; and its awesome finality have the potential to humble as no other reality can. In some instances, it occasions mourning within the African American community, but in others, it has become cause for celebration. Many of the rituals and emotional responses to death are the by-products of African retention that survived the Middle Passage. As one historian posits,

> Belief in afterlife was integral to traditional African religion. But Africans did not view the future world with fear nor as a place of dispensations for rewards and punishments in a Christian sense. In this land of the dead, where life continued, there was no sickness, disease, poverty, or hunger. . . . Death was a journey into the spirit world, not a break with life or earthly beings.[21]

Clearly African views on death, as expressed here, challenge the very premise of certain popular biblical concepts promoted by Christianity: the resurrection, Judgment Day, Saint Peter and the Pearly Gates, Archangel Gabriel, and the belief that upon death, the soul shall either ascend to heaven or be cast down into the fiery inferno of hell for all eternity.

In her account of the painstaking revisions that went into the making of *Fences*, Joan Herrington notes that in earlier versions of the play, Wilson humbled Troy before Jesus. That, of course, implied that Troy was prone to subordinate his will to that of a higher power and that the ground rules for responsibility were determined by Christian ethics rather than by Troy's rugged individualism. In an early draft of *Fences*, when news of Alberta's death reaches him, Troy "rails at Jesus, asking for salvation in the face of his trials."[22] Yet in subsequent revisions, Troy does not even consider Christianity as a source of consolation. In fact, he seems much more preoccupied by the Devil instead.

It is by Wilson's design, then, that Troy avoids Christian references as he faces a series of devastating news. Rather than resort to prayers and supplication when Alberta dies, for example, he braces himself in the face of this tragedy and apostrophizes Death as one would an old acquaintance:

Alright . . . Mr. Death. See now . . . I'm gonna tell you what I'm gonna do. I'm gonna take and build me a fence around what belongs to me. And then I want you to stay on the other side. See? You stay over there until you're ready for me. Then you come on. Bring your army. Bring your sickle. Bring your wrestling clothes. I ain't gonna fall down on my vigilance this time. You ain't gonna sneak up on me no more. When you ready for me . . . when the top of your list say Troy Maxson . . . that's when you come around here. (2.2.77)

Interestingly, Troy's very personalized way of negotiating the profundity of death is informed not so much by concerns about the afterlife where his circumstances may be improved. Instead, he adopts a perspective that seems antithetical to Christian and Africanist concepts, both of which regard death as a sequel rather than as a final chapter. In retrospect, however, Wilson determined that any suggestion that it is God who determines Troy's destiny must be eradicated, for this would weaken the play's emphasis upon its central theme of responsibility. The art behind his efforts at this point was directed toward making Troy the master of his fate and the captain of his soul.

Ironically Troy draws his strength by constructing death as a worthy opponent in battle. Such regard is but an extension of his heightened estimation of himself as one part warrior, one part bluesman. That is, he fears no one and no thing. He conceives of death as a game of chance, much like baseball where the victor is determined not by the circumstances of his birth but by sheer stamina and skill. When Troy likens death to "a fast ball on the outside corner," then, he interprets it by using terms that he understands. This is a context in which winning or losing simply depends upon one's ability to get a chance at bat.

Troy stands in awe of death's finality to the extent that he spends a significant amount of time positioning himself, both mentally and physically, for its inevitable arrival. Much as one would spar before an actual match, Troy practices swinging his bat at a ball of rags that hangs from his tree. This ritual, together with Troy's imaginative embodiment of Death, eases his anxiety about the unknown and lets him at least pretend to have some control over his fate. To Troy, outwitting Death or making contact with that rag ball becomes ultimate tests of his masculinity. Still, Troy's triumph is his ability to resist, to engage in battle, and to fight the good fight. "He was out there swinging that bat," Rose reveals. "I was just ready to go back in the house. He swung that bat and then he just fell over. Seem like he swung it and stood there with this grin on his face . . . and then he just fell over" (2.5.95–6).

Just as Death is the source of a rich vein of African American folklore, images of endeared animals and ominous humans are also the focus of popular lore. In Zora Neale Hurston's *Their Eyes Were Watching God*, for example, Matt Bonner's yellow mule became the focus of numerous store-front conversations of townspeople. So popular was this equestrian-focused pastime, that the skilled group of "mule-talkers,"[23] as they were called, created a body of folklore that raised Bonner's animal to heroic status. The nature of such folklore often begins in competitive verbal jousting about some unassuming, familiar creature and, over time, evolves into myth and legend. What begins as a simple farm animal in *Their Eyes Were Watching God* turns into the protagonist of many a trickster tale and the brunt of numerous jokes.

In *Fences*, Troy accords his trusted dog Blue with similar heroic status. Whereas Matt Bonner's mule becomes a catalyst for collective humor, Blue's revered memory provides balm for one man's pain. The folklore that takes shape around animal subjects functions in a variety of ways, confirming Henry Louis Gates and Nellie McKay's assertion that "African Americans hammered these myriad tales into unmistakably black American shapes and themes. The voices of the stories . . . marked them as African American. So did the particular turns of the plot as well as the particular heroes, dupes, and villains, and their values."[24]

During several of Troy's blues moments, when he pauses long enough to contemplate his tragic plight, he lovingly evokes the memory of a canine companion name Blue. Doing so apparently fills up the gaping space around him left vacant by his now deeply disappointed family members and friend. Six months after he delivers a double blow to his wife, he sits alone on the steps to his home. Noticeably, he does not demonstrate his profound sense of alienation by moaning or crying. Instead, he breaks into song about "a good old dog" named Blue.

> Here it ring! Hear it ring!
> I had a dog his name was Blue . . . .
> > You know Blue was mighty true . . . .
> > You know Blue was a good old dog . . . .
> > Blue treed a possum in a hollow log

(1.4.44)

Apparently by invoking Blue's memory in song, Troy is able to grapple with the nadir of his emotions. Apparently dead for some time (or more likely romanticized as such), Blue is resurrected in the lyrics of an often-chanted song, the substance of which Troy respectfully credits to his father.

In Troy's resurrection of Blue, one gets a glimpse into the genesis and psychology of folklore. One is also able to appreciate Wilson's regard for and skill at capturing nuances of the African American oral tradition in his work. Wilson blends a mixture of verisimilitude and hyperbole in his representation of Blue in an effort to approximate the highly figurative nature of African American oral lore. Just as in his construction of Death as Troy's mortal foe or in the construction of the furniture creditor as an ominous visitor, complete suspension of disbelief is inconsequential. Likewise, the effectiveness of Troy's stories about Death, the dog, or the furniture creditor may not rest solely upon whether he actually wrestled with Death, owned a dog named Blue, or encountered a foreboding stranger. Nor is it of consequence that those listening to him give any credence to these claims. What is more important, however, is the skill of the narrator in teasing his listeners to at least accept some part of his constructions as conceivable and to, in fact, listen to him long enough for him to put his storytelling skills to the test. Success in the eyes of the narrator (i.e., Troy) can be measured in terms of the amount of time an audience finds him engaging before dismissing him and his tale as bogus. Even if this is the case, the storyteller in him still enjoys a measure of success in honing his art. Anna Blumenthal underscores this argument in her essay that explores the art that underlies Troy's stories and Wilson's considerable skill in converting this oral medium to the stage. She asserts, "Troy shapes his narratives with his audience clearly in mind, and his skill is such that he is able to hold his listeners' interest even with extended stories, whether they are built from his past experience or from imagined material."[25]

The art of Wilson's words in *Fences* extends beyond Troy Maxson's frequent figurative allusions to the potentially volatile use of the word "nigger." Much discussion continues to generate around this potentially explosive term, yet Wilson appears less concerned about the word's political correctness than he is about its effectiveness in capturing the verisimilitude of his characters' speech. As was certainly the case during his early years in Pittsburgh, the term was commonplace on the streets in the inner-city urban area where he grew up as well as in its bars, restaurants, and other gathering places that he frequented. Randall Kennedy, Harvard University law professor and author of *Nigger: The Strange Career of a Troublesome Word* (2002), posits some interesting observations about the legacy of this word and the unwavering stigma associated with its continued use. He notes that the word "nigger" "has been the most socially destructive racial epithet in the American language."[26] Nevertheless, audiences who attend performances of *Fences*, or any of Wilson's plays, for that matter, are regularly peppered by the word "nigger"—so much so that they are either mildly irritated or completely appalled by it or else they eventually concede to the communal bond it affirms.

One must note that the utterance of the word "nigger" during a live performance—whether in *Fences* or in any of Wilson's other plays—has an impact that is significantly different from meaning gained by reading it on the page. Other contributing factors that determine whether the word agitates or simply communicates in a live performance are race, class, and gender demographics of the audience. As one might imagine, the most uncomfortable reception of "nigger" might conceivably come from the demographically mixed group. Surely the label "nigger," when released by the roaring, angry voice of a man denied his dream, has the potential to reverberate throughout the theater space, giving a clearer indication of the pain and suffering that Troy feels yet perhaps still causing discomfort among those who agree with Langston Hughes's contention that

[t]he word nigger to colored people of high and low degree is like a red rag to a bull. Used rightly or wrongly, ironically or seriously, of necessity for the sake of realism, or impishly for the sake of comedy, it doesn't matter. Negroes do not like it in any book or play whatso-ever, be the book or play ever so sympathetic in its treatment of the basic problems of the race. Even though the book or play is written by a Negro, they still do not like it. The word nigger, you see, sums up for us who are colored all the bitter years of insult and struggle in America.[27]

In his *Dictionary of Afro-American Slang* (1970), Clarence Major explains the emotional bond between African American males that is sig-naled by the word "nigger." He posits that when the term is bantered about during black-on-black conversations, it becomes "a racial term with undertones of warmth and goodwill—reflecting, aside from irony, a tragicomic sensibility that is aware of black history."[28] Within the context of *Fences*, where the dialogue is, for the most part, driven by African American males who are inclined to speak more openly outside the gaze of white hegemony, the term "nigger" is far from being a racial slur. On the contrary, the prevalence of this label underscores the existence of a magic circle or special brotherhood who, by virtue of their shared experi-ences as black men in America, find it necessary to adopt a privileged, specialized language. That language affords a safe place from which they may speak to power and affirm their masculinity. That language also pro-vides space to get in touch with their sensitive nature without sacrificing what makes them men. When Troy confides in Bono—his friend for much of his life—the word "nigger" is clearly a term of endearment and even more so an acknowledgment of a fraternal closeness spawned by years of shared experiences—both good and bad:

> Bono like family. I done known this nigger since . . . how long I done know you? . . . I done known this nigger since Skippy was a pup. Me and him done been through some times. . . . Hell, I done know him longer than I known you [to Rose]. And we still standing shoulder to shoulder. Hey, look here, Bono . . . a man can't ask for no more than that . . . I love you, nigger." (1.4.57)

Kennedy endorses the fraternal bond that "nigger" may highlight among African American men, but he emphasizes that these closed circles of men do not completely divorce its meaning from its racist history: "Some blacks, for instance, use 'nigger' among themselves as a term of endearment. But that is typically done with a sense of irony that is predicated upon an understanding of the term's racist origins and a close relationship with the person to whom the term is uttered."[29]

But the magic circle suggested by "nigger" is but one facet of its slippery nature in *Fences*. Although "nigger" easily rolls off the tongues of Troy and Bono during moments of nostalgia and alcohol-enhanced banter, the term just as easily signals for members of this inner circle sudden imposed exile and disinheritance. The magic space that at one point in *Fences* affords an unqualified license to use the term "nigger" safely suddenly shifts its course and turns this same word into a preface to a curse. When Cory forgets to add "sir" to "Yeah" to make "Yes, sir," Troy quickly chides him: "Nigger, as long as you in my house, you put that sir on the end of it when you talk to me" (1.3.37). In yet another instance, Troy applies the term "nigger" to Cory to further underscore their irreconcilable differences. Immediately after a very melodramatic moment in the play during which Troy and Bono confess platonic love for each other, Cory comes home fully dressed in football gear. Seeing his son in uniform triggers in Troy immediate disgust at Cory's decision to sacrifice his job at the local A&P in order to play football.

It is interesting to note that mere moments lapse between the scene where Troy uses "nigger" to express the bond that has persisted over the years between Bono and him and the scene where he registers absolute disapproval of Cory's decision to play ball against his iron rule: "The boy lied to me," he tells Rose. "I told the nigger if he wanna play football . . . to keep up his chores and hold down that job at the A&P" (1.4.57). Later, as emotions run high, a climactic confrontation between Cory and his father ensues in the Maxson family's front yard. After several rounds of verbal sparring with Cory, Troy summons all the fury and hatred contained in the word "nigger" to mark a complete denunciation of his adolescent son: "Nigger! That's what you are. You just another nigger on the street to me!" (2.4.87).

Politics aside, the rough edge of Troy's booming voice as he enunciates "nigger" offers an extension of his character, a more appropriate measure of his passion and frustration in a white-controlled scheme of things. Whether used to punctuate his anger, to address a lifelong friend, to dress down a belligerent son, or to jealously rail against token black ballplayers who broke through the color line in major-league baseball before him, the term "nigger" is an important item in Troy's vocabulary.

Fences is the product of August Wilson's mission to prove to himself and to his critics that he could write a better play. *Fences* was also part of his larger political agenda where it is one of a proposed ten-link, decade-by-decade chain of historical narratives about African Americans in the twentieth century. Despite such tall orders, Wilson accepted the challenge, although in the early 1980s when he began writing *Fences*, he was still somewhat of a novice at writing plays for a larger audience and had not quite mastered the art. His understanding of the inner workings of the play was basic: "I'm not sure of all of the rules," he told an interviewer, "but you just intuitively find your way through to the ending."[30] Not only did Wilson find his way through to the ending of *Fences*, but also along the way, he did not become a slave to conventions or rules. Although this Pulitzer Prize–winning work does adhere to recognizable aspects of Western drama, it also bears the unmistakable stamp of Wilson's creative intuition, which frequently operates outside the box of Aristotelian laws about drama and favors Africa as a more culturally appropriate source of inspiration. To his credit, *Fences* represents a marriage of his art, his politics, his life, and his vision for depicting truthfully African American culture.

NOTES

1. August Wilson, preface to *August Wilson: Three Plays* (Pittsburgh: Pittsburgh University Press, 1991), ix.

2. Robert Brustein, "On Cultural Power," *The New Republic*, 3 March 1997, 31.

3. William Kowinski, "The Play Looks Good on Paper—But Will It Fly?" *Smithsonian*, March 1992, 83–84.

4. Gunilla Theander Kester, "Approaches to Africa: The Poetics of Memory and the Body in Two August Wilson Plays," in *August Wilson: A Casebook*, ed. Marilyn Elkins (New York: Garland, 1994), 106.

5. Harry Elam, *(W)righting History: The Past as Present in the Drama of August Wilson* (forthcoming).

6. August Wilson, interview by Joan Herrington, February 1994, in *I Ain't Sorry for Nothin' I Done: August Wilson's Process of Playwriting* (New York: Limelight, 1998), 64.

7. Ibid., 72.

8. Harry Elam, "August Wilson," in *African American Writers*, 2d ed., vol. 2, ed. Valerie Smith (New York: Scribner's, 2001), 847.

9. Ibid., viii.

10. Kim Powers, "An Interview with August Wilson," *Theater Journal* 16 (fall/winter 1984): 55.

11. David Lida, review of *Fences*, by August Wilson, in *Women's Wear Daily*, 27 March 1987, 8.

12. Anna S. Blumenthal, "More Stories than the Devil Got Sinners: Troy's Stories in August Wilson's *Fences*," *American Drama* 9 (spring 2000): 90.

13. Ibid., 78.

14. Ibid., 80.

15. Qun Wang, "Towards the Poetization of the 'Field of Manners,'" *African American Review* 29 (winter 1995): 607–8.

16. Langston Hughes, *The Book of Negro Humor* (New York: Dodd, 1966), vii.

17. Sandra Shannon, *The Dramatic Vision of August Wilson* (Washington, D.C.: Howard University Press, 1995), 202–3.

18. "Folklore," *Webster's New World College Dictionary*, 3d ed., ed. Victoria Neufeldt (New York: Macmillan, 1997).

19. Trudier Harris, "August Wilson's Folk Traditions," in *August Wilson: A Casebook*, ed. Marilyn Elkins (New York: Garland, 1994), 50.

20. Ibid., 51.

21. Margaret Washington Creel, "Gullah Attitudes toward Life and Death," in *Africanism in America*, ed. Joseph E. Holloway (Bloomington: Indiana University Press, 1990), 81.

22. Joan Herrington, *I Ain't Sorry for Nothin' I Done: August Wilson's Process of Playwriting* (New York: Limelight, 1998), 74.

23. Zora Neale Hurston, *Their Eyes Were Watching God* (Chicago: Illinois University Press, 1978), 81.

24. *The Norton Anthology of African American Literature*, ed. Henry Louis Gates and Nellie Y. McKay (New York: Norton, 1997), 102.

25. Blumenthal, "More Stories than the Devil Got Sinners," 78.

26. Randall Kennedy, *Nigger: The Strange Career of a Troublesome Word* (New York: Pantheon, 2002), 30.

27. Langston Hughes, *The Big Sea* (New York: Knopf, 1940), 268–9.

28. Clarence Major, *Dictionary of Afro-American Slang* (New York: International Publishers, 1970), 85.

29. Randall Kennedy, "A Note on the Word 'Nigger,'" *Toward Racial Equality: Harper's Weekly Reports on Black America: 1857–1874*, 1. http://harpweek.com. HarpWeek, LLC, 1999–2000.

30. August Wilson, "The Historical Perspective: An Interview with August Wilson," interview by Richard Pettingill, in *August Wilson: A Casebook*, ed. Marilyn Elkins (New York: Garland, 1994), 222.

7 Reception

Something noticeable happens when August Wilson's *Fences* plays to an African American audience. This play, which has been dubbed universal and thoroughly embraced by both national and international audiences, also speaks to specific cultural concerns that African American men, women, and youth still encounter in a way that forces immediate recognition. Although set in the not-so-distant 1950s, African American men of today know all too well the blues that consume Troy's life as a disgruntled garbageman and would-be major-league baseball player. African American men in today's America can easily substitute their own deferred dreams for similar demons that taunt Troy. Likewise, African American women of the twenty-first century can relate to Rose's subordination of self for the sake of her husband, family, and home, but they can also relate to her transformation from a loving, supportive wife to a decisive, independent, and strongly principled African American woman. Although now living in a drastically different world and facing what, on the surface, appears to be drastically different domestic issues, young African American males today engage in the same ritualistic battles that Cory wages against his domineering father. Perhaps, most familiar to them is Cory's need to step out from his father's shadow and get out of the range of his father's rules to find his own way in the world.

August Wilson is well aware of *Fences*'s tendency to spark moments of recognition among African American audiences. In fact, he insists that one of his most pressing missions in writing *Fences* (as well as in writing each of the plays that make up his twentieth-century history project) is to affirm and celebrate African American culture and to do so in terms discernible to an African American audience. When asked by an interviewer whether black audiences respond differently to his plays than white audiences, he replied,

> I'll never forget one performance of *Fences* in Chicago I was at, the theater was very, very quiet because Gabriel was getting ready to blow his horn, and this black woman is sitting about five seats back from me, and she says just loud enough so the whole theater could hear: "ey don' need you blowin' that horn; he goin' straight to hell." I'll never forget that. The whole audience broke up, the actors had to turn away they were laughing so hard.[1]

Wilson's play had so affected this African American woman that she could not only easily suspend disbelief for the duration of the play, but she could also become so much of an intimate part of the action that she felt compelled to pass judgment even upon its deceased recipient. Moreover, he recalls several similar instances in which African Americans in the audience became so in tuned to the play that they sought to engage the characters in conversation, turning the performance into an interactive session where they freely rendered their thoughts out loud to concerns that provoked them.

In other less-public displays, *Fences* reaches a receptive African American audience. For example, African American critic Brent Staples was so moved by the March 1987 Broadway performance of the play that his review assumed the tone of a passionate editorial rather than an objective critique of a performance. He saw his father in Troy Maxson:

> When James Earl Jones enters into the set of "Fences," tall powerful, clad in my father's green, he carries a sack of potatoes bought from some farmer (my father bought bushels of tomatoes and corn). He is so familiar that I can faintly make out the odor of the man who has sweated all day. He, my father, seems to have come back over 20 years, and in this yard, among these familiar people, we go once again over this battle that seems never to be finished.[2]

Reading *Fences* occasions the same potential shock of recognition for many African Americans. This has been the case for me, in particular, on a number of occasions when I have assigned the play to my African

American students at Howard University. Their passionate responses to the text confirm that they know or have known and lived among people like Troy, Bono, Cory, Rose, Gabriel, and Lyons or that they see themselves in any one of these very same characters. Like them, I continue to share in their mesmerizing affinity with *Fences*. In fact, reading *Fences* in 1987 was my startling introduction to August Wilson. As I note in the preface to *The Dramatic Vision of August Wilson* (Howard University Press, 1995), "I felt that this man had somehow peeped into my own past to reinvigorate a part of my life that had for years lain dormant in my memory. Troy Maxson was my father—crude, domineering, hardworking, hard-loving, and fiercely proud of his ability to provide for his family."[3]

Fences has also fared well in the broader critical realm where its fate rests with scholars, academics, and theater reviewers. The amount and caliber of critical and scholarly responses to *Fences* since the early 1990s are testaments to its enduring stature as a great American play. Corresponding to the frequency with which *Fences* is staged and its increasing popularity in academic settings, serious critical studies on the play are simply a matter of course. An Internet search of August Wilson's *Fences*, for example, yields a list of publications that treat a range of interesting perspective on the Pulitzer Prize–winning play. Sustained critical discussions of Wilson's best known play appear in a variety of electronic and printed media that focus upon a range of issues pertaining to the playwright's craft, the play's informing historical and cultural contexts, and the artistry of its internal workings. As with most plays that initially gain notoriety through performance, *Fences* garnered its most immediate critical treatment at the hands of theater reviewers. Seasoned theater critics, such as Frank Rich, Samuel Freedman, and Brent Staples of the *New York Times* and Clive Barnes of the *New York Post*, have had the distinct privilege of rendering the first public impressions of the work. Perhaps unwittingly, they set a crucial tone for scholarship to follow. In the wake of its March 26, 1987, Broadway opening and an impressive run of 526 performances, *Fences* earned the respect of a number of critics— some of whom, up until then, had reservations about Wilson's skills as a playwright. *New York Times* critic Frank Rich, for example, heaps praise upon the author of *Fences*. He writes, "*Fences* leaves no doubt that Mr. Wilson is a major writer, combining a poet's ear for vernacular with a robust sense of humor (political and sexual), a sure instinct for crackling dramatic incident and a passionate commitment to a great subject."[4] Another *New York Times* critic, Brent Staples, had difficulty maintaining critical distance from the play before him. Attesting to its widespread appeal, he observes, "In *Fences* at the 46th Street Theatre, Mr. Wilson, whose previous Broadway play was *Ma Rainey's Black Bottom,* has turned an interesting trick—he has found the universal in the particular without compromising the latter. He brings us here a naked vernacular language intact, a language from the streets of his native Pittsburgh— though it could be anywhere."[5] Few frontline theater critics were not impressed by *Fences.* The several who did found fault in what they deemed to be excessive pre-performance hype and too much attention given this author still basking in the glow of his previous Broadway hit, *Ma Rainey's Black Bottom.* Others found the play wanting in comparison to its predecessor.

One reviewer irreverently referred to the cast of *Fences* as "drunks and losers"[6] while another complained that the plot was "conventional and overlong."[7] Despite an occasional lukewarm endorsement of *Fences,* the community of frontline theater critics such as the elite group above may be credited with establishing a useful basis for subsequent analyses of the work. Within less than five years of *Fences's* Broadway run, several significant essays appeared in academic journals that essentially set the bar for critical discourse on this signature play. In 1990, Christine Birdwell's "Death as a Fastball on the Outside Corner: *Fences'* Troy Maxson and the American Dream" was published in *Aethlon: The Journal of Sports Literature.* She acknowledges that "Wilson does use baseball's forms and language to carry part of the meaning of the play"[8] and expounds on the various implications of the play's baseball motif as an appropriate context for conveying Troy's severely restricted world. She also equates America's favorite pastime with the inhibiting image of the fence as America fenced African Americans off from society's playing field and as major-league officials ruled to ban African Americans from play. She explains that "[by] focusing on the effects of this lost opportunity on one aging ex-baseball player, Troy Maxson, Wilson shows his audience the heavy cost to blacks of America's long acceptance of racial injustice."[9]

Shorter, less-focused discussions of *Fences* surfaced in a number of journal publications that introduced the oeuvre of Wilson's project to an audience still not quite familiar with the then relatively new playwright. As one might expect, any discussion of *Fences* automatically situates Troy Maxson at the center of its discourse. Eric Sterling accords Troy this place of honor in his 1998 essay "Protecting Home: Patriarchal Authority in August Wilson's *Fences,*" in which he synthesizes the analytical observations of a number of critics who had published their assessments of the play by the late 1990s. Much like Birdwell, Sterling explores the larger meaning of both the fence metaphor and the symbolic relevance of the game of baseball in *Fences*. He argues that "Wilson employs baseball imagery to represent the physical and familial power, as well as the desires and fears, of the African-American patriarch, Troy Maxson."[10] Also, like Birdwell, Sterling provides a close reading of the play, paying particular attention to what he sees as a correlation between Troy's patriarchal role and the pervasive baseball trope. He concludes, "Maxson's baseball tropes reveal his desire to rule as a patriarchal tyrant and denote his refusal to admit that racial barriers are slowly declining."[11]

Although both Sterling and Birdwell's perspectives prove illuminating, their respective discussions do not venture beyond close readings of the text and their reactions to existing criticism on the play. This laxity in early scholarship on *Fences* is counterbalanced by an impressive number of more focused, more culturally grounded, and critically astute discussions in both journal articles and in select chapters published in either of the two collections of critical essays on August Wilson that appeared in 1994 (see Marilyn Elkins' *August Wilson: A Casebook* and Alan Nadel's *May All Your Fences Have Gates: Essays on the Drama of August Wilson*).

Anna Blumenthal's essay, "More Stories than the Devil Got Sinners: Troy's Stories in August Wilson's *Fences*," is part of this trend. In this article, published in 2000, she moves beyond noting the prevalence of Troy's storytelling to posit a theory that demonstrates how his stories facilitate his efforts to impart lessons to his sons. Blumenthal rightfully argues that prior to her essay, no one had taken an isolated look at Troy's stories—both natural and supernatural—and no one had seen in them any value beyond that of sheer entertainment. Although she acknowledges that Wilson endows many of his characters with narrative capabilities, she focuses upon Troy Maxson as one of Wilson's most accomplished storytellers. She simultaneously explores the art that goes into the creation of each of Troy's stories and examines their politics. Acknowledging how Troy manages to sustain attention even as he spins the most absurd events, she supports her argument that an assessment of his verbal skills is intimately bound with how he stretches the tolerance level of his audience. She explains, "For his actual audience, Troy is able to gauge the impact of his stories by the interruptions they provide. They enable him to judge whether his story is being understood and therefore, keep control over the way the story is received."[12] According to Blumenthal, Troy's sons—not Bono nor Rose—are the chief benefactors of his anecdotes. Framed as tall tales and packaged as entertaining anecdotes, Troy's folk wit is the only legacy he has left to will to his children.

The mid- to late 1990s marked a significant peak in Wilson studies. Between 1994 and 1999 six single-authored references on the drama of August Wilson were published by both university and trade presses. Since the words "prolific" and "acclaimed" were now suitable descriptions for Wilson, it became customary that such studies follow a one-chapter-per-play format. This approach, of course, meant more sustained critical discussions on each of Wilson's plays, including, of course, *Fences*. Sandra Shannon's *The Dramatic Vision of August Wilson* chronicles Wilson's career development from poet to playwright and examines each of the plays in his dramatic history of the African American experience. Her extensive chapter on *Fences*, titled "Developing Character," discusses the play as an indication of Wilson's steady mastery of the craft and the art that goes into composing top-notch plays. Although she discusses the play as "a portrait of the artist as a young man," she also delves into a number of its thematic and political issues. She historicizes the father-son rift between Troy and Cory as a manifestation of a cultural legacy extending as far back as slavery, which was bent on sustaining emotional distance between African American men and their sons. She asserts,

> Black men frequently lash out at their sons (or other blacks) as alternate targets instead of confronting head-on the emasculating racism or the social and economic pressures they encounter outside the home. Often their defense is that they must "break the spirits" of these young black men in their charge, just as one might discipline a horse to submission. Some, like Troy Maxson, rationalize that their downright mean treatment of their sons prepares them for the similar treatment that awaits them in society.[13]

Fences not only speaks to a history of detached fathers, but, as Shannon reveals, it also incorporates a good deal of Wilson's experiences with the same issue. Taking care to keep the two dimensions mutually exclusive, Shannon demonstrates how Wilson's own life became an informing text for *Fences*, but not to the extent that the play becomes autobiographical.

In 1995 Kim Pereira published *August Wilson and the African American Odyssey* (Illinois University Press), which also includes an informative chapter-length discussion of *Fences*. Pereira's examination of the play identifies Troy as a relative of the African deity Esu-Elegbara and offers an assessment of his character outside the framework of Western ideals on life, death, marriage, infidelity, fatherhood, and so forth. He explains,

Like Levee in *Ma Rainey*, Troy is a cultural descendant of Eshu. . . .
Like Levee he wants complete satisfaction or nothing at all. . . .
Such an attitude is the prerogative of the self-empowered trickster
whose goals are survival and success, whatever the consequences.
The so-called realities of the social world around him matter little,
for he dances to an internal rhythm, answering a call for self-
authentication that springs from a cultural, even cosmological,
dimension.[14]

Following Wilson's insistence that his characters are, first and foremost,
Africans, Pereira constructs an enlightening African cultural context for
understanding the play as well as seeing Troy's place in a long line of
trickster prototypes. He also demonstrates that Troy's view of the world
corresponds with his blood's memory of Africa along with pressures of living as a black man in 1950s America.

In addition to putting Africa on the agenda for discussing *Fences*,
Pereira foregrounds aspects of the evolving music industry in America.
Again he takes his cue from Wilson's assertion that sports and music—
even though tightly controlled by white establishments—afforded
African Americans the best opportunities to climb out of poverty. In
these two arenas, Wilson has discovered potential sites containing an
abundance of dramatic conflict. Pereira spends significant time in the
opening of his chapter on *Fences* discussing the exponential growth of
blues and jazz along the lines of increased interaction between African
Americans and mainstream American society. "Reflected in their music,"
he observes, "were the complex changes this movement created in their
identity as black Americans."[15] Pereira's appropriate Africanist cultural
reading of *Fences* in general and Troy, in particular, problematize initial
interpretations of *Fences* as a strictly universal play. His consideration of
the slow metamorphosis of black musical forms runs parallel to the play's
suggestions that major political advances for African Americans are
imminent.

Joan Herrington's *I Ain't Sorry for Nothin' I Done: August Wilson's Process of Playwriting* (Limelight, 1998) shifts critical attention away from
thematic issues treated in previous studies of Wilson's repertoire of plays
to a fascinating behind-the-scenes examination of his high-pressure, on-
the-spot editing and revising processes. Perhaps somewhat attributable to
Wilson's intensive summer residency at the Eugene O'Neill Theater Center in 1982, he now embraces the practice of revising under pressure, finding that making immediate decisions during the rehearsal process is more

efficient than contemplating changes to a script alone and after the fact. Herrington, who once served in the capacity as dramaturg for one of Wilson's plays, describes the intricacies of the playwright's craft as he hones *Fences* toward production. Like Pereira, she organizes her study around a Wilson imperative. Accordingly, the force that inspires the playwright's revision of *Fences* for the stage is an insistence that the theme of responsibility remain clearly within focus. All aspects of the play—character portrayals, dialogue, action, and so forth—must highlight this theme. Toward this end, character portrayals of Rose, Bono, Cory, and Lyons are held in strict compliance, and—if deemed off base in this respect— become top priority in Wilson's rewriting process. According to Herrington, "Many of the characters in *Fences*, like those in our lives, make what seem to be irresponsible choices. Wilson's aim was to examine such choices by revealing the pressures that influence each of them, and ultimately to uncover the nobility and dignity of every individual."[16]

Another single-authored work published in 1998 facilitates another research approach to the playwright's work: performance studies. Yvonne Shafer's *August Wilson: A Research and Production Sourcebook* (Greenwood, 1998) documents Wilson's life, his career as playwright, his dramatic output, and the various staged productions of his plays throughout the United States. As such it provides an important foundation for performance-oriented analyses of his work. She assembles here one of the most extensive chronologies of Wilson's plays published to date, including painstakingly detailed, act-by-act and scene-by-scene plot summaries and critical overviews of his plays, performance reviews, and data on various play productions. More than a catalog of archival information, Shafer's work is useful in providing annotations to scholarly articles, chapters, and reviews on *Fences* that were in print as she completed the final phase of her research on this project.

In 1999 Mary Bogumil and Peter Wolfe both published additional single-authored scholarly treatments of August Wilson's plays. The expressed purpose of Bogumil's *Understanding August Wilson* (South Carolina University Press) is to provide the "uninitiated readers" basic understanding of Wilson's plays. As such, she purposefully designs her study to be a companion to the plays rather than a self-contained reference. Although Bogumil describes her important work as such, *Understanding August Wilson* does significantly more than the all-too-familiar Cliffs Notes. Her chapter on *Fences*, for example, discusses Troy within a much larger context than do other competing references. Bogumil situates Troy's character within the tradition of other popular domestic dramas, such as Eugene O'Neill's *Long Day's Journey into Night*, and Arthur Miller's *Death of a Salesman*. She also acknowledges an Africanist perspective operating in the play. Although she does not expand on this presence much beyond citing Harry Elam's position on hints of the African Yoruba ritual, she does acknowledge that "Wilson discovers a distinctive way of exploring the lives of his characters."[17] In keeping with her mission, Bogumil spends much time in this chapter providing a close reading of the characters' doings as well as the motives for their actions. She also explores the symbolic meanings of dominant images and concepts in the play, such as the fence, death, and baseball, and she offers astute observations about factors that lie beneath Troy's enigmatic nature. According to Bogumil, for example, "Troy thinks in terms of the black man's burden in a Jim Crow America, not in terms of an America on the verge of the Civil Rights Movement. . . . Troy blinds himself to the slow progress for equal rights and constructs a psychological fence against any manifestation of that progress."[18]

Peter Wolfe's *August Wilson* contribution to Twayne's series takes a much less formulaic approach to *Fences*. In a chapter titled "The House of Maxson," Wolfe likens the conflict of the play to that contained in Western classics such as *The Iliad*, *Oedipus Rex*, *Othello*, and *The Emperor Jones*. However, his is a more balanced discussion seasoned with references to Lorraine Hansberry's *A Raisin in the Sun* (1959), James Baldwin's *The Amen Corner* (1968), Philip Hayes Dean's *The Owl Killer* (1974), and Ralph Ellison's *Invisible Man* (1952). In wittily coined subtitles, Wolfe delves into Troy's world while taking into account that the "play's resolution comes from Africa, specifically the black African faith."[19] Like Bogumil, Wolfe's approach is eclectic as he seeks to cast a wide interpretive net over the play.

Spurred on by a desire "to find out why Wilson has won the esteem of so many playgoers,"[20] Wolfe puts together a unique study of his works, which pays attention to issues that other works of its kind merely reference in passing. His abundance of meticulous baseball statistics, for example, gives readers a better sense of Troy's game and a glimpse at the competition he would have faced had he been permitted to stretch his talents beyond the Negro Leagues. Moreover, by citing a plethora of baseball trivia, Wolfe attempts to prove that Wilson must have done substantial research on the sport in order to depict a more credible lead character. Aside from this, he believes "these statistics merit attention because, as an ex-Negro-Leaguer living in Pittsburgh, Troy would have been aware of them. To provide access to Troy's rancor, Wilson also mentions in the play's head note that the Milwaukee Braves won the World Series in 1957 (*Fences*, xviii), when most of *Fences* unfolds."[21]

Such things are not coincidental, as Wolfe strongly implies. Thus, he implicitly challenges Wilson's repeated insistence that he eschews research in his creative process.

The year 1999 also marked the publication of Qun Wang's *An In-Depth Study of the Major Plays of African American Playwright August Wilson* (Mellon). As in the previous single-authored studies, Wang's book dedicates an entire chapter to *Fences*. But unlike its predecessors, Wang's study offers even more literary and theoretical models for interpreting the play. In his discussion of how the blues aesthetic informs *Fences*, Wang references Ralph Ellison's *Shadow and Act*, and in discussing Troy's dual conflicts, he consults José Ortega y Gasset's *Man and Crisis*. In addition, he alludes to Arthur Miller's *Death of a Salesman* to gauge the level of Troy's tragic heroism, Alice Walker's *The Color Purple* to describe the oppressive bond between Troy and Cory, French critic Ferdinand Brunetière to expand on the definition of human will, and Robert Frost's poem "Mending Wall" to acknowledge "psychological barriers that people put up to separate themselves from reality."[22] Wang's multiple literary and theoretical applications used in discussing *Fences* put Wilson's play in the company of other great literary works. Moreover, Wang offers a close reading of the play along with helpful insight on Troy's stories, the fence metaphor, the blues, and humor. Interestingly, however, Wang does not reference other research on Wilson that had been published prior to his book, apparently choosing instead to forge what he considers to be new ground in Wilson studies. To his credit, his insight on *Fences* is illuminating and much needed, yet not particularly groundbreaking.

Appearing simultaneously, though sporadically, to single-authored studies that include a chapter on *Fences* were several very solid treatments of the play. These essays found their way into critical collections to which a discussion of Wilson's *Fences* complements a broader thematic approach. Harry Elam's book chapter titled "Of Angels and Transcendence: A Cross Cultural Analysis of *Fences* by August Wilson and *Roosters* by Milcha Sanchez-Scott" (published in 1995 by Peter Lang in *Staging Difference: Cultural Pluralism in American Theatre and Drama*) fits such a mold. Elam's chapter-length discussion pairs *Fences*, a play grounded in the particulars of African American culture with *Roosters*, a play that, while identifiably Hispanic in tone and in flavor, reveals family dynamics that closely resemble those at work in the domestic drama *Fences*. Scholar and theater historian Harry Elam, who has published a number of cutting-edge essays on Wilson's work, here draws cultural parallels between the final scenes in Wilson's *Fences* and Sanchez-Scott's *Roosters*. He interprets Gabriel's "atavistic shouts and dance" just before the end of *Fences* and Angela's levitation at the end of *Roosters* as "both culturally organized and culturally organizing." He explains,

> I classify these moments . . . as "culturally organized" because they reflect specific cultural belief systems and practices. Gabriel's apocalyptic opening of Heaven's gates is not an affirmation of Christian orthodoxy, but rather an action that links Gabriel, Troy, the entire Maxson family to their African roots. His actions visually codify Wilson's preeminent cultural project; to re-establish and re-affirm the "African-ness" in African-American experience.[23]

Among several other perspectives included in this essay, Elam focuses upon the mutual issue of the "problematic patriarch." Although he makes distinctions in the absent versus the present tendencies of both patriarchs, he makes it clear that the overall thrust of each play is reconciliation and restoration. He writes,

> While both *Fences* and *Roosters* repeat the narrative trope of the problematic father, neither play attempts to exorcise the father nor to vilify him for the family's tragic demise. Instead, even as they reveal the faults and frailties of the father, the underlying objective of *Fences* as well as *Roosters* is to reconcile and restore the position of the patriarch within the fabric of the family.[24]

By melding together a discussion of dramatic texts from two different cultures, Elam underscores a universal link between otherwise culturally different people. At the same time, however, he draws attention to the cultural specificity of both ethnic groups.

In addition to his comparative study of the patriarch in plays depicting Hispanic and African American cultures, Elam has to his credit several other works that shed light on *Fences*. For example, in an article published in *Modern Drama*'s summer 2001 issue, he explores the trope he refers to as "racial madness" in each of Wilson's plays. Included among his examples of this character type are Hambone of *Two Trains Running*, Hedley of *Seven Guitars*, Stool Pigeon of *King Hedley II*, and, of course, Gabriel of *Fences*. Elam believes that "[e]ach of these figures' madness results from symbolic or real confrontations with white power structures.

These confrontations cause ruptures and schisms within the experiences of Africans in America. As such, they become representations of collective African American social memories."[25] The frequency with which Wilson relies upon the idiot savant to convey the paradoxical silent noise, the unheeded wisdom, and the ignored truths begs further analysis, and Elam addresses this need admirably.

Elam's very thorough bio-critical essay, "August Wilson," which appeared in *African American Writers* in 2001, is perhaps the most succinct, scholarly sophisticated discussion of Wilson's dramas to date. In addition to summarizing the history of Wilson's life, the evolution of his aesthetic, and various thematic influences within each of his history cycle plays to date, Elam includes a sober discussion of *Fences*. Given Elam's history of critically sound and culturally incisive work on Wilson, his is, of course, understandably most reliable as a basis for subsequent scholarship. His near three-page discussion of *Fences* in this reference delves deeply into the Africanist context of the play and interprets its characters as visible links to Africa. On a much deeper level and on a more sustained basis, he situates individual characters within an African continuum, tying certain of their cultural beliefs and practices to African belief systems. For example, he notes the African resonance of Troy's stories and sees the presence of African tradition in "Gabriel's ritualistic and spiritual enactment."[26]

In 1997 editors Joyce Moss and George Wilson published *Literature and Its Times: Profiles of 300 Notable Literary Works and the Historical Events that Influenced Them* (Gale), which includes an informative entry on August Wilson's *Fences*. Along with obligatory biographical coverage of the playwright's early life in Pittsburgh, this essay examines the baseball culture that flourished in Pittsburgh and that runs parallel to the athletic career of Troy Maxson. Yet more than a bio-sketch, this piece also injects into the discussion of *Fences* the real-life practices of corrupt union officials in order to qualify the success of Troy's challenge to his superiors to divide heavy lifting details equally among both African American and white workers. This entry further contextualizes Troy's experiences alongside events that mark imminent improvements in civil rights for African Americans:

> In 1957 President Dwight D. Eisenhower put federal power behind public school integration in Little Rock, Arkansas, ordering army troops there to ensure that black students would be allowed to enter Little Rock Central High School. . . . In 1957 Milwaukee became

the first baseball team outside New York to, with the help of a black hitter, win the World Series.[27]

Organized according to appropriate subheadings, this essay covers a number of conceivable angles for understanding *Fences*. For example, the writers provide dual historical contexts that consider "Events in History at the Time the Play Takes Place" and "Events in History at the Time the Play Was Written." This double immersion into the historical milieus of both play and playwright proves especially useful in imagining the extent of Troy's oppression. In addition, these concomitant histories seem to validate the pain of Troy's suffering and, at the same time, promote empathy among reading and spectating audiences.

Although not usually regarded in the academy as a scholarly enterprise, one particularly insightful interview appeared in a 1985 issue of *Theater Journal*. Here, interviewer Heather Henderson conducts a candid and revealing conversation with two very prominent cast members who starred in the spring 1985 Yale Repertory Theatre production of *Fences*: James Earl Jones and Mary Alice, original creators of Troy and Rose Maxson. Jones and Alice received stellar reviews for their credible performances and spoke intimately with Henderson about Wilson's powerful script. When asked about their experiences in trying to breathe life into their roles, both acknowledged the play's power as well as Wilson's brilliance in drawing their conflicting characters. In response to Henderson's curiosity about possible difficulties in portraying Troy's character, for example, Jones confessed,

> It's been hard to modulate Troy's levels of energy, to measure the extent to which he is just loud-mouthing. I have not found yet where his depths and highs are. He's like a manic-depressive; he's up and he's down. His relationship to his son is the most complicated one— I don't believe I have yet solved that. The love relationships he has with Rose, with Bono, and even with the older son are a lot easier to achieve than those he has with his younger son and his daughter. That is probably because an actor draws from his own experience, and unless you have things in your own life that can enlighten you, you have to search and search until you understand it.[28]

Mary Alice, in like manner, expresses the challenges she faced playing the role of Troy's wife: "Basically I just started with what had been given by the writer, what Rose says, what is said about her. I suppose I somehow used women that I knew, women I knew in 1957."[29]

What Jones and Alice add to the critical discourse on *Fences* is an appreciation and understanding of the nuances of the play from a performance perspective and of the degree to which Wilson had mastered the creation of complex, three-dimensional human characters—characters who come to life on stage as well as on the page. They also engender an appreciation for the crisp, accurate manner in which Wilson captures the speech patterns of his characters. Moreover, it is particularly relevant that Jones and Alice, both of whom are African American, readily identify with the cultural and gender-related issues with which African Americans had to contend half a century ago and, to a certain extent, still encounter. At the risk of essentializing their roles, the strength of Jones's and Alice's characters lie in the fact that they can relate to Troy and Rose on the often-intersecting levels of culture, race, and gender—levels that far exceed those made possible through the controversial practice of color-blind casting. Jones's and Alice's affinity with Troy and Rose comes from their concepts of blackness and their obvious identity as African Americans. Thus, for one who wishes to go beyond the text to explore the performative aspect of *Fences*, consideration of the comments from such seasoned, respected actors as Jones and Alice are likely to prove beneficial in their research.

One other source that falls outside conventional scholarly responses to *Fences* and that is useful in considering the far-reaching impact of the play is Margaret Booker's published account of her experiences as director of an all-Chinese production of *Fences* in Beijing, China, in the winter of 1997. Booker's recollections of her easy rapport with members of the cast of Beijing People's Art Theatre and the ease with which they slipped into the demanding roles confirm the play's truly universal scope. Also facilitating this successful introduction of *Fences* to audiences in Beijing was (and still is) the climate that prevailed among the country's youth and that gave rise to a disturbing irreverence toward tradition. China—at the time of the play's Far Eastern production—was especially sensitive to issues that involved a noticeable restlessness among a new generation of nationals. That restlessness had begun to manifest in increasing tendencies among nonconforming youth to question their elders' authority as well as to ignore established Chinese cultural practices. Understandably, then, Booker saw *Fences* as a test-case project, for it addressed this sensitive issue from another cultural perspective. *Fences* explores surprisingly similar family dynamics though its audiences are clearly oceans apart.

The father-son conflict at the heart of *Fences* was thus perceived as a microcosm of the country's conflict.

During her eight-month stay in the Chinese capital, Booker gained somewhat of an insider's view of the culture and its people. That knowledge was put to use as she groomed the cast of the play toward production. Booker set forth her own theory for the play's reception:

> China in the '90s wants to be a member of the modern world and economic community, yet still tries to preserve its intellectual tradition and social values. Nowhere could the clash between old and new be more apparent. ... I believe that *Fences*, set in the social upheaval of the civil rights movement and revolving around a father/son conflict, would suit both the rapid societal change in China as well as the Beijing People's Art Theatre.[30]

Booker's experiences in China mirror what Harry Elam's conveys in his comparative essay "Of Angels and Transcendence" (see previous discussion) in which he examines how family dynamics in *Fences* suggest uncanny similarities to domestic issues that surface within the Hispanic family. Booker's aptly titled essay, "Building Fences in Beijing," which also juxtaposes the experiences of two distinct cultures, reveals some surprising commonalities.

Well before the publication of each of the existing single-authored studies on Wilson's oeuvre, two critical collections of essays on the same were released simultaneously in 1994. Responding to Wilson's increasing popularity in print and on stage and heeding the demands of a reading public that sought a closer look at this artist, Marilyn Elkins and Alan Nadel brought together in two separate sources an array of noticeably more critically sophisticated and refreshing perspectives. Some eight years after the initial publication of *Fences*, editors Nadel and Elkins published, respectively, *May All Your Fences Have Gates: Essays on the Drama of August Wilson* (Iowa University Press) and *August Wilson: A Casebook* (Garland). These two welcomed sources introduced essays that take closer looks at fairly general observations about *Fences*. While the majority of the essay lineup in *May All Your Fences Have Gates* merely references *Fences* as part of a balanced treatment of all of Wilson's plays, two, in particular, feature more sustained and more focused discussions of his 1950s play. For example, in essays titled "August Wilson's Women," "The Ground On Which I Stand," and "August Wilson's Gender Lesson," Harry Elam, Sandra Shannon, and Missy Dean Kubitschek, respectively, briefly reference *Fences* in their overarching discussions of Wilson's entire body of dramatic works. Shannon draws attention to the strengths of Wilson's portrayals of African American women even as they are perceived as victims. About Rose of *Fences*, she writes, "Rose Maxson is a woman who chooses to direct her energies toward being a wife, a mother, and a homemaker. . . . Rose initiates her own brand of female consciousness that allows her to remain in control throughout the play. She also comes to some conclusions about what constitutes victimization."[31] Harry Elam, who also does a sweeping analysis of Wilson's African American female characters, asserts a similar argument in "August Wilson's Women": "The representation of black women by August Wilson, thus, offers a complex and intriguing dialectic. He presents independent women who assert feminist positions, but who, either through their own volition or as the result of external social pressures, ultimately conform to traditional gender roles and historical expectations."[32] Missy Dean Kubitschek investigates what she calls "gendered interactions in the black community" in "August Wilson's Gender Lesson." She asserts that *Fences* forcefully demonstrates the spiritual alienation of men and women from one another, and of men from their children. The play shows men and women speaking different languages, reflecting different understandings of the spiritual cosmos.[33]

Fences moves more toward the center of discourse in Alan Nadel's *May All Your Fences Have Gates* with his essay, "Boundaries, Logistics, and Identity: The Property of Metaphor in *Fences* and *Joe Turner's Come and Gone*" and in Michael Awkward's "The Crookeds with the Straights: *Fences*, Race, and the Politics of Adaptation." Regarding the fence metaphor that is embedded in the play, Nadel couches his argument in post-structuralist terms. He views the idea of a fence as infinitely more significant than the physical boundary it initially suggests. Nadel argues that the metaphoric fence "separates human properties from non-human ones" and cites as examples how such beliefs were used historically to "separate blacks from humans."[34] He further validates this argument in references to the Mason-Dixon Line and the Dred Scott Decision, both of which are based upon clear demarcations between the white hegemony and the African American subject.

Michael Awkward's "*Fences*, Race, and the Politics of Adaptation" examines the conflicting premise of Wilson's controversial and highly publicized demands in 1990 that the film version of *Fences* be directed by a black director. Using this cause célèbre as the jumping off point of his discussion, Awkward turns to *Fences* to lend philosophical support to his position because, in his estimation, its dynamics of cultural specificity closely mirror the sticking points of Wilson's argument. He notes,

> I want to investigate the play's examination of the possibilities of erecting protective fences around black familial space in terms of the quite different trajectory of Wilson's efforts to find a black film director in order to protect his creation from potentially contaminating caucacentric forces. While the playwright orchestrates the search primarily for what are ideologically justifiable reasons, its perspectives appear on the surface at least to be at odds with Fences' inquiry into the advisability of protectionist imperatives.[35]

Implicitly Awkward suggests that Wilson's adamant demands for a black director appear hypocritical and contradictory to the dramatic lessons *Fences* imparts.

Marilyn Elkins describes the objective of her twelve-essay collection, *August Wilson: A Casebook* (Garland, 1994) as an attempt "to adumbrate the multiple perspectives that can be brought to bear upon August Wilson's work and to attest to its multi-layeredness."[36] Toward that end, she assembles an eclectic assortment of essays that represent a range of ideas from literary and cultural influences to applications of contemporary cultural theory.

Like Nadel's *May All Your Fences Have Gates*, Elkins *Casebook* on August Wilson does not single out *Fences* for investigation. Rather, Wilson's 1950s play receives the same cursory examination as it does in Nadel's scholarly product. However, one essay, in particular, takes an exclusive behind-the-scenes look at the making of *Fences* through an exposé on Wilson's work as "craftsman, reviser, collaborator."[37] Joan Fishman's "Developing His Song: August Wilson's *Fences*" analyzes five of Wilson's early drafts of *Fences* and "looks at the way in which these changes allow Wilson to reinforce his theme without sacrificing the unity of the play."[38] Her essay, which obviously becomes the basis for her future book *I Ain't Sorry for Nothin' I Done: August Wilson's Process of Playwriting*, is performance-based in nature, providing a step-by-step narration and analysis that demonstrate Wilson's faithfulness at keeping the theme of responsibility at the center of *Fences's* conflict and thereby reveal his commitment as an artist.

Fences moves a little more to the periphery in Gunilla Theander Kester's "Approaches to Africa: The Poetics of Memory and the Body in Two August Wilson Plays." It is Kester's contention that *Fences* (and *Joe*

Turner's Come and Gone) highlights the metaphoric relationship between African American history and the black body. She expands upon this postmodernist premise to suggest that in *Fences* Wilson creates what she refers to as "the poetics of memory." She asserts that "by refocusing on the black body as a locus of a new and dynamic metaphorics of African American history, he [Wilson] attempts to reformulate the African American poetics of memory."[39] Kester's theoretical framework presents a rather esoteric analysis of *Fences*. Indeed, as theater critic Paul Carter Harrison vehemently protests, "[S]he makes a cumbersome effort to apply post-modern analysis to the cultural metalanguage of gesture in *Fences*."[40]

Kim Marra's feminist analysis, "Ma Rainey and the Boyz: Gender Ideology in August Wilson's Broadway Canon," is an effort to address what its author deems as "a critical blind spot" in published discourse on the politics of gender in Wilson's plays. Admitting that her ideas emerge from the perspective of "a middle-class white feminist critic,"[41] Marra, rather awkwardly, applies principles of a white feminist aesthetic to the gender dynamics that she perceives to be at work in male-female relationships among August Wilson's African American characters. *Ma Rainey's Black Bottom* and *Fences* become proving grounds for this application. At the center of Marra's contention is her belief that since Wilson has achieved such a high profile, "the perceptions of women disseminated in his plays have influential power and thus merit critical attention."[42] Having stated this as her mission, she explores the paradoxical nature of gender representation in five plays that reflect a combination of societal norms and the male author's subjective, masculinist constructions. About *Fences* she asserts,

> The primary focus, once again, is on the male hero, Troy Maxson's, quest for manhood, with the major female character, his wife Rose, drawn primarily according to how she affirms or thwarts his endeavor. Though following a similar overarching pattern of gender relations as in the plays set in earlier decades, this work offers greater complexity in the characterization of the female lead who is accorded more consciousness than her predecessors of her own and her male cohort's motivations. Her consciousness foregrounds not only the dynamics of racism and sexism which oppress all African Americans, but those which divide them male from female. The most far-reaching and insurmountable "fences" in this play . . . prove to be those of gender.[43]

Marra shifts emphasis from Troy as the pivotal tragic figure of *Fences* to the dynamics of the African American male-female relationships.

Fences moves readers in much the same way that it impacts its audiences. Whether these audiences or readers are African Americans, Asian Americans, Chicano Americans, or white Americans, the play has a proven record for touching lives. Brent Staples took off his hat as a theater critic to reminisce about the play's uncanny images of his father, and journalist Bill Moyers admitted to Wilson that he wept during one of its performances. In response to the infectious power of the play, academic critics bring to bear a number of critical paradigms to tap the mysteries of *Fences*. Cultural criticism, feminist criticism, new historicism, poststructuralism, and postmodernism are just a few of the magnifying lenses that have been held up to the play. As a result of the ability of *Fences* to speak across boundaries of race, age, and gender, it continues to intrigue those who experience the play. As a result of the intrigue that it stimulates, critics are attracted to it as the focus of their scholarly inquiries. As a result of the growing body of scholarship generated about *Fences*, the play has been canonized and assured the title "classic."

NOTES

1. August Wilson, interviewed by Roger Downey, April 1988, in *Microsoft Encarta Africana*, Microsoft Corporation, 1999.

2. Brent Staples, "'*Fences*': No Barrier to Emotion," *New York Times*, 5 April 1987, 1, 39.

3. Sandra Shannon, *The Dramatic Vision of August Wilson* (Washington, D.C.: Howard University Press, 1995), vii.

4. Frank Rich, "Theater: Family Ties in Wilson's 'Fences,'" *New York Times*, 27 March 1987.

5. Staples, "Fences," 39.

6. Martin Kihn, "Wilson Builds Second Sturdy *Fences* at Rep," *Yale Daily News*, 8 May 1985.

7. Douglass Watt, "'Fences' Is All over the Lot: But James Earl Jones Is Its Saving Grace," *Daily News*, 3 April 1987. In *New York Theatre Critics' Reviews*, 1987, 316.

8. Christine Birdwell, "Death as a Fastball on the Outside Corner: *Fences*' Troy Maxson and the American Dream," *Aethlon: The Journal of Sports Literature* 8 (fall 1990): 88.

9. Ibid., 87.

10. Eric Sterling, "Protecting Home: Patriarchal Authority in August Wilson's *Fences*," *Essays in Theatre* 17 (November 1998): 53.

11. Ibid.

12. Anna S. Blumenthal, "'More Stories than the Devil Got Sinners: Troy's Stories in August Wilson's *Fences*," American Drama 9 (Spring 2000): 78.

13. Shannon, *Dramatic Vision*, 100.

14. Kim Pereira, *August Wilson and the African American Odyssey* (Urbana: Illinois University Press, 1995), 38.

15. Ibid., 35.

16. Joan Herrington, *I Ain't Sorry for Nothin' I Done: August Wilson's Process of Playwriting* (New York: Limelight, 1998), 77.

17. Mary Bogumil, *Understanding August Wilson* (Columbia: South Carolina University Press, 1999), 42.

18. Ibid., 40.

19. Peter Wolfe, *August Wilson* (New York: Twayne, 1999), 73.

20. Ibid., ix.

21. Ibid., 62.

22. Qun Wang, *An In Depth Study of the Major Plays of African American Playwright August Wilson* (New York: Mellon, 1999), 66.

23. Harry Elam, "Of Angels and Transcendence: An Analysis of *Fences* by August Wilson and *Roosters* by Milcha Sanchez-Scott," in *Staging Differences: Cultural Pluralism in American Theatre and Drama* (New York: Lang, 1995), 287.

24. Ibid., 290.

25. Harry Elam, "August Wilson, Doubling, Madness, and Modern African American Drama," *Modern Drama* 43 (winter 2000): 9.

26. Harry Elam, "August Wilson," in *African American Writers*, 2d ed., vol. 2, ed. Valerie Smith (New York: Scribner's, 2001), 848.

27. "Fences by August Wilson," *Literature and Its Times: Profiles of 300 Notable Literary Works and the Historical Events that Influenced Them*, eds. Joyce Moss and George Wilson (New York: Gale, 1997), 148.

28. Heather Henderson, "Building Fences: An Interview with Mary Alice and James Earl Jones," *Theater Journal* 16 (summer/fall 1985): 68.

29. Ibid.

30. Margaret Booker, "Building Fences in Beijing," *American Theatre*, May/June 1997, 50.

31. Sandra Shannon, "The Ground On Which I Stand: August Wilson's Perspective on African American Women," in *May All Your Fences Have Gates: Essays on the Drama of August Wilson*, ed. Alan Nadel (Iowa City: Iowa University Press, 1994), 154, 155.

32. Harry Elam, "August Wilson's Women," in *May All Your Fences Have Gates: Essays on the Drama of August Wilson*, ed. Alan Nadel (Iowa City: Iowa University Press, 1994), 164.

33. Missy Dean Kubitschek, "August Wilson's Gender Lesson," in *May All Your Fences Have Gates: Essays on the Drama of August Wilson*, ed. Alan Nadel (Iowa City: Iowa University Press, 1994), 183.

34. Alan Nadel, "Boundaries, Logistics, and Identity: The Property of Metaphor in *Fences* and *Joe Turner's Come and Gone*," in *May All Your Fences Have Gates: Essays on the Drama of August Wilson*, ed. Alan Nadel (Iowa City: Iowa University Press, 1994), 87.

35. Michael Awkward, "The Crookeds with the Straights: *Fences*, Race, and the Politics of Adaptation," in *May All Your Fences Have Gates: Essays on the Drama of August Wilson*, ed. Alan Nadel (Iowa City: Iowa University Press, 1994), 215.

36. Marilyn Elkins, introduction to *August Wilson: A Casebook*, ed. Marilyn Elkins (New York: Garland, 1994), xii.

37. Ibid., xvi.

38. Ibid.

39. Gunilla Theander Kester, "Approaches to Africa: The Poetics of Memory and the Body in Two August Wilson Plays," in *August Wilson: A Casebook*, ed. Marilyn Elkins (New York: Garland, 1994), 105.

40. Paul Carter Harrison, review of *August Wilson: A Casebook*, ed. Marilyn Elkins, *African American Review* 35 (winter 2001): 674.

41. Kim Marra, "Ma Rainey and the Boyz: Gender Ideology in August Wilson's Broadway Canon," in *August Wilson: A Casebook*, ed. Marilyn Elkins (New York: Garland, 1994), 123.

42. Ibid., 124.

43. Ibid., 147.

8 Bibliographical Essay

The most important studies of August Wilson's *Fences* are those that proceed from a distinct African sensibility—not just because this approach is *en vogue* or politically correct, but because it represents the abiding cultural premise on which Wilson bases his entire cycle of plays about the African American experience in the twentieth century. African American theater critic Paul Carter Harrison refers to this fundamental context as "a culturally specific African American cosmological world view forged from ancestral memory that informs the aesthetics of his works."[1] Armed with a sensibility and regard for African underpinnings in the play, critics, such as Harry J. Elam and Harrison, have proven to be most adept and best equipped to communicate Wilson's African-based aesthetic. As no book-length study on *Fences* has yet been done, the most important critical work on the play in this regard exists in the form of essays and chapter-length discussions.

Some important jewels of intellectual thought on *Fences* are interspersed throughout several excellent published overviews on Wilson. In such works, relatively brief discussions of *Fences* appear chronologically according to the date of its publication or its position in Wilson's decade-by-decade narrative. Paul Carter Harrison's essay "August Wilson's Blues Poetics" in *August Wilson: Three Plays* (Pittsburgh University Press, 1991) belongs to this class. In 1991 when scholarship on August Wilson's dramatic works had not yet caught up with the success of his plays on stage, Harrison was in the forefront as one of the few academic critics to give his work serious attention. As if cognizant of this unique status, Harrison reveals Wilson's ancestral landscape by situating his plays squarely within African and African American traditions, citing literary and cultural predecessors, such as W.E.B. DuBois, Jean Toomer, Langston Hughes, Zora Neale Hurston, Ralph Ellison, Leadbelly, Amiri Baraka, Ishmael Reed, Alice Walker, Adrienne Kennedy, Toni Morrison, and Thelonious Monk, who clearly shape his agenda.

According to Harrison, Troy Maxson is part of an unmistakable African continuum. That legacy directly links him to the trickster prototype and thus thwarts any attempts to pin him down as a victim of racist schemes. As a descendant of the Yoruba trickster, Eshu, Troy, as Harrison argues, transcends blame, defies Western logic, and appears driven by this African deity's "phallocentric legacy."[2] While it is most likely that initial responses to Troy will not see past his sexual indiscretions, Harrison offers an alternative to conventional wisdom. This alternative reading of Troy more closely aligns him with Wilson's model of the African warrior whose greatest quality is his persistence in rebelling against institutional norms and various forms of racial oppression—unfortunately, not in faithfulness to his marriage.

In Kim Pereira's *August Wilson and the African American Odyssey* (Illinois University Press, 1995), Africa also becomes a powerful referent for discussing *Fences*. As is also indicated in Harrison's "Blues Poetics," Troy's transgressions suggest a kinship with images of the invincible, uncompromising African warrior, refusing to adhere to any accepted communal codes for family relationships. Pereira identifies Troy as a "cultural descendant of Eshu" and notes that this heritage confers upon him "a sense of indestructibility."[3]

In addition to situating Troy within the African continuum, Pereira discusses how *Fences*, as part of Wilson's larger dramatic agenda, conveys African American cultural themes of separation, migration, and reunion. He argues,

> Since reunion with lost family members was not always possible in a country so vast, Wilson elevates this theme to a new, mystical dimension by suggesting that black migration is ultimately a quest for self-authentication and empowerment. Therefore, his characters cannot be defined within the narrow framework of the social roles they are forced to accept in an inimical society, for they are seeking spiritual unification with the mythological aspects of their greater cultural identity as Africans.[4]

Pereira's structuralist reading of Wilson's larger agenda invites readers to appreciate the playwright's "big picture." At the same time, he demonstrates the place that *Fences*, as well as other Wilson plays, occupies on the expansive landscape on which he works.

Harry Elam has been perhaps most consistent in publishing work that advances Wilson's African-based aesthetic. In three important sources, he carefully demonstrates Amadou Bissiri's contention that "Wilson's sense of identity looks emphatically toward Africa, and carries a large part of his ideological program."[5] In his forthcoming book *(W)righting History: The Past as Present in the Drama of August Wilson* (Michigan University Press, 2003), Elam does an intertextual reading of Wilson's body of works and explores critical thematic issues pertaining to Wilson's commentary on music, gender, madness, and African spirituality. In a chapter titled "Ogun in Pittsburgh: Ritual of Resurrection," Elam provides one of the most cogent and culturally sensitive discussions of African spirituality in Wilson's work done to date. His premise is that "Wilson's African-influenced, diasporic spirituality fundamentally concerns processes of healing as it connects the everyday trials and tribulations of black life to the forces of the divine—a spirituality that speaks to the fully realized depth of black sacrifice."[6] Elam describes the hybrid spirituality that characters, such as Troy Maxson, adapt after realizing that "conventional faith in Christianity proves insufficient in addressing their social ills and racial injustices."[7]

The presence of Africa in *Fences* is most recognizable in Gabriel. Harry Elam attests to this in several well-placed, culturally sensitive discussions of the play. In addition to the above-referenced chapter, "Ogun in Pittsburgh: Rituals of Resurrection," Elam approaches the subject of Gabriel's Africanness in an essay titled "August Wilson, Doubling, Madness, and Modern African American Drama" (*Modern Drama*, 2000), and in a reference article titled, "August Wilson" (*African American Writers*, 2001). In both sources, Elam emphasizes that Gabriel's actions are far from the absurd, dismissive labels so freely heaped upon him in hasty critiques of the *Fences*. Prior to Elam's enlightening work, Gabriel was regarded as a "dimwit," as an "idiot savant," or, worse, as a "madman." Indeed, much misinformation has been imparted on the significance of Gabriel. One may recall that so baffling was Gabriel's relevance to the play that Broadway producer Carole Shorenstein waged an all-out battle against Wilson. Rescuing him from total marginalization, then, Elam frames his ideas on Gabriel, which he expresses in each essay, within Yoruban cultural concepts. He explains, "Gabriel's ritualistic and spiritual enactment is an exhibit of a syncretic cosmology, the presence of African tradition within New World religious practice."[8] Gabriel's significance in this regard is not fully realized until the play's finale when he unsuccessfully attempts to issue forth sound from his horn to cue open the gates of Heaven for his brother.

Because the term "mad" is used so freely to describe individuals such as Gabriel, Elam seeks to demystify and defamiliarize its stigma in "August Wilson, Doubling, Madness, and Modern African American Drama." For any who have read at least two of Wilson's dramatic works, the recurring "fool" character prototype becomes immediately recognizable. He or she is a familiar fixture within society, yet that same familiarity is ironically also the cause of their invisibility. Society does not expect wisdom from these least likely sources. According to Elam, Wilson problematizes this stereotype. He writes,

> The madness of each of these figures' madness results from symbolic or real confrontations with white power structures. These confrontations cause ruptures and schisms for the characters that parallel primal scenes of loss, rupture, and schism within the experiences of Africans in America. Thus, they become representations of collective African American social memories.[9]

Read as African American historical memory, Gabriel is a manifestation of the fragmented, scarred, disconnected African American psyche. Such an interpretation establishes a kind of cultural sensitivity that surpasses emphasis upon Gabriel's role and may unlock other obscure aspects of the text.

Of lesser importance are analyses of *Fences* that limit themselves to the box of Western ideology. Although discussing how the play both adheres to and departs from Aristotelian prescriptions for tragedy may be one of many salient approaches to the text, it is also infinitely more useful to discuss the tensions that emerge in *Fences* when Western thought and cultural norms clash with those that evolve from an African cosmology. What new knowledge is gained? What do these encounters reveal about the ongoing cultural shock that the Maxsons face as Africans in America? To critique *Fences* as the African American version of Arthur Miller's *Death of a Salesman*, to view Troy as a cousin to Shakespeare's Hamlet, or to pair Rose with the long-suffering Mary Tyrone of Eugene O'Neill's *Long Day's Journey into Night* constitutes an unfortunate form of naiveté that is all too symptomatic of a monolithic view of the world.

Critics who choose this course far too often come to Wilson's work with an agenda of their own that has less to do with illuminating the text and more to do with testing (or forcing) theoretical paradigms that simply are not applicable. Trudier Harris calls this practice "dabbling" and has cast a disparaging eye upon alarming numbers of such culturally untrained violators of African American literary criticism:

> They are simply appropriating the literature as a means of quick aca-demic capital, in what they perceive to be the going fad. What they do amounts in effect to cultural rape, to the commodification of and exploitation of African American literature—commodification by using it merely to advance their positions, exploitation in the lack of respect for the people, the history, the circumstances out of which the literature was produced.[10]

Harris's indictment of the dabblers is not to be misconstrued as an attempt to "fence off" Wilson's work from critics who are members of racial groups other than African Americans or—to put it more bluntly—to imply that only African American critics can and should critique African American works of literature. Rather, as she argues, it is a desire to "fence in" meaning that reveals itself most fully through cultural spe-cific readings of the play. That requires that one discusses the play mind-ful that the dynamics of its various conflicts are neither racially nor culturally interchangeable, despite widespread contentions about the uni-versal quality of *Fences*.

In his very unsettling 1996 speech, "The Ground On Which I Stand," August Wilson—among other things—sets the bar on a high rung for drama critics. He points out that "a stagnant body of critics, operating from the critical criteria of forty years ago, makes for a stagnant theatre without the fresh and abiding influence of contemporary ideas. It is the critics who should be in the forefront of developing new tools for analysis necessary to understand new influences. The critic who can recognize a German neo-romantic influence should also be able to recognize an American influence from blues or black church rituals, or any other con-temporary American influence."[11] Such prescribed standards must be applied across the board—not only in essays in journals or critical collec-tions that illuminate *Fences* but also in the analysis of all forms of African American literature and culture.

In addition to important studies on *Fences* that interpret the play through the lens of an imperative Africanist aesthetic, essays that take other interesting approaches also deserve this discriminating label. These include critical discussions that explore from multiple angles the tragic dimensions of the play's protagonist as Wilson's marvelously complex yet tragically flawed hero. Recognizing that one of Wilson's most pressing motivations for writing *Fences* was to develop a fully blown individual character, authors who take this approach concentrate upon how the playwright transforms Troy from a garbageman to a character whose concerns engage a universal audience. For example, Anna Blumenthal explores the multiple functions of Troy's stories in her essay "More Stories than the Devil Got Sinners: Troy's Stories in August Wilson's *Fences*." She interprets Troy's catalog of anecdotes, tall tales, and recollections of memorable events from his personal past as instructional devices—Troy's indirect means of imparting life's lessons to his sons. She argues that much about Troy's character is reflected in his boastful rhetoric and believes that "a thoughtful examination of the stories Troy tells increases the reader's respect for Troy because study of the stories brings to light his emotional self-control and his effectiveness as a teacher and guide; that is, his sense of duty toward his family."[12] Blumenthal problematizes possible interpretations that some may proffer about Troy's stories as the continuation of the folksy tradition popularized in Joel Chandler Harris's Uncle Remus stories. She challenges such essentialist assumptions through her intriguing psychoanalysis of the role of storytelling in Troy's life beyond simple entertainment and amusement.

Social scientist Anthony Bibus III, whom Blumenthal references more than once in her essay, proves that *Fences* has both literary as well as sociological merits. In an essay titled "Family Metaphors in Three Plays by August Wilson: A Source of Deeper Cultural Sensitivity," *Fences* is one of a trilogy of Wilson plays used to support Bibus's thesis that "Social workers' understanding of African American families can be deepened through an analysis of the metaphors Wilson uses as his characters experience family life, especially metaphors relating to primary issues in child welfare policy and practice such as placement prevention, permanency planning, and family-based services."[13] Because the play is set in what Bibus refers to as "family-centered years for Americans"[14] (a.k.a. the 1950s), its emphasis upon family relationships is more pronounced.

Also important are essays that situate and discuss *Fences* at length within the historical context of the 1950s time frame. Such works create a solid and credible backdrop of—what was for African Americans—a pivotal decade. Critics who come to the text of *Fences* fully informed of the world that African Americans inhabited during the postwar 1950s—

and, just as important, the period immediately following Emancipation—are more apt to grasp and comprehend the very real pressures that the Maxson family faced during the pre–civil rights era. Their concerns over issues of employment, education, and finances assume a greater sense of urgency when critics consider also the times that influence their attitudes and their decisions. Three references prove especially useful in this regard: "Fences by August Wilson" (*Literature and Its Times*, 1997); *August Wilson* (Twayne, 1999); and *The Dramatic Vision of August Wilson* (Howard University Press, 1995). Editors Joyce Moss and George Wilson, whose work appears in the 1997 reference volume *Literature and Its Times*, go to great lengths to provide what is the most thorough discussion of the historical and political contexts that inform *Fences*. Using the subheadings "Events in History at the Time the Play Takes Place" and "Events in History at the Time the Play Was Written," they provide two important historical frameworks for analyzing and understanding the complexities of the play's conflict. Beginning with a snapshot of Wilson's hometown, the essay moves to a detailed discussion of the conditions of "Black Pittsburgh" that *Fences* re-creates. Noted is the city's vibrant steel industry that attracted hundreds of black laborers up North: "Pittsburgh's steel and coal industries had reached the peak of their productivity around the same time that European immigration had been cut off by the war, and Northern mills and factories hired and even recruited black laborers for the first time."[15] Also explored are the historically divisive conditions of home ownership in Pittsburgh among African Americans. In addition editors apprise readers of corrupt practices of labor unions, noting, "In real life, the city's black workers responded enthusiastically to nonracist unions but also had reasons to mistrust organized labor. Corrupt union officials who accepted bribes or made deals with the management were not uncommon."[16] Equal attention is given to the prevailing racial climate in sports and the background of Negro League teams.

Interestingly, this essay also takes into account what influences may have impacted the playwright when he actually composed *Fences*. Whether the fact that in 1985 Rand McNally named Pittsburgh "the most livable city in the United States" had any bearing on Wilson's thoughts is certainly debatable. However, such information can be helpful as ports of entry for discussing *Fences* from a contemporary perspective. In addition to this bit of real-estate propaganda, the study reveals the following milieu that enveloped Wilson as he put together this classic work: "Industrial activity had slackened, and as a result, the city's rivers, buildings, and air were cleaner than they had been fifty years before.

Architecturally, the city was a jumble of old and new: many old buildings had been preserved, others had been replaced by plain, functional ones, and aluminum siding covered the exteriors of older homes, which were made of wood and brick." African Americans made up a much higher percentage of professional athletes; colleges admitted more African American athletes to their programs and responded to criticism about low graduation rates by beefing up support services. Amid all of these positive changes, racism still lifted its head. In the late 1980s, CBS sports commentator Jimmy "the Greek" Snyder lost his job because he made an offensive racial remark about the physiology of African American athletes. It is certainly conceivable, if not likely, that these events may have filtered through to Wilson's consciousness and, in some fashion, influenced his writing of *Fences*.

Sandra Shannon's *The Dramatic Vision of August Wilson* (Howard University Press, 1995) emphasizes *Fences* as a generational play. As such, the historical landscape that she describes for the play extends back to the era of Troy Maxson's father: the Reconstruction years—a time shortly after the freeing of masses of enslaved African Americans. Because the Maxson male lineage does not double back across the Atlantic, she acknowledges the indelible influence of North American slavery upon the African American male psyche:

> *Fences* reminds us that the politics of racial hatred that endured long past slavery continues to drive wedges between black men and their sons. Black men frequently lash out at their sons (or other blacks) as alternate targets instead of confronting head-on the emasculating racism or the social and economic pressures they encounter outside the home.[17]

Shannon argues that Troy is carved from a past that has not only shaped his concepts of fatherhood, but also his ideas on the institution of marriage and his thoughts of his own mortality. She delves into the frustrating world of the sharecropper and the tenant farmer of the antebellum south to provide some clues for his enigmatic behavior.

Closely associated with historicizing *Fences* are critical discussions that pay close attention to the Jim Crow status of baseball in America during the 1940s and 1950s, and the closely related proliferation of Negro League teams also brings to the forefront major contributing factors behind the conflict of *Fences*. Although Mills and Wilson also spend time on this issue, so too does Peter Wolfe, author of the Twayne series installment on August Wilson. Titled, not surprisingly, *August Wilson*, Wolfe's book-length study includes a chapter on *Fences* that contains an abundance of baseball facts. Wolfe does more than list statistics, however. His baseball acumen allows readers to measure Troy's capabilities among major-league players of his day, many of whom his talents would have eclipsed. Wolfe writes,

> Troy was a great hitter, fully deserving of the chance to become a major leaguer. A friend's statement, that only Babe Ruth and Josh Gibson hit more home runs than Troy (F, 9), though possibly an exaggeration, attests to Troy's prowess as a slugger. Most of his prowess, though, ran to waste. . . . Such data improve our understanding of Troy. Not only has his exclusion from major leagues poisoned his psyche for the last 17 years. His dying act consists of playing an imaginary game of baseball in his backyard.[18]

Rose Maxson also commands considerable attention in *Fences*, both as an individual character and as a partner in a seemingly unilateral relationship with an egocentric, tyrannical husband. Her story demands closer scrutiny apart from the cast of other characters who essentially orbit around the central figure Troy. Several attempts have been made to either point out Rose's victimization at the hands of Troy and (whether warranted or not) to diagnose her circumstances according to feminist thought. Interestingly, yet conversely, other attempts have been made that emphasize her unequivocal compliance in the matter. In Alan Nadel's *May All Your Fences Have Gates: Essays on the Drama of August Wilson*, Harry Elam, Sandra Shannon, and Missy Dean Kubitschek contribute essays that explore gender issues in the body of Wilson's work. In "August Wilson's Women," Elam asserts,

> The representation of black women by August Wilson, thus, offers a complex and intriguing dialectic. He presents independent women who assert feminist positions, but who, either through their own volition or as the result of external social pressures, ultimately conform to traditional gender roles and historical expectations."[19]

Sandra Shannon's essay titled "The Ground On Which I Stand: August Wilson's Perspective of African American Women," uses as its focus comments from a 1991 interview with August Wilson in which he states emphatically that he is not bothered by charges that African American women are voiceless and underrepresented in his plays. Proceeding from this blameless position, Shannon argues in discussions of each of Wilson's cycle plays that although his plays are male centered, his portrayals of African American women are sensitive and honorable. "Although individually his feminine portrayals tend to slip into comfort zones of what seem to be male-fantasized roles," she writes, "collectively they show Wilson coming to grips with the depth and diversity of African American womanhood."[20] Shannon advanced this same argument in "The Fences That They Build: August Wilson's Depiction of African-American Women" (*Obsidian II: Black Literature in Review*, summer 1991). Here she asserts, "Wilson not only places African-American women in traditional roles, such as nurturing wives, mothers, organizers, and pillars of strength, but he also portrays free-wheeling, independent sides of them which are skeptical of men and the demands of marriage and family."[21] Shannon credits Rose with coming up with her own version of feminism that allows her to retain her capacity to nurture but, at the same time, recognize and repudiate exploitation.

While Elam and Shannon distinguish between Rose Maxson as victim and Rose Maxson as a woman in charge, Missy Dean Kubitschek sees Rose as both alienated and victimized. She regards Troy's use of baseball metaphors as exclusionary jargon meant to further shut out or, more appropriately, "fence out" Rose. She makes much of the uneven circumstances in their marriage, arguing that "the play shows men and women speaking different languages, reflecting different understandings of the spiritual cosmos."[22] Kubitschek echoes a similar uncompromising position more fully explored in feminist critic Kim Marra's essay "Ma Rainey and the Boyz: Gender Ideology in August Wilson's Broadway Canon." Here Marra does not qualify what she perceives as Troy's sexism toward his wife Rose. She writes rather emphatically,

> The primary focus, once again, is on the male hero, Troy Maxson's, quest for manhood, with the major female character, his wife Rose, drawn primarily according to how she affirms or thwarts his endeavor. . . . The most far-reaching and insurmountable "fences" in this play . . . prove to be those of gender.[23]

Marra's feminist position on Rose's alienation challenges the ground on which August Wilson stands as a male writer. She rejects the notion that Rose "has chosen her bed to lie in" and directs her attention instead toward Troy's unbridled sexism: "She [Rose] comes to realize that he

[Troy] sees her not as an individual entitled to pursue her own needs but as a functionary who fulfills expected roles, including that of passageway for the realization and release of his frustrated dreams."[24]

Considering that it is widely understood that the poet in Wilson has much to do with his reliance upon metaphor in *Fences*, several essays, chapters, and longer studies that linger on the relevance of three dominant figurative images in the play are especially illuminating: (1) the fence and the process of its construction; (2) the game of baseball whose codes Troy adapts to express his conflict; and (3) the personification of Death, Troy's most respected adversary. Explorations of meaning of these figurative images in both abstract and concrete terms provide helpful sites of entry for discussing the play's meaning more fully. It is important to note also that any one of Wilson's characters—in particular, Gabriel— may also function in a symbolic capacity beyond his or her literal, one-dimensional identity as human.

Eric Sterling and Sandra Shannon provide fundamental interpretations of the ubiquitous fence image in *Fences*. In his essay "Protecting Home: Patriarchal Authority in August Wilson's *Fences*," Sterling sees the fence as but a component of the larger symbolic framework of the baseball diamond that is at work in the play. He reasons, "If the Maxson home signifies home plate, the fence that stands at the boundary of the house symbolizes the fence at the confines of a baseball field."[25] Sterling adopts the dynamics of the game in making sense of the pressures Troy faces. However, he also reveals a number of other interpretations for this symbolic barrier. For example, he refers to the fence as "the symbolic boundary defining his [Troy's] social power" and as a "metaphor for the barrier he creates between Cory and himself."[26] In a chapter exclusively on *Fences* in *The Dramatic Vision of August Wilson*, Shannon notes that the fence "raises issues ranging from economic and professional deprivation to emotional and moral isolation."[27] She moves from the abstract, figurative meaning of *Fences* to a discussion of the literal impact that numerous barriers had on the dreams of the Maxson family clan.

Building upon Shannon's and Sterling's discussions of the figurative significance of the fence metaphor, Alan Nadel and Michael Awkward provide post-structuralist analyses of the fence that speak to larger issues regarding racial and cultural boundaries. For instance, in "Boundaries, Logistics, and Identity: The Property of Metaphor in *Fences* and *Joe Turner's Come and Gone*," Nadel regards the fence as a demarcation used centuries ago to justify, for purposes of slavery and disenfranchisement, classifying African Americans as nonhumans. He extends this logic to explain the racist implications of the familiar Mason-Dixon Line, which, according to Nadel, "became the universal metaphoric fence that marked the properties of race as criteria for inhuman treatment."[28] At the core of Michael Awkward's essay "The Crookeds with the Straights: *Fences*, Race, and the Politics of Adaptation" is the "I-want-a-black-director" controversy of 1990, which became a celebrated cause within the arts world. Awkward draws parallels between the fence metaphor in *Fences* and Wilson's demands for a culturally sensitive, African American director for a screen version of the same. To advance his position, Awkward points to what he regards as similar aspects of his argument embedded in the conflict of *Fences*. His objective is "to investigate the play's examination of the possibilities of erecting protective fences around black familial space in terms of the quite different trajectory of Wilson's efforts to find a black film director in order to protect his creation from potentially contaminating caucacentric forces."[29]

Because the interconnectedness between fences and baseball is such a given, critics have not resisted the impulse to explore the game in somewhat similar restrictive terms. Take, for example, Christine Birdwell, whose essay "Death as a Fastball on the Outside Corner: *Fences'* Troy Maxson and the American Dream" demonstrates how Wilson conveys the fundamental meaning of *Fences* through baseball metaphors. Birdwell argues that "the fences of the title are both real and metaphorical, both defenses and obstructions. . . . They are not the white picket fences in the front yards of American Dream homes. Instead they are the racial barriers keeping blacks, even great hitters who can slam balls over any ballpark fence, from realizing their potential."[30] Qun Wang argues in his essay "Towards the Poetization of the 'Field of Manners'" that the blues have developed in Wilson "an interest in finding apt metaphors to express his thematic concerns."[31] Those "apt metaphors" in *Fences* turn out to be Troy's baseball bat and the fence that surrounds the Maxson house. Wang sees Troy's bat as "a constant reminder of Troy's unfulfilled dreams, and the fence a manifestation of the consequences."[32]

On Death personified, Anna Blumenthal, author of "More Stories than the Devil Got Sinners: Troy's Stories in August Wilson's *Fences*," provides one of the best discussions of the omnipresence of Troy's pesky archenemy. She traces the initial summoning of this image in Troy's deathbed story to his final swing of the bat just before he dies in his own backyard. Blumenthal references Death in her larger discussion of the function of Troy's prolific stories in *Fences*.

In a lengthy biographical essay that delves into the life of Wilson and provides thorough commentary on each of his plays, Harry Elam examines the implications of Gabriel's final obscure actions in *Fences*. Drawing upon traditional African beliefs about the otherworld view on retentive memory, he explains Gabriel's mission to "[invoke] racial memory, an African inheritance. His actions again reinforce the impact of the past on the present as the family's African heritage provides a benediction for their African American present."[33]

Finally, discussions of Wilson's fascinating creative process are important sources for those interested in studying the work/art of a much-acknowledged master craftsman. The importance of such discussions lies in their potential to inspire future artisans and to enlighten lay audiences on what goes into the making of a classic, such as *Fences*. Joan Herrington stands alone in this category with her thorough study *I Ain't Sorry for Nothin' I Done: August Wilson's Process of Playwriting* (Limelight, 1998). Her chapter on *Fences* is a study in discipline and commitment, for it chronicles Wilson's efforts during the painstaking evolution of *Fences* from a flawed, unfocused script to one precisely tuned to convey the theme of responsibility. From Herrington's work, readers get to appreciate August Wilson as a perfectionist, as a taskmaster, as a serious artist who continues to earn every bit of the recognition that has been lavished upon him and his dramatic work. *I Ain't Sorry* also helps readers to realize that, contrary to romantic notions of muse-inspired art, here is an instance where diligence and hard work rule.

NOTES

1. Paul Carter Harrison, review of *August Wilson: A Casebook* by Marilyn Elkins, *African American Review* 35 (winter 2001): 674.

2. Paul Carter Harrison, "August Wilson's Blues Poetics" in *August Wilson: Three Plays* (Pittsburgh: Pittsburgh University Press, 1991), 305.

3. Kim Pereira, *August Wilson and the African American Odyssey* (Urbana: Illinois University Press, 1995), 37.

4. Ibid., 3.

5. Amadou Bissiri, "Aspects of Africanness in August Wilson's Drama: Reading *The Piano Lesson* through Wole Soyinka's Drama," *African American Review*, 30 (spring 1996): 99.

6. Harry Elam, *(W)righting History: The Past as Present in the Drama of August Wilson* (Michigan University Press, forthcoming).

7. Ibid., 378.

8. Ibid., 440.

9. Harry Elam, "August Wilson, Doubling, Madness, and Modern African American Drama," *Modern Drama* 43 (winter 2000): 616.

10. Trudier Harris, "Miss-Trained or Untrained? Jackleg Critics and African American Literature (Or, Some of My Adventures in Academia)," in *African American Literary Criticism: 1773 to 2000*, ed. Hazel Ervin (New York: Twayne, 1999), 462.

11. August Wilson, *The Ground On Which I Stand* (New York: Theatre Communications Group, 2001), 43.

12. Anna S. Blumenthal, "More Stories than the Devil Got Sinners: Troy's Stories in August Wilson's *Fences*," *American Drama* 9 (Spring 2000): 76.

13. Anthony A. Bibus III, "Family Metaphors in Three Plays by August Wilson: A Source of Deeper Cultural Sensitivity," *Social Work in Education* 14 (1992): 1.

14. Ibid.

15. Joyce Moss and George Wilson, eds., "Fences by August Wilson," in *World War II to the Affluent Fifties (1940–1950)*, Literature and Its Times: Profiles of 300 Notable Literary Works and the Historical Events that Influenced Them, vol. 4 (New York: Gale, 1997), 144.

16. Ibid., 145.

17. Sandra Shannon, *The Dramatic Vision of August Wilson* (Washington, D.C.: Howard University Press, 1995), 100.

18. Peter Wolfe, *August Wilson* (New York: Twayne, 1999), 55–56.

19. Harry Elam, "August Wilson's Women," in *May All Your Fences Have Gates: Essays on the Drama of August Wilson*, ed. Alan Nadel (Iowa City: Iowa University Press, 1994), 183.

20. Sandra Shannon, "The Ground On Which I Stand: August Wilson's Perspective on African American Women," in *May All Your Fences Have Gates: Essays on the Drama of August Wilson*, ed. Alan Nadel (Iowa City: Iowa University Press, 1994), 151.

21. Sandra Shannon, "The Fences That They Build: August Wilson's Depiction of African-American Women," *Obsidian II: Black Literature in Review* 6 (summer 1991): 2.

22. Missy Dean Kubitschek, "August Wilson's Gender Lesson," in *May All Your Fences Have Gates: Essays on the Drama of August Wilson*, ed. Alan Nadel (Iowa City: Iowa University Press, 1994), 183.

23. Kim Marra, "Ma Rainey and the Boyz: Gender Ideology in August Wilson's Broadway Canon," in *August Wilson: A Casebook*, ed. Marilyn Elkins (New York: Garland, 1994), 147.

24. Ibid., 148.

25. Eric Sterling, "Protecting Home: Patriarchal Authority in August Wilson's *Fences*," *Essays in Theatre* 17 (November 1998): 55.

26. Ibid., 56.

27. Shannon, *Dramatic Vision*, 108.

28. Alan Nadel, "Boundaries, Logistics, and Identity: The Property of Metaphor in *Fences* and *Joe Turner's Come and Gone*," in *May All Your Fences Have Gates: Essays on the Drama of August Wilson*, ed. Alan Nadel (Iowa City: Iowa University Press, 1994), 88.

29. Michael Awkward, "The Crookeds with the Straights: *Fences*, Race, and the Politics of Adaptation," in *May All Your Fences Have Gates: Essays on the Drama of August Wilson*, ed. Alan Nadel (Iowa City: Iowa University Press, 1994), 215.

30. Christine Birdwell, "Death as a Fastball on the Outside Corner: *Fences'* Troy Maxson and the American Dream," *Aethlon: The Journal of Sports Literature*, 8 (fall 1990): 88.

31. Qun Wang, "Towards the Poetization of the 'Field of Manners,'" *African American Review* 29 (winter 1995): 607.

32. Ibid., 609.

33. Harry Elam, "August Wilson," in *African American Writers*, 2d edition, vol. 2, ed. Valerie Smith (New York: Scribner's, 2001), 848.

Works Cited

African American Performance and Theater History: A Critical Reader. Edited by Harry Elam and David Krasner. New York: Oxford University Press, 2001.

Africanisms in American Culture. Edited by Joseph Holloway. Bloomington: Indiana University Press, 1991.

Anderson, Telia U. "Calling on the Spirit: The Performativity of Black Women's Faith in the Baptist Church Spiritual Traditions and Its Radical Possibilities for Resistance." In *African American Performance and Theater History: A Critical Reader*. Edited by Harry Elam and David Krasner. New York: Oxford University Press, 2001.

Awkward, Michael. "The Crookeds with the Straights: *Fences*, Race, and the Politics of Adaptation." In *May All Your Fences Have Gates: Essays on the Drama of August Wilson*. Edited by Alan Nadel. Iowa City: Iowa University Press, 1994.

Baker, Ray Stannard. *Following the Color Line*. New York: Harper & Row, 1964.

Barbour, David. "August Wilson's Here to Stay." *Theater Week*, 18–25 April 1998, 8–14.

Barnes, Clive. "Fiery 'Fences.'" *New York Post*, 27 March 1987.

Bennett, Lerone. *Confrontation: Black and White*. Chicago: Johnson Publishing, 1965.

Bibus, Anthony. "Family Metaphors in Three Plays by August Wilson: A Source of Deeper Cultural Sensitivity." *Social Work in Education* 14 (1992): 1–10.

Birdwell, Christine. "Death as a Fastball on the Outside Corner: *Fences'* Troy Maxson and the American Dream." *Aethlon: The Journal of Sports Literature* 8 (fall 1990): 87–96.

Bissiri, Amadou. "Aspects of Africanness in August Wilson's Drama: Reading *The Piano Lesson* through Wole Soyinka's Drama." *African American Review* 30 (spring 1996): 99–113.

Blumenthal, Anna. S. "More Stories than the Devil Got Sinners: Troy's Stories in August Wilson's *Fences*." *American Drama* 9 (spring 2000): 74–96.

Bogumil, Mary. *Understanding August Wilson*. Columbia: South Carolina University Press, 1999.

Booker, Margaret. "Building Fences in Beijing." *American Theatre*, May/June 1997, 50–52.

Brustein, Robert. "On Cultural Power." *The New Republic*, 3 March 1997, 31–35.

———. "Unity from Diversity." *The New Republic*, July 1993, 29–30.

Call and Response: The Riverside Anthology of the African American Literary Tradition. Edited by Patricia Liggins Hill. Boston: Houghton Mifflin, 1998.

Conteh-Morgan, John. "African Traditional Drama and Issues in Theater Performance Criticism." *Comparative Drama* 28 (1994): 3–18.

Conwill, Kinshasha H. Introduction to *Memory and Metaphor: The Art of Romare Bearden*. New York: Oxford University Press, 1991.

Creel, Margaret Washington. "Gullah Attitudes toward Life and Death." In *Africanisms in America*. Edited by Joseph E. Holloway. Bloomington: Indiana University Press, 1990.

Dean, Philip Hayes. *The Owl Killer*. In *The Best Short Plays: 1974*. Edited by Stanley Richards. Radnor, PA: Chilton, 1974.

Dictionary of Literary Biography. Vol. 228: Twentieth-Century American Dramatists Series, 2d ed. Edited by Christopher J. Wheatley. New York: Gale, 2000.

DuBois, W.E.B. *The Souls of Black Folks*. In *Three Negro Classics*. New York: Avon, 1965.

Elam, Harry. "August Wilson." In *African American Writers*, 2d edition. Vol. 2. Edited by Valerie Smith. New York: Scribner's, 2001.

———. "August Wilson, Doubling, Madness, and Modern African American Drama." *Modern Drama* 43 (winter 2000): 611–32.

———. "August Wilson's Women." In *May All Your Fences Have Gates: Essays on the Drama of August Wilson*. Edited by Alan Nadel. Iowa City: Iowa University Press, 1994.

———. "Of Angels and Transcendence: An Analysis of *Fences* by August Wilson and *Roosters* by Milcha Sanchez-Scott." In *Staging Differences: Cultural Pluralism in American Theatre and Drama*. New York: Lang, 1995.

———. *(W)righting History: The Past as Present in the Drama of August Wilson*. Michigan University Press (forthcoming).

Elkins, Marilyn. Introduction to *August Wilson: A Casebook*. Edited by Marilyn Elkins. New York: Garland, 1994.

Ellison, Ralph. "Richard Wright's Blues." In *Shadow and Act*. New York: New American Library, 1964.

Gantt, Denise. "Letter from Denise A. Gantt." *The Next Stage at Center Stage* (Playbill for *Seven Guitars*) 3 (1996–1997): 1.

Gates, Henry Louis. *The Signifying Monkey: A Theory of African-American Literary Criticism*. New York: Oxford University Press, 1988.

Gordon, Joanne. "Wilson and Fugard: Politics and Art." In *August Wilson: A Casebook*. Edited by Marilyn Elkins. New York: Garland, 1994.

Hansberry, Lorraine. *A Raisin in the Sun*. New York: Signet, 1959.

———. *To Be Young, Gifted, and Black: Lorraine Hansberry in Her Own Words*. Adapted by Robert Nemiroff. New York: New American Library, 1970.

Harris, Trudier. "August Wilson's Folk Traditions." In *August Wilson: A Casebook*. Edited by Marilyn Elkins. New York: Garland, 1994.

———. "Miss-Trained or Untrained? Jackleg Critics and African American Literature (Or, Some of My Adventures in Academia)." In *African American Literary Critics: 1773 to 2000*. Edited by Hazel Ervin. New York: Twayne, 1999.

Harrison, Paul Carter. "August Wilson's Blues Poetics." In *August Wilson: Three Plays*. Pittsburgh: Pittsburgh University Press, 1991.

———. Review of *August Wilson: A Casebook*. Edited by Marilyn Elkins. *African American Review* 35 (winter 2001): 674–77.

Henderson, Heather. "Building Fences: An Interview with Mary Alice and James Earl Jones." *Theater Journal* 16 (summer/fall 1985): 67–70.

Herrington, Joan. *I Ain't Sorry for Nothin' I Done: August Wilson's Process of Playwriting*. New York: Limelight, 1998.

Hewitt, Barnard. *Theatre U.S.A.: 1665 to 1957*. New York: McGraw-Hill, 1959.

Holman, C. Hugh and William Harmon. *Handbook to Literature*, 6th ed. New York: Macmillan, 1992.

hooks, bel. *Yearning: Race, Gender, and Cultural Politics*. Boston: South End, 1990.

Hughes, Langston. *The Big Sea*. New York: Knopf, 1940.

———. *The Book of Negro Humor*. New York: Dodd, 1966.

Hurston, Zora Neale. *Their Eyes Were Watching God*. Chicago: Illinois University Press, 1978.

Kauffman, Stanley. "Bottoms Up." *Saturday Review* 11 (January/February 1985): 83, 90.

Kennedy, Randall. *Nigger: The Strange Career of a Troublesome Word*. New York: Pantheon, 2002.

———. "A Note on the Word 'Nigger.'" *Toward Racial Equality: Harper's Weekly Reports on Black America: 1857–1874*. http://harpweek.com. HarpWeek, LLC, 1999–2000.

Kester, Gunilla Theander. "Approaches to Africa: The Poetics of Memory and the Body in Two August Wilson Plays." In *August Wilson: A Casebook*. Edited by Marilyn Elkins. New York: Garland, 1994.

Kihn, Martin. "Wilson Builds Second Sturdy *Fences* at Rep." *Yale Daily News*, 8 May 1985.

Kowinski, William. "The Play Looks Good on Paper—But Will It Fly?" *Smithsonian*, March 1992, 78–87.

Kubitschek, Missy Dean. "August Wilson's Gender Lesson." In *May All Your Fences Have Gates: Essays on the Drama of August Wilson*. Edited by Alan Nadel. Iowa City: Iowa University Press, 1994.

Lida, David. "Fences—A Review." *Women's Wear Daily*, 27 March 1987, 8.

Logan, Rayford. *The Negro in American Life and Thought: The Nadir, 1877–1901*. New York: Dial, 1954.

Major, Clarence. *Dictionary of Afro-American Slang*. New York: International Publishers, 1970.

Marks, Carole. *Farewell—We're Good and Gone: The Great Black Migration*. Bloomington: Indiana University Press, 1989.

Marra, Kim. "Ma Rainey and the Boyz: Gender Ideology in August Wilson's Broadway Canon." In *August Wilson: A Casebook*. Edited by Marilyn Elkins. New York: Garland, 1994.

May All Your Fences Have Gates: Essays on the Drama of August Wilson. Edited by Alan Nadel. Iowa City: Iowa University Press, 1994.

Mills, Alice. "The Walking Blues: An Anthropological Approach to the Theater of August Wilson." *Black Scholar* 25 (spring 1995): 30–35.

Moss, Joyce, and George Wilson, eds. "Fences by August Wilson." In *World War II to the Affluent Fifties (1940–1950). Literature and Its Times: Profiles of 300 Notable Literary Works and the Historical Events that Influenced Them*, vol. 4. New York: Gale, 1997.

Moyers, Bill. *A World of Ideas*. New York: Doubleday, 1989.

Nadel, Alan. "Boundaries, Logistics, and Identity: The Property of Metaphor in *Fences* and *Joe Turner's Come and Gone*." In *May All Your Fences Have Gates: Essays on the Drama of August Wilson*. Edited by Alan Nadel. Iowa City: Iowa University Press, 1994.

Neal, Larry. "The Black Arts Movement." In *The Black Aesthetic*. Edited by Addison Gayle. New York: Doubleday, 1971.

Norton Anthology of African American Literature. Edited by Henry Louis Gates and Nellie Y. McKay. New York: Norton, 1997.

Pereira, Kim. *August Wilson and the African American Odyssey*. Chicago: Illinois University Press, 1995.

Peterson, Robert. *Only the Ball Was White*. Englewood Cliffs, NJ: Prentice-Hall, 1970.

Pointsett, Alex. "August Wilson: Hottest New Playwright." *Ebony*, 24 November 1987, 68+.

Powers, Kim. "An Interview with August Wilson." *Theater Journal* 16 (fall/winter 1984): 50–55.

Reed, Ishmael. "In Search of August Wilson: A Shy Genius Transforms the American Theater." *Connoisseur*, March 1987, 92–97.

Rich, Frank. "Theater: Family Ties in Wilson's 'Fences.'" *New York Times*, 27 March 1987.

Richards, David. "The Powerful Confines of *Fences*." *Washington Post*, 27 April 1990, D4.

Richards, Lloyd. Interview by author, New York City. 1 June 2000.

Rocha, Mark. "August Wilson and the Four B's." *August Wilson: A Casebook*. Edited by Marilyn Elkins. New York: Garland, 1994.

Rothstein, Mervyn. "Round Five for the Theatrical Heavyweight." *New York Times*, 15 April 1990, 1–8.

Shannon, Sandra. *The Dramatic Vision of August Wilson*. Washington, D.C.: Howard University Press, 1995.

———. "The Fences That They Built: August Wilson's Depiction of African American Women." *Obsidian II: Black Literature in Review* 6 (summer 1991): 1–17.

———. "The Ground On Which I Stand: August Wilson's Perspective on African American Women." In *May All Your Fences Have Gates: Essays on the Drama of August Wilson*. Edited by Alan Nadel. Iowa City: Iowa University Press, 1994.

Staples, Brent, "'Fences': No Barrier to Emotion." *New York Times*, 5 April 1987, 39.

Sterling, Eric. "Protecting Home: Patriarchal Authority in August Wilson's *Fences*." *Essays in Theater* 17 (November 1998): 53–62.

Walker, Alice. *In Search of Our Mothers' Gardens*. New Brunswick: Rutgers University Press, 1994.

Wang, Qun. *An In Depth Study of the Major Plays of African American Playwright August Wilson*. New York: Mellon, 1999.

———. "Towards the Poetization of the 'Field of Manners.'" *African American Review* 29 (winter 1995): 605–13.

Watlington, Dennis. "Hurdling Fences." *Vanity Fair*, April 1989, 102–13.

Watt, Douglass. "'Fences' Is All over the Lot: But James Early Jones Is Its Saving Grace." *Daily News*, 3 April 1987. In *New York Times Theater Critics' Reviews*, 1987, 316.

Weales, Gerald. *American Drama since World War II*. New York: Harcourt, Brace & World, 1962.

Webster's New World College Dictionary. 3d ed. Edited by Victoria Neufeldt. New York: Macmillan, 1997.

Wilson, August. "Characters behind History Teach Wilson about Plays." *New York Times*, 12 April 1992, sec. H, p. 5.

———. *Fences*. New York: New American Library, 1986.

———. *The Ground On Which I Stand*. New York: Theatre Communications Group, 2001.

———. "The Historical Perspective: An Interview with August Wilson." Interview by Richard Pettengill. In *August Wilson: A Casebook*. Edited by Marilyn Elkins. New York: Garland, 1994.

―――. Interview by Roger Downey April 1988. In *Microsoft Encarta Africana.* Microsoft Corporation, 1999.

―――. Interview by David Savran. In *In Their Own Words: Contemporary American Playwrights.* New York: Theatre Communications Group, 1988.

―――. "I Want a Black Director." In *May All Your Fences Have Gates: Essays on the Drama of August Wilson.* Edited by Alan Nadel. Iowa City: Iowa University Press, 1994.

―――. *Joe Turner's Come and Gone.* New York: Plume, 1988.

―――. *Ma Rainey's Black Bottom.* New York: New American Library, 1985.

―――. Preface to *August Wilson: Three Plays.* Pittsburgh: Pittsburgh University Press, 1991.

Within the Circle: An Anthology of African American Literary Criticism from the Harlem Renaissance to the Present. Edited by Angelyn Mitchell. Durham, NC: Duke University Press, 1994.

Wolfe, Peter. *August Wilson.* New York: Twayne, 1999.

Index

African American Writers, 64
African spiritualism, 73, 75, 145
Africanisms in American Culture, 104
Africanist aesthetic, 1, 98, 103–108, 175, 176–178
Alberta, 4, 41, 64, 136, 141
Alice, Mary, 165–166
The Amen Corner, 22, 161
American Dream, 118
American Gothic, 8
Anderson, Telia, 120
Apartheid, 91–92
August Wilson (Wolfe), 161–162, 181, 183
August Wilson: A Casebook, 157, 167, 169
August Wilson: A Research and Production Sourcebook, 160
August Wilson and the African American Odyssey, 158–159
Awkward, Michael, 115, 168, 185

Baldwin, James, 86
Baraka, Amiri
  on the blues, 3, 25
  influence on *Fences*, 88, 92, 176
Barnes, Clive, 124
Barton, Floyd, 117

Bearden, Romare, influence in *Fences*, 7–10, 52, 92, 134
Bedford, David, 53–54, 55, 85, 90
Bell, James "Cool Papa," 17
Bible Belt, 80
Bibus, Anthony, 180
Birdwell, Christine, 156, 186
Bissiri, Amadou, 177
Black Arts movement, 24, 70, 89, 97
"Black Arts Movement," (Neal), 25
Black Horizons Theatre, 89
Black nationalism, 92
Black Power movement, 88
Blood memory, 92
Blue, legendary dog's significance in *Fences*, 147
Blues, influence in *Fences*, 71–71, 162
Blues People, (Jones, LeRoi), 3
Blumenthal, Anna, 139, 148, 157, 180, 186
Bogumil, Mary, 160–161
The Book of Negro Humor (Hughes), 141
Booker, Margaret, 11, 166–167
Borges, Jorge Luis, 69, 92
Brunetiere, Ferdinand, 162
Brustein, Robert, 10, 20, 26–27, 129, 130
Bullins, Ed, 25

Call and Response: The Riverside Anthology of the African American Literary Tradition, 15, 19
Cat on a Hot Tin Roof, 21
Chicago Defender, 80
Christian church, as symbol of white oppression, 75
Christianity, 3–75, 145
Civil War, 52
The Coldest Day of the Year (Wilson), 138
The Color Purple, 162
Color-blind casting, 11, 84
Continuities (Bearden), as catalyst for *Fences*, xii, 8, 52–53, 85, 134

Dean, Philip Hayes, 25, 88, 89, 161
Death, African and African American cultural responses, 144–146
Death of a Salesman, 21, 27
    parallels to *Fences*, 84–85, 132, 161, 162, 178
Deprivation of possibility, 16, 59–60, 110–111, 116, 117, 118, 119
Dictionary of Afro-American Slang, 149
The Donna Reed Show, 21
The Dramatic Vision of August Wilson, 155, 158, 181
Dred Scott Decision, 168
DuBois, W.E.B., 14–15, 100, 176

Edmonds, Randolph, 70
Elam, Harry, 7, 53, 55, 56, 86, 103, 117, 120, 133, 162, 167, 168
    on madness, 178, 183–184, 187
    Wilson's Africanist context, 175, 176–178
Elder, Lonne, 25, 88
Eliot, T. S., 5
Elkins, Marilyn, 167, 169
Ellison, Ralph, 3, 161, 162
The Emperor Jones, 161
Eshu (Esu Elegbara), 73, 100, 105, 176
Eugene O'Neill Theater Center's National Playwright's Conference, 49, 50, 130, 159
Evers, Medgar, 24

Father Knows Best, 21
Faustian legend, 87
Fences
    African intertextuality, 103–108
    autobiographical parallels, 54–56
    Beijing, China performance, 11–13
    blues influence, 3–6
    favorite text for aspiring performers, 130
    film version, 121–123
    generational play, 14–15, 54–55, 65–66
    language, 58
    meaning in play's title, 105, 115–116
    memory play, 133–134
    myth of irresponsible black man, 51–52
    postwar drama, 21, 23
    power in performance, 58
    revision process, 134
    strategic positioning in Wilson's ten-play cycle, 64–68
    subversive narrative, 20, 22
    well-made play, 83
Florence (Childress), 22
Folklore, 141–142, 146
Food
    as cultural signifier, 78–79, 107–108
    as dramatic device, 79
Four Revolutionary Plays (Baraka), 88
Franklin, Aretha, 24
Freedman, Samuel, 155
French, Samuel, 53
Friendship among African American men, 114–115
Frost, Robert, 162
Fugard, Athol, 91, 97
Fuller, Charles, 15, 16
Fullerton Street (Wilson), 63

Garvey, Marcus, 84
Gates, Henry Louis, 72, 85, 100, 146
Gibson, Josh, 17, 18, 27
The Glass Menagerie, 132
Gordon, Joanne, 91
Great Depression, 64
Great Migration, 64, 79–81

Gregory, Montgomery, 70
Grim Reaper (Death), 76, 142, 144
Ground on which he stands (recurring
    Wilson theme), 1, 25–26
"The Ground on Which I Stand" (The-
    atre Communications Group confer-
    ence speech, June 1996), 87, 121,
    179

Halfway Art Gallery, 23
Hamlet, 87, 178
Hansberry, Lorraine, 2, 3, 68, 161
Harlem Renaissance, 64, 70
Harris, Joel Chandler, 77, 180
Harris, Trudier, 142, 144, 179
Harrison, Paul Carter, 86, 105, 170, 175
Henderson, Heather, 165
Herrington, Joan, 49, 52, 69, 134, 135,
    145, 159–160
Hewitt, Bernard, 20, 27
Holloway, Joseph, 104, 108
Hooks, bell, 120
Hughes, Langston, 141, 148, 176
Hurlyburly (Rabe), 87
Hurston, Zora Neale, 146, 176

I Ain't Sorry for Nothin' I Done: August
    Wilson's Process of Playwriting, 52,
    159, 169
Ibsen, Henrik, 87
The Iliad, 161
An In Depth Study of the Major Plays of
    African American Playwright August
    Wilson (Wang), 162
In Search of Our Mothers' Gardens
    (Walker), 60, 118
Inge, William, 21
Invisible Man, 161

Jim Crow laws, 77, 100, 182
Jitney, 90, 110
Job (Old Testament), 87
Joe Turner's Come and Gone, 66, 67
Jones, James Earl, 51, 165–166

Kennedy, Adrienne, 176

Kennedy, Randall, 148, 149
Kester, Gunilla, 133, 169–170
King, Reverend Martin Luther, Jr., 23–24
King Hedley II, 163
Kittel, Frederick August. See Wilson,
    August
Knight, Etheridge, 25
Kubitschek, Missy Dean, 167, 168,
    183–184

Leadbelly, 176
Leave It To Beaver, 21
"Leftovers from history," 102
Lida, David, 138
Literature and Its Times, 164, 181
Locke, Alain, 70
Long Day's Journey into Night, 161, 178
Loomis, Herald, 143

M. Butterfly (Hwang), 87
Ma Rainey's Black Bottom, 2, 3, 111, 117,
    138, 170
Macbeth, 111
Major, Clarence, 149
Man and Crisis (Ortega y Gasset), 162
Marks, Carole, 81
Marra, Kim, 170–171, 184–185
Mason-Dixon Line, 116, 168, 186
Master Class (McNally), 87
Maxson, Cory
    confrontation with Troy, 45
    effects of move north, 114, 141
Maxson, Gabriel, 33
    campaign to purge his character from
        script, 56
    effects of move north, 114
    failed attempt to blow trumpet, 47–48,
        74
    importance to Fences, 101–103
    as spectacle character, 74
    as symbol of African cosmology, 74, 76
Maxson, Lyons, 32
    as antithesis of responsible black man,
        135
    visited by sins of his father, 113
Maxson, Raynell, 136–137

Maxson, Rose, 31
  challenge to 1950s profile of black
    women, 42, 117–118
  as symbol of Christian tradition, 75
  desire for nuclear family, 113
  as example of responsibility, 135–136
Maxson, Troy
  African identity, 86–87, 104–106
  Baraka's influence, 89
  historicized within postwar 1950s,
    19–21
  nature of his tragedy, 60–61
  philosophy on death, 142–146
  storyteller, 77, 105, 138–148
May All Your Fences Have Gates: Essays
    on the Drama of August Wilson, 157,
    167, 168–169, 183
McKay, Nellie, 146
Melting pot, 98
Middle Passage, 102, 143, 144
Miller, Arthur, 21, 22, 161, 162
Mills, Alice, 104, 105, 107
Monk, Thelonious, 176
Moss, Joyce, 164, 181
Moyers, Bill, 89, 171
Muhummad, Elijah, 84
Murphy, Eddie, 124

Nadel, Alan, 116, 157, 168, 183, 185,
    186
National Association for the Advance-
    ment of Colored People (NAACP),
    20
National Association of Black Ball Play-
    ers (NABBP), 17
Neal, Larry, 25
Negro League, 16–18, 17, 30, 182
Negro Problem, 14–15
New Republic, 129
Nigger, as rhetorical device in Fences,
    148–150
Nigger: The Strange Career of a Trouble-
    some Word, 148
"Nobody Can Bake a Sweet Jelly Roll
    Like Mine" (Bessie Smith), 23

Oedipus, 111

Oedipus Rex, 161
O'Neill, Eugene, 22, 87, 161
Only the Ball Was White (Peterson), 17
Oral tradition, 77
Ortega y Gasset, Jose, 162
Othello, 161
The Owl Killer (Dean), 89, 90, 161
Ozzie and Harriet, 21

Paige, Satchel, 17
Paramount Pictures, 121
Parks, Rosa, 23
Penny, Rob, 24
Pereira, Kim, 73, 75, 86, 158–159, 160,
    176–177
Peterson, Robert, 17
Picnic (Inge), 21
Pittsburgh Public Theatre, 91
Pittsburgh's Center Avenue Poet's The-
    atre Workshop, 23
Postmodernism, 92, 103

Racial madness, 163
Rainey, Gertrude "Ma," 138
A Raisin in the Sun, 2, 15, 16, 21, 22, 67,
    68, 122, 161
Randolph, A. Philip, 16
Reconstruction, 14–15, 133, 135
Recycle (Wilson), 138
Reid, Ishmael, 176
Rich, Frank, 155
Richards, David, 87
Richards, Lloyd, 6, 27, 56, 59, 64, 97,
    111, 116, 122
Richardson, Willis, 70
Rickey, Branch, 18
Robinson, Jackie, 18, 27, 117
Rocha, Mark, 85, 92
Roosters (Sanchez-Scott), 162–163
Ruth, Babe, 27

Sanchez, Sonia, 15
Sanchez-Scott, Milcha, 163
Savran, David, 108
Schafer, Yvonne, 160
Selkirk, George, 106
Seven Guitars, 117, 163

Shadow and Act, 162
Shakespeare, William, 87, 130, 141
Shannon, Sandra, 167, 168, 182,
    183–184, 185
Shorenstein, Carole, 56, 101, 177
Sizwe Bansi Is Dead (Fugard), 91
Snyder, Jimmy "The Greek," 182
A Soldier's Play, 5
Spectacle character, 74, 101
*Staging Difference: Cultural Pluralism in
    American Theatre and Drama*, 162
Staples, Brent, 154, 155, 171
Sterling, Eric, 156, 185

Take a Giant Step (Peterson), 22
Talented Tenth, 70
Teer, Barbara Ann, 25, 88
Theatre Communications Group (TCG),
    10, 26, 108
Theatre Journal, 165
Their Eyes Were Watching God, 146
Toomer, Jean, 176

Turner, Nat, 83
Two Trains Running, 163

Uncle Remus, 77, 143, 180
Understanding August Wilson, 160

Vesey, Denmark, 83
Vietnam War, 24

Walker, Bynum, 143
Wang, Qun, 141, 162, 186
Warrior spirit, 92
Wilson, August
    language skill, 137–148
    one-play playwright anxiety, 49–50
    realistic dialogue, 90
Wilson, Daisy, 55–56
Wilson, George, 164, 181
Wolfe, Peter, 10, 87, 160, 161–162, 182

Yale Repertory Theatre School, 97, 165
Yale School of Drama, 27

About the Author

SANDRA G. SHANNON is Professor of African American Literature at Howard University. Her previous books include *The Dramatic Vision of August Wilson* (1995), and her essays have appeared in such journals as *African American Review, College Language Association Journal,* and *MELUS.*